EXPLAINING SOCIAL CHANGE HOW INFLUENCE AMAZON DEVELOPMENT

JOHN LOK

Made with ♥ on the Notion Press Platform
www.notionpress.com

Contents

Preface

Introduction

Nowadays, many businesses had begun to apply internet to operate their online businesses. So, online business model will be very popular to let global online buyers can apply internet channel to buy any kinds of products, they are living far away from themselves countries. It implies that future e-commerce market competition will be very serious. However, some businessmen still feel shops and online-stores both sale mode may be attractive sale channels to let consumers to choose their products to buy. On another side, some businessmen only feel online-stores sale channel is the best sale mode or another side, some businessmen only feel visiting shop method is only the traditional best sale mode.

In my this book, I shall indicate the most famous Amazon e-commerce organization will face what kinds of marketing competitive challenges, how Amazon ought implement its management and marketing both strategies to solve Amazon future possible competitive challenges.Also I shall explain why and how social development and consumer purchase need change which may help Amazon success. I believe that Amazon is global the best famous and successful e-commerce organization. It needs to solve how to persuade online buyers to prefer to click its web-stores to choose to buy any kinds of brands products as well as how to persuade its any kinds of brands of sellers to choose to apply its online purchase channels to instead themselves online purchase channels. I hope my readers can have more clear understanding whether future what challenges that Amazon may face and how it can implement strategies to solve its future competitive challenges.

Prologue

Table of content

CHAPTER ONE

Amazon Knowledge innovation strategy

There are both kinds of knowledge innovation influences to Amazon ecommerce organization develops in success, one is e-commerce technological knowlegde as well as another is social innovation knowledge. I shall explain the reasons why these both knowledge may cause Amazon e-commerce organization grows in success as below:
E-commerce technological knowledge innovation
What does knowledge innovation mean? Why and how does Amazon ecommerce organization need to continue to innovate its online shopping knowledge sale channel? Can knowledge innovation impact positive online shoppers number grow to Amazon? Why does Amazon ecommerce organization apply knowledge innovation strategy to grow itself organization to achieve global online buyers number in success? In fact, when we can prepare to innovate our knowledge to be perfect. Consequently, it can help our social development more success, e.g. non manual driving vehicle, e-commerce, construction houses on water skill, hospital new robocit surgeon equipment, manufacturing robotic technology , even space touriusm leisure development etc. different kinds of technology innovation, they are depended on how human can attempt to learn to innovate or improve ourselves traditional old knowledge to be changed to any kinds of new or not discovered unique knowledge. So, human ought need to continue to learn how to innovate our old traditional knowledger to be more perfect. The question concerns how human can continue to change our old knowledge to innovate in succeed. I shall attempt to indicate how Amazon ecommerce organization can apply knowledge management innovation strategy to improve itself online puchase and sale platform to attract global many online buyers number choose its any kinds of product online purchase channel in preference as below:
What does knowledge innovation mean? The role of knowledge innovation means that knowledge management assists in building competencies required in the innovation process. Though knowledge accessibility and knowledge flow to organization, staff memebers are able to increase their skills levels and knowledge both formally and informally. An increase in skills can improve the quality of innovation as well as in society. When the country have many people can attempt to learn how to change and knowledge old knowledge to new knowledge, then they my bring their societies to develop more rapidly. So, it seems that knowledge innovation may help society, organization and individual to bring new knowledge to attribute to our future societies easily. It wil be a very important factor influence human future development in success.
However, knowlege innovation concept is not just represented by introducing or implementing new ideas or methods. The definition of meaning of innovation can be defined as a process, but involves multiple activities to uncover new ways to do things. Innovating helps developing original concepts and is to driver of optimizing operations. The purpose of innovation is to come up with new ideas and technologies that increase productivity and generate greater output with the same input on organizational aspect.
So, knowledge innovation may be applied on organization aspect, such as Amazon ecommerce organization, even individual and social aspects. On Amazon ecommerce organizational knowledge innovation aspect, innovation secures tomorrow's revenue, lowers costs and differentiates companies from the market. However, a good business model that only provides a brief market advantage and disappears after a year is not the right approach. Hence, organizational knowledge innovation aims to help the organization to raise competitive effort in long term.
Does knowledge provide innovation in Amazon ecommerce organization? Knowledge managment creates a culture conductive to tacit knowledge creation, sharing ideas in the organization, which plays an important role in the innovation process. Is knowledge management ncecessary for innovation? Beside the financial basis knowledge

is the most important resource for innovations, in order to lead a company successfully, systematic handling of " knowledge", becomes more important. Today, the increase in value develops from the productivity and the innovation in business society.

What is the role of knowledge for individual? Knowledge is important for personal growth and development, knowledge sharpens our skills like reasoning and problem solving. A strong base of knowledge helps brains function more smoothly and effectively. We become smarter with the power of knowledge and solve problems more easily. Hence, innovation is about knowledge creating new possibilities through combining different knowledge sets. These can be in the form of knowledge about what is technically possible or not particular configuration of this world meet an articulated or latent need.

For Amazon knowledge innovation can bring the positive effects of technology improvement example, there are just a few of the ways in which technology may positively affect our physical and mental health. Health apps to track chronic ilnesses and communicate vitual information to doctors , health apps that anyone tracks diet, any kinds of sport exercise and mental health information . Hence, technololgy innovation had been applied to health apps smart phone product to help we to track our health from ourselves smart phone apps equipment easily any time.

What impact did this innovation have on daily life? It increased the regional differences among various groups of people across the country, it become a major method of long distance commnication to many years. It allowed people to sign documents from across the country. So, innovation can be applied to administive tasks aspect. Also, it can increase productivity and brings citizens new and better goods and services that improves our overall standard of living.

The benefits of inovation are sometimes slow to materialize. They often fell broadly across the entire population. According to Krathwohl (2002), he indicated that knowledge can be categorized into four types: (1) factual knowledge (2) conceptual knowledge (3) procedural knowledge and (4) metacognitive knowledge. So, if human hopes to implement knowledge innovation in success, we need to know how to learn these 4 types of knowledge innovation elements. For organizational knowledge management components example, the best four components are people, process, content/ IT and strategy.

Regardless of the industry size or knowledge needs of Amazon ecommerce organizations, organizations always need people to lead, sponsor, and support knowledge sharing. Sharing knowledge innovation how influences social development. Social innovation includes social processes of innovation, such as open source methods and techniques and also the innovation which have a social purpose, like activism , virtual volunteering, or distance learning. Social innovation may include the social processes of innovation. However, social innovation is important because it can provide a unique opportunity to step back from a narrow way of thinking about social enterprise, business engagement and to recognize instead the interconnectedness of various factors and stakeholders. For science and technolgical social innovation example, science and technology can help a nation's process and development science and technology innovation are connected with development because they have hostorical record of bringing advances that have led to healthier, longer, weathler and more productive lives and they are key ingredients to solutions to the most serious poverty and economic development challenges.

Social knolwedge innovation

So, social innovation may bring human benefits, such as providing food and lifestyle products world wide with focus on environmental and social innovation , giveing every child in the world the chance to learn code and helping the visually impaired interact with their surroundings. Hence, social innovation means new solutions (products, services, models, markets, processes etc.) that stimultaneously meet a social need (more effectively than existing solutions) and lead to new or improved capabilities and relationships and better use of assets and resources. However, a social innovation process consists of a sequence of activities that seals to find solutions to a special challenge. The process itself brings a new approach that has social impact in its means (process) and ends (solution).

There are 6 keys characteristics of a social innovation, as told by Colombian social enterprises, they include: Adresses real needs of people in a community, requires a deep understanding of the problem, localizes and humanizes the problem, builds trust and collaborates with the community in need, is sustainable and scalable and adapts

constantly. Hence, every one may attempt to learn in social innovation. You will learn what social innovations are and understand how they are help solve societal problems. You will get an overview of important literature and debates on social innovation. You will also learn and apply methods to develop , implement and scale social innovations.
How can social innovation be improved to apply to Amazon ecommerce organization case? Major cross business/ cross functional projects should also have social innovation objectives include: leadership programs that include volunteering activities may help employees develop their skills and lead to greater innovations during their daily work in any organizations. How does the idea of social innovation connect with social needs? We define social innovations as new approaches to addressing social needs. They are social in their means and in their ends. They engage and mobilize the beneficiaries and help the transform social relations by improving beneficiaries' access to power and resources.

For social innovation on education aspect, teaching technological literacy, critical thinking and problem, solving through science education gives students the skills and knowledge, they need to succeed in school and beyond. The essence of how science and technology contributes to society in the creation of new knowledge , and then utilization of that knowledge to boost the prosperity of human lives, and to solve the various issues facing society. Hence, when many consumers believe online shopping channel is one kind of convenient visa card payment and safe purchase , rapid goods transport to different countries, many different kinds of products choice channel. Consequently, global societies will be influenced to accept online shopping method / mode to replace traditional shops visting purchase mode. This kind of social online purchase knowledge innovation may influence Amazon ecommerce organization develops in success in long future days.

Amazon ecommerce organization warehouse products transport process and workplace innovation

How Amazon needs to consider warehouse goods delivery service tasks ?

Why does Amazon need to innovate its wareshoise products transport process to raise rapid products delivery service to different countries consumers as well as let buyers can view any products photos to feel their good quality, good design shape to attract customers consideration from its websites/ web stores in short time? What advantages will be bought to Amazon after Amazon warehouse delivery products had been innovated in success? Can products innovation help the product to improve its market image to Amazon? Can product innovation raise Amazon growth? I shall attempt to indicate reasons to explain above questions?

In our business societies, any products ought need to be concerned how to innovate them to be good quality. The key practical benefits of innovation may include: Improved productivity, reduced cots, increased competitivenesss, improveed brand recognition and value, building new business partners relationship, helping the business to increase turnover and improved profitability.

So, it seems that product innovation may bring positive impact more than negative impact to any businesses. In fact, after the buysiness innovates itself products, innovation ought may help the business to charge higher prices for new products before competitors products come on the market. Being innovative good for the firm's reputation, even people naturally interested in its future products, if they have been first in the past as well as innovations in processes can add value to existing products/ services.

So, the meant is by product innovation, it means that a product innovation is the introduction of a good or service that is new or significantly improved with respect to its characteristics of intended uses. Maninly, these reasons can explain why innovation is important: Innovation grows business, increasing profit, innovation helps any businesses stay ahead of the competitiion, innovation helps businesses take advantage of new technologies, such as Amazon ought need to innovate its warehouse products delivery service to let global buyers feel Amazon can provide rapid products delivery service to themselves homes after they paid visa card to buy any Amazon products from its web stores rapidly. On organizational benefit aspect to Amazon warehouse products delivery service innovation, innovation may help Amazon organization differentiates its 3 rd parties sellers themselves products when they decide to display their products photos on Amazon webstores, e.g. if your organization is using innovation on its processes, its because doing so will save your time, money, or other resources, and give your organization a competitive advantage over other companies stuck in their system.

In common, innovation may include four types. Incremental, disruptive , archihectural and radical, they help illustrate the various ways that companies can innovate. For technological innovative advantages, it increases productivity and brings citizens new and better goods and services that improve their goods and service that improve their overall standard of living.

The benefits of innovation are sometimes slow to materialize. They often broadly across the entire population. Hence, the advantage of product innovation may include: Growth, expansion and gaining a competitive advantage. A business that is capable of differentiating their product from other businesses in the same industry to large extent will be able to reap profit. Examples of product innovation in improved products involves introducing beter or more functionality to existing products, e.g. electric and gas lawn mower, GPs in car , battery car, non-manual driving auto car etc. So, product innovation is the creation, development and implementation, a new product, process and service, with the aim of improving efficiency, effectiveness or competitive advantages. Such as Amazon case, it needs to make products AI warehouse delivery service innovation, e.g. chaning to artificial intelligent products delivery service from workers delivery service in order to raise its goods can delivered to different countries buyers homes in the shortest time rapidly every day.

How does innovation help Amazon ecommerce organization grows its online buyers number? In fact, one of the major benefits of innovation is its contribution to economic growth. Simply put, innovation can lead to higher productivity, meaning that the same input generates a greater output. As productivity rises, more goods and services are producted. In other words, Amazon online buyers number grows.

Instead of innovation on product aspect, innovation is also important in the workplace, it can help staffs to raise efficiency. Innovation is vital in the workplace, because it gives companies an edge in penetrating markets faster and provides a better connection to developing markets, which can lead to bigger opportunities, especially in rich countries or developed countries.

However, when an organization decides to implement innovation before it implements , it needs to concern these possible risks of innovation. Operational risk, e.g. failing to meet your quality, cost or scheduling requirements, commercial risk, e.g. failing to attract enough customers, financial risk,, e.g. investing in unsuccessful innovation projects. But, when the organization decides to implement any innovation, it may hope innovation how contribute to success. Especially as customers become more demanding. Entrepreneurs need an innovation to survive to boost your business productivity, growth and profitability more easily.

IN simple, innovation may improve sales and customer relationship, reduce waste and costs boost your market position, improve employee relations. What does the right time to organizations make decisions to innovate ? When the firm discovers its customers use the product and they field praise and complaints. And they probably have ideas, however, that can be refined into a better product. Innovative companies make it clear they want ideas, that the door is open and there is always a friendly ear for changes, then they will start to come it. It may be right innovation time, when customers have any unique idea to concern the product after they use.

What is required to introduce innovation in an organization, such as Amazon ecommerce organization? To successfully implement innovation, you need to know exactly what makes an innovative organization as well as how it contributes to its growth. Our organizaitons also need to require an innovative culture where everyone is able to think independently . So, these reasons can explain why our organizations ought need to innovate, being bold in taking on the innovation challenge build people's readiness and receptivity to change, assisting people to resolve their unconscious biases and resistance to it, developing both customer intimacy and customer empathy. However, although innovation can bring positive impact in a business, but it is so difficult to implement because new ideas and initiative depend on the people who work for the organizations. It is a lot harder to achieve desired results. Innovation is not about optimizing gross margins , but about attempt how finding new ways to create more value for yourselves profit image to attract more customers consideration.

Innovation is difficult to implement, because no system, process, or industry knows how to change, more innovations are worth exploring for many. Technology for example, can be re-purposed into new innovative solutions provide your customers with new value. The challenge is that when it comes to disruptive innovation, it almost always involves " higher risk" compared to incremental changes and thus can not be managed the same way as regular business projects are managed.

Hence, maintaining quality and product improvement and process development often involves standardization, whereas innovation can rarely be standardized . Also, new innovationds can not be measured using the same metrics and value drivers as the existing products and services . To overcome this major barrier to innovation, companies should approach disruptive innovation differently compared to how they are used to approaching regular projects. This, any organizations need to understand that they may fail to innovate. In the beginning, innovation and most specifically disruptive kind, is inferior to the existing products and services on the market. Because product improvement takes a lot of time and requires multiple iterations, the value for the customer at this point is minimal , when distuptive innovation initally caters only to a small and not so profitable customer base, established organizations are focused on serving more demanding, high and customers using their existing value channels. This is where it typically has higher profit margins, which is why established companies with rational decision-making processes usually choose not to invest in disruptive initiatives in the easrly stages. The problem ocurs when incumbents attempt to apply new technologies to trheir existing value networks or refuse moving into new markets because they are seen as too small to drive growth goals or are simply perceived to have too low margins. So, for organizations that prioritize reaching scale through operational efficiency, it makes more sense to focus on growing the business through incremental means, such as invest in risky and uncertain innovations.

On conclusion, in reality, however, Amazon ecommerce organization needs to do both simultaneously improve the core business and exploit new business opportunities . Hence, when Amazon organization decides to innovate its 3 rd party sellers their product, on warehouse goods AI delivery processing or AI workplace safe working environment . Amazon needs to find a balance between different types of innovations to choose which is the most effective goods delivery and warehouse workplace safe and efficient goods delivery innovation, which is a lot more sustainable may be stay in the Amazon e-business growth in the long term to in order to implement Amazon AI warehouse goods delivery service and warehouse working environment efficient and safe workplace innovation in order to let its all warehouse workers to feel comfortable and safe feeling and raise their goods delivery tasks efficiently.

CHAPTER TWO

AI creates Amazon efficient service growth

How does (AI) technological development will influence Amazon develops in success ?

(AI) robotic automation technology can bring Amazon warehouse goods delivery service task more efficient Future, (AI) robotic automation technology can be applied to Amazon warehouse goods delivery tasks in order to help it to shorten goods transport time to be delivered to overseas different countries buyers homes in the shortest time rapidly every day. For example, nowadays, UK computer and space explore technology had reached the mature stage. It means that UK government ought not need to continue spend much resource to research these two kind technologies. Otherwise, the (AI)robotic automatic manufacturing technology, e.g. human intelligence new product. It has need to develop because human intelligence machines will bring beneficial to satisfy human everyday life need, e.g. hospital patients' activities need, if the patent who can not walk easily, but the human intelligence machine can assist the patient walk to anywhere conveniently. So, he/she does not need to sit on wheel chair and apply the human intelligence machine man to help him/her to drive on the intelligence automatic driving vehicle to go to anywhere conveniently.

Otherwise, increased automation in low wage countries, e.g. China, Korea, Africa, Hong Kong etc. which have traditionally manufacturing firms, could use automatic technological manufacturing to bring lose cost advantage and potentially lose their ability of achieving rapid economy growth by shifting workers to factory jobs. So, UK government and businessmen needs to consider automation technology development, i.e. 3D printing manufacturing industry will encourage UK companies to move manufacturing process, closer to gain the biggest advantage from this 3D automation technology development.

A growing concern of premature de-industrialization in energy and developing countries could require new models and a need un-skillful the UK workforce. In the future, the best way toward for UK cities will reduce their exposure to automation is to boost their technological dynamic and attract more UK skilled workers. Automation technology progress can give UK manufacturers' employee benefits, such as long term healthy productivity improvement, raising productivity efficiency and product quality, macroeconomic and microeconomic effects of automation technological change, it's change will be beneficial to UK society, i.e. automation active labor market policies, which could help UK job seekers find jobs from training to incentive to support self-employment to create high technological job employment chance in UK society. So, raising science, technology, engineering and math subjects update skills level are needed to UK any universities, which can be increasingly important in UK society, these factors could complicate the ability of UK high automation technology education to adopt to the UK automation manufacturing technological change. A talent mismatch already exists in UK, with many well UK educated workers can find employment in lower-skilled jobs. To combat this, greater coordination will be needed between the education, training and employment sectors in UK society.

Why are high automatic technology product development models needed to improve to Amazon warehouse goods delivery improvement service ? UK government and manufacturers need to consider how to achieve high technology product development models. According to Hauser et al. (2006) indicated the high technology (high tech.) development process, is influenced by the innovative process, bringing products on exception value which stimulate product market demand. Innovation provides products the specific basis for which world economies compete with each other on the global market. Able to find new solutions, innovations generate significant changes in existing markets, destroy them, or create new marketing (Hauser et al. 2006). So, UK manufacturers need to concern on any manufacturing high technology product development process because which can influence any new products development to manufacture to sell to any overseas or domestic both markets successfully.

What does high tech. product warehouse goods delivery transport service improvement mean? Mohr et al. (2010) argues that there are two reasons why it is important to clarify and specific high technology : (1) due to the impact of technologies on the economy, attempts are made to classify economic production and incomes ; (2) due to the impact of high tech. on the environment. Standard marketing strategies are being modified and adopted , therefore, it is necessary to know the products to focus on. Why does Amazon need to consider warehouse high technological product delivery transportation process? Nowadays, high tech. products are complex, advanced, requiring specific technical knowledge, which is technologically not discontinued and being produced at the companies which have twice as many technical personnel and invest twice as many in scientific research and development than other companies. Moreover, these products are time-sensitive as scientists are continuously searching for new approaches for invention of more advanced technologies which make all preceding ones lower-ranking. The most important, nowadays global consumers will adopt the particular technology. It means that Amazon needs to improve high technological goods delivery service process to avoid the delay when global any online shoppers choose to buy any kinds of high technological products from Amazon web stores.

Anyway, nowadays customer individual needs in high tech. environments are characterized by sudden changes related to unpredictable fashion. Even, consumers concern about how to preserve new product' competitive technological standard is completely incompatible with technological uncertainty. The most important factor is the prevalence rate of any new products development process, which is influenced by slower than of traditional products. In many cases high-tech. automatic product market are being materialized slower than which are expected. The technological uncertainty challenges will exist in development process, such as uncertainty related to the timetable for development of the question whether the new product will be function as promised. In automatic high-tech. industries, the time requires for product development is difficult to predict as , commonly, it takes longer than expected , uncertainty related to unanticipated consequences and uncertainty about the product life cycle related to competition products. In conclusion, these factors will influence future Amazon any kinds of new automatic technological product warehouse delivery process to avoid to delay to deliver to different countries buyers themselves homes rapidly every day.

Future economists predict automatic technology how to influence future ecommerce goods efficient delivery service

Before, all over the world presented picture of demonstrate in London on the occasion of the meeting of the G20. Some economists indicated disastrous economy consequences will occur to any one of Western country , such as UK, so if any one of Western country did not consider automatic technology development to itself country. They indicated one example, such as material incentives to produce disappeared throughout Russia and, when Society leadership called off the experiment, the country faced industrial output reduced to 10% of what had been registered in 1914 and agricultural output reduced to such low levels as to cause widespread famine.

Why would UK encounter disastrous economy consequences if UK government did not encourage manufacturers spend money to invest to innovate automatic technology industry, such as Amazon online goods global delivery service case? According to a variety of anthropological studies, a collectivity is unable to operate efficiently with everybody giving talent workers have chance to devote whose best effort to manufacture any high technological products, e.g. human intelligence vehicle or airplane. Hence, economic incentives are needed to manufacturers to invest high technological automatic industry development. Because the economists predict future ecommerce organizations will have many talent worker numbers, their number will be more than a certain number of normal effort workers, due to technological education level is very excellent to provide to train many young technological manufacturing students to find this kind of high technological manufacturing job. So, the high technological manufacturing job seekers need to future ecommerce market in order to raise ecommerce any organizational development.

Assuming that future UK ecommerce market will have high technological automatic manufacturing workers who would desire only to introduce changes in the workings of the international e-commerce economic order and policies of countries participating in the present economic order rather than change the order itself, what will be UK manufacturers their specific economic preferences in the future? It implies tnat either concentrate on spending more investment to automatic high technological development, e.g. human intelligence automatic high technological products or still concentrate on spending more investment to common traditional technological products to future UK ecommerce market.

However, UK was a developed Western country which had had strong automatic high technological development effort very long time. Otherwise, it compared to some developing countries, such as Asian China, Hong Kong, Korea etc. Asian countries their future economic growth rate will show un- surprising , different patterns, so the Asian countries has weak effort to invest high automatic technological product development, such as human intelligence technological development. The catching-up process suggests low economic growth rate in the high automatic technological product development to the Asian developing countries in the future.

Hence, the future economists predict that it views as probable successors of the Western world economic leadership if any Western country , such as UK manufacturers who prefer to invest to any high automatic technological products development , e.g. developing on human intelligence automatic technological products more than traditional common technological products development. On the one side, but it seems important to stress that two very poor countries among the challengers-China and India-are examples of countries that changed their institutions and economic policies from no or little economic freedom to more economic freedom. Because there two countries whose governments prefer to lend loans to encourage their country manufacturers prefer to invest high automatic technological products manufacturing. On the other side, attitudes toward foreign direct investment (FDI) have undergone change since the 1960 s and a large majority of less developed countries, e.g. China and India are now competing strongly among themselves and with developed market economies for direct investment from multinational companies. So, UK will face China and India high automatic technological product competitors in the future. And in fact, all countries that joined Western developed economies did that without much (if any) external inflow of public resources. It is right time that UK government needs to lend loans to encourage domestic manufacturers to invest high automatic technological products to raise whose international high technological products sale effort to win its future competitors. So, machine resources will be increased demand to o UK manufacturers if who chose to spend machine resources to innovate to manufacture any new and high technological automatic products to raise human daily life needs in the future. It means that it is right time UK manufacturers need buy much machines to prepare to manufacture many future high technological automatic products when these machine prices are low. Because the future global machine prices will possible be raised if many China and India manufacturers will also buy many machines in the future. For example, USA government had provided much financial support to assist sugar cane producers to develop their businesses. And they are dependent to a much larger extent than sugar cane producers and sugar processors in the USA on government. Without very high subsidies to renewable energy generation, they would not have survived at all. So, USA government had been the first country which could lent much financial assistance to encourage domestic renewable energy generation manufacturers to develop high technological energy manufacturing business. So, UK government needs follow USA to lend financial assistance to encourage domestic high technological automatic industry development.

Future economists also predict China and India will be competitors for future leadership in the global e-commerce economy, special high technological products. China has been the media and analyst's favorite for quite some time. Quantitative projections have seemingly supported such expectation. Such as China and India had manufactured many high technological new space rockets products, ocean war large ships etc. Moreover, China has become one of the major world trade players in the early twenty-first century.

Many long-term forecasts, assuming similarly high economic growth rates in the decades ahead, predict that China will surpass the USA in terms of aggregate GDP somewhere between 2020 and 2030 or later, say between 2030 and 2050 year. The future economists conclude on the basis of these predictions that China will not only pass the USA in aggregate product (GDP), but its economy and economic policies will influence the rest of the world to a similar extent that the USA does at present.

I stressed a very important point to future global ecommerce organization growth, namely that the UK future high technological automatic product competitor China and India, namely that economies not only grow, but in the process change their structure. China and India have been industry very rapidly (the first transition) and building the physical infrastructure that accompanies industrialization changes to technology in the future. However, at a certain per capita GNP level the two countries, such as China and India will face another structural shift when which technological development will reach the mature stage in the future. China and India had been primarily historical pattern of economic development because the shift in the role of engine of growth from industry to services is to a much greater extent a qualitative shift. Both higher and different skills are required. And, even more importantly, interactions generating ideas driving the highly human-capital-intensive service economy require a much freer environment, not only in the economic area. Chinese exports have been heavily labor-intensive. This being the case, they contributed to the expansion of industrial employment, offering for the first time in the history of China a taste of (very modest) prosperity to more than 100 million new industrial workers and their families. This is the major component of the success accomplished by Chinese economic growth. Richer trade partners create room for more trade, so the Chinese should hope that intra-South trade, that is, trade between the emerging economies of Asia, the Middle East, Africa and Latin America, will open up new and growing opportunities. I presume that if Western economy , such as UK did not developed high technological automatic industry to stable their social welfare, so thoroughly slowed down their economic growth.

Will it allow China to accomplish the transition to a mature, innovation, service-sector-based ecommerce market economy? It has allowed the economy to industrialize much more successfully, even if the labor shift from agriculture to industry has not yet been completed. But it is a long way off the next major test: the second high technological industry transition of the economic structure to China. Bear in mind that Russia attempted it twice and failed at both attempts.

But even, assuming that China at some point in the future does succeed in accomplishing the second transition, will it be able to supersede the USA, for example, as the main global high automatic technological innovation center if it wants to become the No.1 global high technological industry ecommerce economy? Given the nature of the centralized state and its stability to collect financial resources , China's ability to increase research and development expenditure to high automatic technological products and to hire a mass of researchers, engineers, technicians and other specialists should not be doubted. This process in already taking place.

But , again, Soviet Russia already exceed the USA in the R&D/GDP ratio in the 1970s, long before the communist collapse, with no effects on its innovativeness. Inputs matter less than outputs, quantity in the innovation process mean much less than quality. The latter characteristics depends importantly on economic, civic and even political institutions. Otherwise, independent India had three options open to it in 1946s. It could pursue spontaneous economic development, with some state intervention to be sure, along the lines of basically free market capitalism; it could turn the clock back and try to recreate the rural-agricultural and handicraft based. The dominant way of thinking was Society -style priority to industrialization and , within industralization , priority to heavy industry. In other words, not textiles and clothing, which has been developing well in India since the mid- nine teen century, but production of sewing machines and , even better, production of machines the produce sewing machines.

The results were only to be expected. The heavy stress on the expansion of capital-intensive heavy industries in a very poor country quickly strained the ability of the Indian economy to generate adequate savings. Moreover, some of these industries were above the level of industrial competence of an underdeveloped economy. Thus, the amount of required resources (capital, skilled labor) was usually larger per unit of output than in the same industries in more mature, richer industries economies. In another view point, India will develop light industries, just as any other poor country with a great deal of unskilled labor, had a comparative advantage and no less importantly, an economy in which, due to their low capital/labor ratio, light industries could employ many more people, spreading prosperity more widely in a poor country. So, it explain that why China will have more effort to develop heavy high technological industry in the future. Thus, India got less economic efficiency, less employment than in a spontaneously developing economy, less ability to compete internationally in light industries suitable for an underdeveloped economy and finally got heavy industry unable to compete even on the domestic market and, therefore requiring no less heavy a dose of protection. Overall India got an underperforming economy, in particular in its relations with the rest of the world.

To conclude by comparing the performance of the traditional sectors of the Indian economy and the performance of its modern, human -capital-intensive subsector of manufacturing and skill intensive service sector. The latter both employ workers with high-and medium -high skillful level (in branches ranging from computer software and biotechnology and pharmaceutical high technological light industry). India is ahead of China in terms of the output and export of such products and services. Thus, it implies that Amazon ecommerce organization ought concentrate on developing high automatic heavy high technological warehouse goods delivery service industry, e.g. human intelligence technological warehouse delivery products because these industry is not better development to other many countries' strong effort , such China and India large population countries, they still have weakness to develop warehouse AI delivery service skills in themselves ecommerce organizations.

CHAPTER THREE

Amazon successful leadership management behavior

How Amazon leader be one successful CEO?
If it is not, what are the unique personal characteristics between one general CEO and one successful CEO ? Instead of personal characteristics, which kinds of skills to any successful CEOs, they will need? Why do some CEOs encounter fail to manage themselves companies? Why do some CEOs feel difficulties to manage themselves companies? This book can indicate some evidences to explain what factors can influence the person can be successful CEO to let readers to understand. Readers can learn whether what personal factors can help general CEO to become excellent CEO in any organizations.

The different characteristics between common CEO and successful CEO
The characteristics of common CEO
What are the common characteristics to general CEO? IN general, CEO person specification includes: High level of self-motivation, creativeness high level of self confidence. So, In general, qualitiies and traits of a chief executive officer, he /she may have courage, passion , but an excellent CEO is draw to change and effective action. Also CEO needs have resillence and drive ability. It means theat the CEOs, leaders ought know that taking risks and making large-scale changes can lead to organizational growth or can fall dramatically.
A CEO must posses certain traits to be an effective leader, e.g. ability to learn from the past experience, strong communication skills, buildinh relationship, realistic optimism, easily understanding, listening people and adapting to necessary managment styles.
What makes a good CEO leader? At a leader, a common CEO needs to posses strong communication skills. From motivating your employees to meeting set deadlines. You should have the ability to communicate your needs, when you hope to become a common CEO. If you want to be a good CEO, you must be consistently clear in your communication. But, some succesful executives may have these 7 perdsonality traits, such as visioning, in-depth problem solving and analysis, attapting change, driving for results, influencing and persuading, managing others, organizational resources allocation.
Hence, it seems that it is not all people these 7 successful Ceo. In fact, many companies own common CEOs more than successful CEOs in human resource view. In general, an organizational leader (CEO) , he /she does not need special management train, he /she depends on his/her past working experiences training to climb up to become the company's leader. SO, taking risks and acceptance fail or acceptance attempt, they may be general CEO personal characteristics . All of these personal characteristics, it is not difficult to own to general CEOs in any organizations. But if the organization hopes to help the business owner to manage himslef/herself overall organizational different departmental operation more effectively and efficiently. The CEO must own unique personal characteristics and excellent managing ability in order to gelp his/her boss to manage whole organization excellently. Hence, one successful CEO must own unique personal skills or abilities and personal judgement characteristics to compare common or general CEOs in any organizations.
For example, when one organization has serios financial resource allocation to provide different departments challenges, it is the best chance to examine the CEO how to apply shortage financial resource to provide to

different departments in order to still keep efficient operation aim. If the CEO can know how to arrange shortage financial resource to provide to salespeople salaries expenditure , shop or office rent, water , electricitiy , telephone fee etc operational expenditure, factory workers salaries and factory machines productive energy expenditure, product manufacturing processing material expenditure etc. resource managment expenditure allocation effectively. Consequently, the overall organizational performance can still keep positive growth, or profit can still raise. Then, I believe that this organization leader may be one successful CEO , he/she does not ne one common CEO or failure CEO role to this organization.

The characteristics of successful CEO

What factors cause the CEO can be one successful leader to his/her organization? What are this CEO personal unique characteristics own? I believe that any successful CEOs must oen unique personal characteristics that common CEOs must not own, I shall explain as below:

Usually , any successful CEO must need time from common CEO to become. Every successful CEO must communicate with their employees using concise, easy-to-understand language, open-mindedness, approachability, growth mindset, ethics, decisiveness. All these characteristics may need to any successful CEO. A chief executive officer (CEO) is the highest-ranking executive in a company , whose primary responsibilities include: making major corporate decisions, managing the overall operations and resources of a company, acting as the main point of communication between the board of directors (the board) and these corporate .

Hence, a successful CEO needs have these 5 key managerial skills: Technical skills, conceptional skills, interpersonal and communication skills, decision-making skills. The roles that a manager plays in the organization require having some skills. Hence, one successful CEO must need to know how to supervise and manage stsffs for his / her overall organization. A successful CEO also needs to understand every part and function of the business: accounting, finance, HR, marketing , legal , operation supply chain, sales and information technology. Also, one successful CEO also needs to consider organizational cultural fit, industry understanding , building good soft communication skills between staffs and him/her or between customers and its sale service staffs. Moreover, a successful leader with a CEO mindset has a clear direction for the future, and is not afraid to share it. Do not be scared to set yourself, when you are the organizational CEO and your team, ambitious and exciting goals, sure that you have smaller, achieveable steps in these as well. So you can maintain motivation.

For next example, if you are your firm's CEO, you can help your firm shareholders grew in power and their demand for booming stock prices led to booming pay. It means that you 's CEO salaries increase or decrease, it depends on share price driven salaries, when your organization's share price can often keep high price position to compare similar competitors ' share prices. Then, you 's CEO salary may keep increase, because your can manage firm's share price often keeps on high price position in share market. However, one successful CEO must need to own there managerial skills in order to help his/her organization can grow rapidly. The managerial skills may include as below:

Technical skill, it means that the abilities, knowledge, or expertise required to perform specific, job-related tasks. Technical skills are related to jobs in science, engineering, technological, manufacturing or finance. They are learnt through on-the-job experience or structured learning, e.g. data analysis, project management, technical writing, software proficiency, programming languages, artificial intelligence, machine learning, data engineering, visualization, network and information security, cloud computing.

The next is conceptual skill, a successful CEO also needs have conceptual skill, it is the ability to analyze and evaluate whether a company is achieving its goals and its business plan. Conceptual skills are skills that enable individuals to identify , conceptualize and solve problems. It is important in the workplace because it allows professionals to think and woth though abstract ideas and come up with multiple solutions to complex issues. Hence, conceptual skills include the ability to view the organization as a whole, understand how the various parts are interdepentend, and assess how the organization relates to its external environment. These skills allow managers to evaluate situations and develop alternative courses of actions. Conceptual skills may include: abstract thinking, analytical skills, congnitive skills, communication, contextualizinf, creative thinking, critical thinking, decision making. Hence, one successful CEO may be a conceptual person, who is one conceptual thinker, he /she has an understanding of why something is being done. The conceptual thinker can think at an abstract level and easily applythe CEO himself/herself insights to the suitation. So, any comon CEO may attempt to improve conceptual thought processing and increase work performance by these methods:

Observe leadership. using challenges as case studies, seeking outside knowledge, staying up-to-date on the industry, applying new practices, disucssing concepts with colleagues, finding a mentor, learning about the organization. So, one successful CEO needs to own critical thingking skills: Analysis, interpretation, inference, explanation, self-regulation, open-mindedness and problem solving, strategic thinking includes careful and deliberate anticipation of threats to guard against and opportunities to pursue.

Ultimately strategic thinking and analysis can help CEO to lead to a cleear set of goals, plans, and new ideas have abstract thinking and feeling, it is the ability to understand concepts that are real, such as freedom. So, analytical skills refer to the ability to collect and analyze information , problem solve and make decisions. Successful CEO can know how to use analytical skils when detecting patterns, brainstorming, observing , interpreting data and making decisions based on the multiple tailors and options available to you, such as the organizational CEO, e.g. creative thinking visual art, communication skills and open-mindedness to any one successful CEO, he /she ought own.

Finally, successful CEO needs have excellent interpersonal communication and decision making skill. Why is decision making and communication an important skill? It can help any CEo to raise the ability to make a decision of good leadership skills. Decision making is an on-going process in every organization, large or small. Having critical thinking skills allow the CEO to ascertain the problem and come up with a solution that is benefical to the company and its employees. So, one successful CEO needs to own soft and hard skils both.

For making decision for the organization, the successful CEO must have decision making skill to find the best solution to the challenge in process. He /she can define the problem, challenge or opportunity clearly, generate of possible solutions or responses, evaluates the costs and benefits or pros and associated with each option, selects a solution or response and knows how to implement the option chosen clearly.

Any CEO can learn how to improve decision making in workplace, such as following these steps: starting with the desired outcome, or goals, rely on data and insights to spot patterns, use S.W.O.T analysis, simulate the outcomes, trust your instincts and identify your cognitive biases. Identifying critical factors which will affect the outcome of a decision, evaluate options accurately and establish priorities, anticipate outcomes and see logical consequences, navigate risk and uncertainty,, reason well in requiring quantitative analysis. On conclusion any one CEO must need time to improve his/her hard and soft skills in order to become one successful CEO to his /her organization.

What skills to one successful CEO owns

We can learn that it is difference between one common CEO and unique successful CEO personal characteristics. Then, it beings this question: What are the skills that one successful CEO ought own? I believe that one successful CEO ought own these skills that one common CEO he /she won't own.

Building excellent communication skill:

Top performing CEO, ough know that strong communication skills are the secret to influence final success. Successful CEOs understand that influence is required if they are to inspire people to willingly act upon what they have to say. Highly influential CEOs deliver on these communication skills daily as below:

Successful CEOs understand the importance of clear, concise communication. They recognize that in the absence of simplicity comes confusion. For example, one organizational CEO sent an email to his employees listing only three objectives he wished for the company to focus on : " customers, team and execution". Instead of providing a dozen areas of opportunity . This CEO also maintained a short list of objectives that were clear. He kept employee goals concise, guiding them to focus to perform excellent services to let customers feel satisfactory. Such as this case, it explains that where one CEO focuses on concise and clear communication, he makes it easier for others to follow. This level of influence ensures that others remember what was said and are inspired to act accordingly.

Top CEOs are known for their sharp minds, and business acumen. They know that frequent communication between employees and senior leadership to be very important in their ability to stay engaged. For conference discussion case, when a successful CEo discusses ongoing company objectives and action items. he begins each all by sharing status updates of previous discussions, including what the executive staff is doing to secure the company's future. Each call concludes with a 30 minute open question forum, where all empllyees have the chance to ask questions and on ideas the executives discussed. Allowing employees to collaborate and share ideas creates a sense of ownership . It permits insight into the company's goals and encourage employees to engage in its success with ideas of their own.

By creating an atmosphere, successful CEOs encourage employees to share ideas. As a result, CEOs build stronger relationships and deepen trust in leadership . For example, when one CEO maintains an open-door policy and is known for frequently visiting employees on the floor, no matter the department or position. As a result, the CEO builds personal relationships that foster trust and candidacy that only comes with real influence. So , the difference between the successful CEO's communication skill and common CEO's communication skill is that a common CEO has influence based solely on his /her title may intimidate employees to act on direction, but successful CEO is a leader who influences others to act willingly has establish the trust and credibility necessary for lasting success. Unfortunately, too may ledaers fail to share this level of detail with their staffs leading employees to question their intention. They neglect communication weaknesses that need improvement . As a result, the entire organization will benefit from improved performance and communication . When leaders admit they are not perfect and are willing to improve, employees follow suit.

What makes a CEO successful? Findings from a database of 17,000 c-suite assessments reveal that successful CEOs demonstrate four specific behaviors that prove critical to their performance. They are decisive, they engage for impact, they adapt proactively, and they delive reliably. So, as a leader, you need to posses strong communication skills. From motivating your employees to meeting set deadlines, you should have the ability to communicate your needs and even show your employees how things are down. If you want to be a good CEO, you must be consistently clear in your communication.

What is the most important skill to a CEO? In short, the single important role of a CEO is to make absolutely certain that the right CEO is running the company and then do what is necessary to encourage that CEO's effectiveness, strategy, vision, culture shareholder value, all crucial and all within the scopr of the CEO's role. Hence, successful CEO needs to know whether what he/ she actually does. A chief executive officer (CEO) is the highest ranking executive in a company, whose primary responsibilities include making major corporate decisions, managing the overall operations and resources of a company, acting as the main point of communication between the board of directors. Hence, CEO needs to report to the board of directors, with most CEOs being members and sometimes chair of the board, president, they report to the CEO and the board of directors and cometimes they are board members.

Hence, a CEO needs to understand every part and function of the business: accounting, finance, HR, marketing, legal , operations, supply chain , sales , information technology . In business speak, the CEO's job is to define the mission (purpose), strategy (direction), and metric (pace and performance). These three elements provide the essential elements that a growing company needs to be able to perform. So, a successful CEO must need to find the effective strategy to help his/her company to solve any challenges in ay time. When the chairman technically has higher level power, the CEO is indeed the boss of a company. The CEO does by the law answer to their board of directors, which is ultimately headed by the chairman. In general., the CEO job starts when the organization reaches about 20 employees, prior to 20 employees, the job resembles more of a product management role. CEOs at this stage are trying to develop a visable product and generate some revenue.

In general, successful chief executives tend to demonstrate four specific behaviors that prove critical to their performance. For example, holding people accountable and the ability to motivate a team, high-performing (CEO) do not necessarily stand our for making great decisions all the time, rather they stand our for being more decisive. They make decisions earlier, faster, and with greater conviction. Also, they do so consistently, even with incomplete information, and in unfamiliar domains . Interestingly, the highest IQ executives , they are intellectual complexity, when the quality of their decisions is often good, because of their pursuit of the perfect answer, they can take tool ong to make choices or set clear priorities and their teams pay a high price. These smart but slow decision makers, their teams either grow frustrated , which can lead to the attrition of valuable talent ot become overcautious themselves.

Moreover, high-performing CEOs understand that a wrong decision is often better than no decision at all. It means that a bad decision was better than a lack of direction. Most decisions can be undone, but a successful CEO has learnt to move with the right amount of speed. To that end, successful CEOs also knows when not to decide, whether a decision should actually be more lower down in the organization and if delaying, it is a week or a month time, would allow important information without causing harm.

Hence, strong performers balance keen insight into their stakeholders' priorities with focus on delivering business results. They start by developing an understand of their stakeholders' needs and motivations and get many people on board by driving for performance. So, CEO needs to bring others along plan and execute disciplined communications and influencing strategies. Indeed, the skilled CEO gains the support of their colleagues by confidence that they will lead the team to sucess, even if that means taking uncomfortable or unpopular moves. These CEOs do not shy away from conflict in the pursuit of business goals. The ability to handle different viewpoints significantly faster than average.

Factors Influence CEO Success Or Fail

In fact, any CEOs will be influenced to succeed or how how to manage their organizations by personal psychology and personal skills or knowledge and external environment factors. However, CEO is such leader role to any organizations. Can owning high level leadership skillful CEOs manage their organizations more eaily to compare owning low level leadership skillful CEOs? May leadership skill be main factor to influence any one CEO's person success or fail? I shall attempt to explain as below?

In fact, I feel any CEo must need have these kinds of leadership skills. They ma y include: First, recognizing strengths, everybody with an organization has their strengths, and it is essential that you are able to identify the strengths of individuals, and recognizing weaknesses, second, reacting to employee needs, third, clarity and fourth, willingness to make tough decisions and conflict managment skill. Why does every CEO need have leadership skill? Effective leaders have the ability to communicate well, motivate their team, handle and delegate responsibilities, listen to feedback and have the flexibility to solve problems in an ever changing workplace. Hence , in CEO personal psychological view, an excellent CEO is drawn to change and effective action, courage , passion and resilence and drive attitude . A good leader knows that taking risks and making large-sacle changes can lead to organizational growth or can fall dramatically.

Why is CEO leadership important to the performance of a firm? Research evidence provides overall support for the positive relationship between leadership and firm performance (Lowe et al, 1996). CEOs with transactional leadership can successfully manage goal accomplishment and contribute to the enhancement of the firm performance. So, it seems that CEO's leadership has indirect or direct relationship to inflience his / her whole organizational performance whether it can grow up rapidly or slowly, even fall fown rapidly or slowly, because if the firm's CEO can not manage different department teams cooperate efficiently. Then, the firm's leader personal leadership effort may influence whole organization different department teams to cooperate smoothly. Although, CEO must not need to contact all department staffs every day, but he /she needs to contact any department managers in order to know whether their departments have any challenges , when managers feel difficulties to solve. If the CEO had low level leadership ability, he /she won't discuss with any department managers to conclude the best opinions to solve the challenges more easily. For example, when financial budget department manager discovered that his organization had deficit challenge recently. If he can not solve lack of cash available problem. Then, his organization's deficit will be increased easily. Consequently, it will influence staffs salaries can not pay on time, it won' t have cash to buy enough manufacturing material to prepare to be supplied to manufacture to provide products to provide to market to sell, factory can not have enough money to buy new productive machines to replace old productive machines etc. different kinds of organizational operational needs.

However, if the CEO owning high level leadership skills, he may know hoe to lead this financial budget manager to solve " deficit" challenge. Although, deficit seems to be simple matter, but if this financial budget manager can not know how to manage cash available in order to allocate to different departments operations, e.g. allocating the limiting amount of cash to urgent departments to use in prior. Then, deficit challenge will increase cash shortage number more seriously. So, high leadership skill mist need to any one organizational CEO in order to help his/ her organization can solve any challenges more efficiently and easily. Otherwise, low leadership effort owning CEO only influences his/her organization can not grow up more rapidly, even it can fall down rapidly. Consequently, the organization will only liquidate or it will be sold out rapidly.

What does excellent leadership skill need to CEO? Many psychologists indicate excellent leadership may include these essential elements: Integrity, ability to delegate, communication, self - awareness, gratitude, learning agility, influence effort, empathy.In common, characteristics of a good leader, he / she can help staffs and makes the essential large-sacle decisions that keep the organization can operate efficiently and reduce challenges occur. Integrity is especially important for top-level executives who are charting the organization's actions and making countless other significant decisions. Ability to delegate , delegating is one of the core responsibilities of a leader, the goal enables the CEO's direct reports, facilitate teamwork, provide autonomy, lead to better decision making and help the CEO's direct reports grow. Effective leadership and effective communication are intertwined.

So, any CEOs need to be able to communicate in a variety of ways, from transmitting information to coaching your staffs (managers). Any CEO must be able to listen to , and communicate with, a wide range of staffs across roles, social identities and more. The quality and effectiveness of communication across the CEO's organization directly affect trhe success of the CEO's business strategy. So, better communication skill can actually improve the CEO's organizational culture. Self-awareness is focuses skills for leadership. The better leadership skill to the CEO , he / she can understand himself / herself managing ability, the more effective , he /she can do. Do you know how other people view you or how you show up at work?

Gratitude can lead to higher self-esteem, reduced depression and anxiety, learning agility is the ability to know what to do when you do not know what to do. So, great leaders are great learners, with strong learning agility to get started , when you are one organization's CEO in beginning, you must need to learn how to influence your whole organizational staffs behaviors to be the perfect.

" Influence" may be through locial , emotional or cooperative appeals, is a component of being an effective leader, influence is quite different from manipulation, and it needs to be done and it requires emotional intelligence and trust. Empathy is correlated with job performance and is a critical part of emotional intelligence and leadership effectiveness. A successful leadership CEO needs have empathetic behaviors towards his / her direct reports, empathy can be for improving workplace conditions. Courage is such that when the CEO wants to voice a new idea, provides feedback to a direct report or flag a concern for someone above him / her. That is part of the reason courage is a key skill for good leaders. Rather than avoiding problems or allowing conflicts to faster, courage enables leaders to step up and move things in the direct direction. A workplace with high levels of psychological safety and a strong coaching culture will further support truth and courage. Finally CEO needs to know how to treat people with respect on a daily basis is one of the most important things . A leader can do that it will ease tensions and conflict, create trust, and improve effectiveness.

On conclusion, when the CEO can know how to build these psychological and emotion feeling, then the CEO can be trained to improve leadership skill in order to know hoew to manage his / her organization efficiently and effectively.

Can training provision raise CEO leadership

Any organizational CEO is the top level managerial position. So, it is one job to anyone. Any organizational positions may have training provision in order to improve the staff personal job skills, e.g. organizations can provide internal accounting training to accounting clerk, even accounting manager training in order to let they can learn company's accounting policy in order to improve their accounting tasks more proficient, or a law firm can provide legal draft training to general law clerks in order to improve their legal draft writing skils, or one company's data processing department can provide data processing training to improve data processor typing speed to learn more proficient to type its documents, or property agent firm can provide property sale speaking training to its property sale agents to improve their property sales presentation skill or insurance agent firms can provide insurance sale speaking training to its insurance sale agents to improve their insurance sales skills.

Hence, it seems that any organizational positions may apply training methods to improve any staff individual performance in any organizations. So, it brings this question: Can organizations provide training to improve CEO performance to achieve more proficient? To answer this question, we need to suppose same kinds of business CEO positions , they ought be trained to improve their performance. If it is true, whether what kinds of businesses CEO positions, they may be applied training method to improve their managerial skills? How and why to these kinds of business CEO positions, they can be trained to improve their proficiency? I shall attempt to answer as below:

In fact, general CEO typically have a bachelor's or master's degree in business administration or a fiels related to their industry. Some CEO positions require that candidates have a master's or even depending on the industry , education, for instance. So, one university CEO or president, he /she needs have education psychology master or doctorate level to any kinds of degree. They need have high educational level to do university leader. Hence, CEO, training can focus on learning or educational aspect, e.g. certified CEO program is general education certification course designed for business leaders globally (CEO senior managers) and aspiring business leaders who are looking to build upon existing qualifications and business experience.

What does CEO coach training method mean?

However, every CEO needs a coach in organization , because a coach suports the CEO to manage conflict effectively often decisoin of the CEO please one group and displease another. The CEO needs a partner who the CEO can be open with, one who is going to be sensitive, and objective, honest and respectful. Hence in any organizations, a coash can teach the CEO these managing skills to manage their organizations more easily, e.g. flexibility, value driven decision making, delegating, leadership, clear vision implementation.

Hence, in general, coach training needs ususally take 2 to 3 years to complete. The organizational CEO will does on the-job-training and spend time with a training provider. Employers will set their own entry requirements. So, in popular, many CEOs use a CEO coach over the course of their career. No athlete would be embarrassed they use a coach. Yet, CEOs believe they do not need a coach of their own. However, any organization is the final deicion making person, when the organization feels that the CEO's managerial effort is poor, it can attempt to provide a proficient managing experience coach to train this CEO's management skill in order to achieve this organization's CEO ability requirement within 2 to 3 years. For example, a CEO peer group training, interchangably called CEO peer groups or networks, these organizations generally arrange reqular meetings in confidential environments where CEOs can share ideas, best practices, experiences and advice together to attempt how to improve their managerial skills.

So, executives look for in a coach, a good executive coach does not need to have the exact background or experience as the CEO , but a familiarity will help him or her better understand the CEO thinking and needs. More importantly, the CEO coach needs skills, the CEO either does not have and wants to attain, or ones that can help strength the CEO opportunity areas.

In general, what leaders want from coaching. Coaching empowers leaders to do expectional work. Coaches establish and advantageous relationship that uncovers hidden strengths and weaknesses within the leader. Goals will be created to enable leaders to indicate their weaknesses and track their progress. What is better up coaching? Coaching training can address the CEO must pervasive organizational challenges with the organizational unique combination of coaching to achieve a growth approach to mental fitness and organizational health more effectively.

Have a CEO coach is similar to the executive or leadership coach , but with the added responsibility of working with the CEO who is working in the firm. So, coach can attempt to help the CEO potentially make the most significant difference in the company's success and lives and careers of those who work for the company. Hence, any organizations can provide executive or leadership coach to improve the CEO's leadership skills by these 5 caoching styles, such as below:

Democratic coaching, this method gives the term freedom and accountability, with the coach stepping in only when meeded to keep the process going, or authoritarian coaching, holistic coaching, authcratic coaching and vision coaching training methods, for example, entrepreneur coach can help new and existing business owners with any number of tacks to foster their entrepreneurship. In fact, entrepreneurship is not about having a business, but about having an entrepreneurship mind. So, CEOs can be trained from any style of coach in order to improve their management and leadership skills to more proficient in their organizations. So, it means that coaching training is one kind of effective training method to improve CEO's performance in any organizations.

On conclusion, I believe that it is only one kind of training method to train any organizational CEOs to become proficient CEO, it is coaching training method, instead of providing general educational level to the CEO for leadership knowledge, because coach training is one kind of organizational leadership practice training, it can satisfy any CEOs to raise leadership effort effectively to help the CEO to manage his/her organization easily.

Amazon leader / founder owns new business foundation strategies mind

Any new business founders, they ought hope their new businesses can run long time. The question concerns that how they can help their new businesses run long time, e.g. at least above 5 years . I shall attempt to apply behavioral economic theory to solve this common challenge as below.

Keeping a new business is in difficult economic time is challenging. Every new business is different and each carries its own risks and rewards in behavioral economy view. These sifferences cause some new business founders attempt to copy another similar new business founder strategy. Still, these are save general strategies business owners can follow to help themselves new businesses to copy another similar new business strategy succeeds in possible.

However, some of these copying another new business founder strategy's owner still feels their sopying another new business founder strategy may help them to succeed. So, they still have risk or they may encounter failure, if the another similar new business founder strategy can not be suitable to be adopted to themselves new business similiarly. So, it explains that why some new business founder can not keep their new businesses can run long time, because they feel the other similar new business founders their strategies can help to develop their new businesses succeed together. But in fact, there are may new business founders their copying strategy decisions are wrong. They feel their copying another new business founder's strategy can help them to develop in success. So, their new business strategies ought also help their new businesses to develop or grow long time. However, there are many new businesses can not run above 5 years, due to there new business founders choose the wrong copying strategies from another similar new business or old business competitors.

New business founder needs to look at the big picture, it means that long term customer behavior change picture. Because consumer behaviors must often change suddenly in any time. So, any new business founder ought attempt to discover whether what their product buyers behaviors will change after 5 years, even 10 years in predicting. People have a tendency to attack the most obvious immediate prodblems without hesitation. That's understandable and might make good business sense in some suitations. However, it is also advisable to step back and look at the big picture to see what is still working and what might need changing.

Its an opportunity to better comprehend the size and the scope of exciting problem and further understand your new firm's decision model, determining how its strengths and weaknesses come into play. What is a business model? The term business model refers to a firm's plan making a profit. It identified target market, e.g. which is age customer group, where is the geographical sale place, and anticipated expenses. However, business models are improtant for both new and established businesses. They help new developing companies attract investment, recruit talent, and motivate management and staff. Establishing businesses should reguarly update their business plans or they will fail to anticipate trends and channelgens. So, business models both levers are pricing and costs. It is a high -level plan for profitably , a business in a specific marketplace. A primary component of the business model is the value proposition. This is a description of the goods or services that a new business offers and why they are desirable to customers, ideally stated in a may that differentiates the products or services from its competitors.

A new business enterprise's business model should also cover projected startup costs and financing sources, the target customer base for the new business, marketing strat egy , a review of the competition, and projections of revenue ans expenses. It may also define opportunities in which the new business can partner with other established companies, e.g. the new business model for an advertising business may identify benefits from an arrangement for referrals to and from a printing company. So, successful new businesses need have good business models that allow them to fulfill client needs at a competitive price and a sustainable cost. Over time, many new businesses revise their business models from time to time to reflect changing business environments and market demands. However, the business model may not tell new business founder everything about a company's prospects, but the investor who underatands the business model can make better sense of the financial data.

New business founder also needs to consider organizational internal matter, e.g. suppose a new business founder discovers that two employees are making mistakes with inventory that cause certain supplies to be overstocked or understocked. When a initial reaction might be to fine those employees. It might be wiser to examine whether the manager who hires and supervises them properly trained time. If the manager is to blame, that person could be fired, but this might not be the best solution. If the manager's relationship with client have a history of bringing in repeat business and substantial revenue. They are likely someone, you would want to keep. However, retraining might be a better alternative than termination.

Infact, by thoroughly reviewing the strengths and weaknesses of the employees, the owner is looking at the issue from a top-down perspective, reducing or eliminating the chance that the problem will occur when avoiding a change that could adversely impact future sales. Hence, a similar kind on analysing how youe new products or services fit into the marketplace in your new business beginning stage, how the economic crisis has affected your customers and suppliers and all the other key aspects of your new business. You need to know how well your new business model fits the current environment and forecast what various alternative scenarios of the future mighr mean for it.

For one interesting new business behavioral economic view to recuriting new employees view example, any new business owners or large corporational founders tend to be either wise or follish when they hire the least expensive workers sometimes, the productivitiy of these workers may be suspect. Hiring one worker who costs 20% more than the average workers, but works 40% more effectively make of crisis. By seeking resumes and interviews from new applicants. New business founders can make change to new staff when needed to increase efficiency. So, how to choose any department new staff recruitment , it is very important to influence the new business furher develops for long time. Don't sacrifice quickly, keeping a handle on costs is crucial in tough times. Owners need to stay on the offensive and get employees on board with changes that are being made. However, any one new business founders need have good sense to predict when their new products or new services need to be changed in order to adopt customer behavioral changing environment.

ON conclusion, so any new business founders hipe to keep themselves new businesses can run long time, they must need to know " consumer behavioral psychology" how and why to cause their change in order to implement the most effective new business strategy to improve their sale methods to achieve the most satisfactory level to their potential clients' purchase needs or service needs in long time. Consequently , their new businesses ought keep long running time in this old and new product / service competitor market.

Avoiding new business low value method

Internet marketing promotion strategy

Any new business founders do not hope their new business market worth falls rapidly or share price falls rapidly. What facors may cause new business share price or market value falls rapidly? What methods to help new businesses keep the same share price is stable long time or market value can be kept in the stable worth, even share price can be influenced the rise or market value can be influenced to rise? I shall attempt to explain some useful methods, they may influence new business market value to avoid falls down, or share price can rise more easily.

TO avoid new business low value, these ways may be used in developing new business. They may include: Knowing what your client individual actual need, e.g. rice cooker product, cooking rice function must need , but avoiding to spend long time or short time to cook rice rapidly, big rice cooker size to cook more rice, long time keeping rice warm function. All these factors may influence rice cook buyers individual choices. Some housewives also need the kind of rice cooker has above all these functions, before they make rice cooker purchase decision. So, knowing what your clients real needs, they are essential to product manufacturers, offering great customer service, e.g. repair sevice, after sale enquiry (following up equiry to the client, nurture existing customers and look for new sale need opportunities, use social media attending networking events, give back to your community, measure what works and refine your approach as you go. So, if the business founder can manage sale and customer, service both teams to achieve the best service performance to let clients feel , then they may persuade many clients continue choose to continue to buy their products more easily. So, salespeople and customer service staffs training method may be one main influential factor to help the organization to raise market share value. If the organization can design useful training course to raise its salespeople sale skills or customer service staff service performance.

Which businesses can be started with less investment? For India country example, these low investment business wil be helped the new business founder to earn the most profitable, e.g. dropshipping is one of the most successful business in India, because in India, even global there are many tall offices need dropshipping equipment to transport window cleaners to clean tall office windows. So, dropshipping cleaners'window ability may influence India deopshipping firm share price changes to rise up or fall down. Because India dropshiping companies window clean workers window cleaning performance can bring property management company clients to make dropshipping window cleaning service provider choice.

I mean that India dropshipping office window or global dropshipping office windoe clean service providers, their new business market value or high stable shar e price value, their value is depended on whether their dropshipping window cleaners clearning window skills or window clean priperty management clients' window clean needs. So, for dropshipping office cleaning service provider case example, how to improve dropshipping office window cleaning workers' windows clean ability, it is only one influential method to influence dropshipping office window cleaning firm service providers their shares prices whether they can keep stable market position, even share price can be risen easily. How to improve dropshipping office cleaning workers' office windows cleaning skill is very important to influence dropshipping office window service providers' shares prices are at the stable high price level. For courier company example, how to improve courier service performance, e.g. shorten the document / goods delivery time between the document or goods sender countey and the document or goods country receiver, when the document or goods can not bt delayed to send to the overseas receiver whose home from the another country sender, e.g. From US sends the document to China in common general couriers need 5 days , but the US courier company can send the documents to China, it only needs 2 days delivery time. Then, it may attract many China goods or documents receiving clients to choose the US courier service providers. So, how to keep the US new courier servier providers, or market value or share price value, it depends on whether it may help its overseas documents or goods receiving clients to reduce how long time to let they can receive the documents or goods from US. So, the avoiding delivery time delay is the import factor to influence courier goods / documents delivery service provider new business market value.

Moreover, any one new business founder may promote themselves new business in a low budger. These methods may include: posting amazing content on your new firm's blog, creating a google my new business account, building a free or cheap email list, contributing an article to an industry magazine, attending local networking events, co-sponsor a contest. So, internet channel may help any new business to build a rapid promotion network to let many people to know that this kind of new business exist, it aims to let potential clients number increases in short time in possible. So, internet may be a kind of new promotion tool to help any new business market share value rises in short time, the internet strategies for effective promotion of new business, e.g. creating a website, geting listed on google, advertise on facebook, email customers, and potential customers use google Adwords, paid media advertising , social networks and viral marketing, internet marketing, email marketing, direct selling, point-of-purchase marketing, co-branding, cause marketing , conversational marketing .

All of these internet promotion methods may help new businesses to rise market growth value or share price in short time. Hence, internet promotion method is preferable to choose to compare general TV, advertising , newspaper, advertising, magazine advertising, radio adverting, sales promotion, general selling, publicity promotion methods because internet promotion marketing is one kind method, it may bring the new product or new service providing message to let many potential clients to know from the new firm's email ot website in short time rapidly. It is one kind of new global promotion method for any kinds of new busienss development in beginnning.

So, any new business founder may prefer to choose internet promotion method in orde to let many potential cients to know their new products ot services are existence. So, attracting new customers method may use social media optimizing the new business founder's social media account, improves website and engage with loyal customers, give branded gifts , referral discounts, social media contects, and giveways, sending email to survey customers, researching your competitors and finding out who their customers are, target email advertisement, smart social media, responding to every email, tweet , facebook comment, e-publish user reviews from internet media channel. All of these new internet promotion strategies may help any kinds of new businesses to promote their products or services to let clients to know in short time rapidly from internet media promotion channel. The internet promotion marketing strategy is one kind of low cost promotion strategy, low cost marketing stragtegy for startups, cheapest new businesses to start and focused low cost strategy company.

Why internet promoting strategy can help new business to avoid low market value? The reason is simple, because when the new firm sends one email message to let any one country's email user to know. This new product or new service email message can let global any one emaill user to know that this new product or new service business is existence in market. When the email user receives the new business' semail message, it may keep in itself email box. So, the email user won't lose the one email message and it can often remember this new product, or new service provider is existence in market. So, any one email user when he/she receives new product or service provider 's email, this email is such as the private advertisment between the new business founder and the email receiver. So, email advertising is different general product magazine, TV, newspaper , radio advertisment. It is public promotion advertisement.

Hence, the feeling of private advertisment, it is the most influential factor to persuade potential consumers to choose to buy the new product or use the new service from this provider, because when the potiential client receives the email promotion from the new product/ new service provider, he /she may feel surpise to raise interest to click the advertismeent email to see whether what benefits can be given ti him/her if he /she chooses to buy the new product or use the new service. If one say, the new product / new service provider can send about 1,000 promotion email to let global 1,000 different countries possible potential clients to know its new product/new service is existence in market. Consequently, this email network promotion method can help this new business founder to advertise his / her new product /new service to let global 1,000 email users to know in one day. When, its potential clients number increases, it implies that its new product or new service market existence value will be possible to influence to rise up. Hence, emial promotion method may influence any kinds of new businesses to rise market value in short time in possible, because when may email receivers become to the new business potential clients. Consequently, the new business's share price may be influenced to riase up then its market value may also be follow to influence to rise up. So, it seems that email promotion method may be nowadays a kind of the most effective promotion method to help any new businesses to raise up share price or raise market value in short time.

Becoming talent human how influences social changes

Nowadays we tend to think about social and digital technology more from a personal or consumer perspective than their business or professional applications, but as the Digital Era continues to progress, many of technology's most profound impacts are likely to be in the world of work. In addition to changes in product and business development, knowledge management, data analysis, and other operational processes, transforming talent management will be a key priority for organizations striving to be employers of choice.

- Digital technology encourages to create talent human

Why does digitial technology encourage to create talent human or excite human to learn new things ? The human capital implications of social and digital technologies impact virtually everyone, regardless of the type of organization they work for, their profession, their functional area, or their career stage. That means that the talent management functions in all organizations, as well as the professionals who staff and lead them, have a critical role to play in ensuring the efficient and effective transition and transformation from Industrial Era models and processes to their Digital Era upgrades.

It's no surprise that talent management has already become more "high tech." Many employment related activities have been digitized, and there has been a corresponding increase in employee self-service. It's important to remember, however, that digitization is not the same thing as digital engagement, and that the rise of "high tech" solutions doesn't necessitate the loss of a "high touch" approach to managing an organization's human assets. Transforming talent management requires digitization, to be sure, but it also involves leveraging social and digital technologies in ways that promote and enhance communication, collaboration, and engagement - not just between an employee and the organization, but between and among employees themselves.

Talent Acquisition

The logical place to start when talking about the impact of social and digital technologies on talent management is talent acquisition, where the greatest advances have been made. Anyone who has searched and applied for jobs in the past 10 years is very familiar with how technology has transformed the application process, which in most organizations (and virtually all large ones) is now almost completely digitized and automated. However, there are other ways in which social and digital technologies are impacting talent acquisition that may not be as well-known or commonly understood. Social media sites in particular (such as Facebook, YouTube, and Pinterest) are a great way to promote an employer's brand and offer realistic previews of work life, people and culture in organizations. Online games and simulations can also be used to get a sense of what working for an organization would be like, and give organizations themselves an opportunity to determine if a prospective candidate would be a good cultural fit and potentially successful.

On organizational working environment aspect, some employers are recognizing the value of digital alumni networks or communities to maintain strong relationships with former employees. One of the primary motivations for doing this is that the employees may return one day and/or make referrals to or from their personal and professional networks. Similarly, talent networks enable organizations to establish and maintain relationships with professionals in key areas like IT and engineering, even when there isn't a current opportunity to have those folks be a part of the organization. Moreover, social media can bring positive influence to impact organizations to encourge employees to attempt or feel needs to learning new things for their tasks needs. Due to social media has actually transformed every stage of the recruiting process in significant ways - so much so that the traditional recruiting funnel can be recast in "social" terms. At the top of the funnel are activities like social advertising (i.e., placing job ads on social networks like Facebook), social sourcing (i.e., searching for candidates who meet certain criteria on networks like LinkedIn), and social referrals (i.e., having current employees share position openings with their online personal and professional networks). And at the bottom of the funnel is social screening (i.e., reviewing a candidate's public activity in social networks to identify potential hiring risks).

● Learning management is needed to feel needs to any organizations

Learning management is probably the another most advanced area when it comes to adopting and adapting to new technologies. As with recruiting and other processes, the initial advances are in the area of digitization, with social software applications evolving next. One of the obvious digital impacts is the increased use of elearning and online learning platforms with self-paced study. There are also countless instructional videos on the web, both free and fee-based, that address a virtually unlimited range of topics. And we can't forget MOOCs - massive, open, online courses - which have proliferated in the past couple of years. Finally, many organizations have also started to leverage tablets and other mobile devices for learning, as well as using simulations and games to help employees develop specific skills. In addition to offering training through a variety of multimedia channels, organizations are increasingly using a range of digital tools for assessing employees' skills. They're also allowing employees to play an enhanced role in identifying their key skill sets and training needs, and can even have them create their own learning and development plans. Allowing employees to take a more active role in their own learning and skills management enables organizations to develop and maintain a more complete and accurate knowledge and skills database, which in turn enables them to maximize the value of the workforce in which they've already invested.

1. Formal learning management systems and platforms are also beginning to incorporate social technologies in a variety of ways. Promoting connections and interactions among participants, as well as with the instructor, can enhance the learning experience both during and after a course. Creating course-based cohorts that allow people to continue to interact with each other via a digital community - even when their shared learning experience is face-to-face - can promote both knowledge transfer and retention, in addition to increasing commitment and engagement through interpersonal connections.

2. Informal learning - which is now also referred to as social learning - is greatly enhanced by social technologies as well. In fact, this is probably the greatest opportunity and area of growth for organizations of all types and sizes. Through private social networks, intranets and other internal platforms that have incorporated social technology elements, organizations are better able to facilitate employee learning as they perform their job duties and complete work activities. Along with the networks themselves, features like advanced search, identified subject matter experts, digital communities of practice, wikis and more enable employees to access and learn from colleagues who are not just next door or down the hall, but even in another city, state or country!

As organizations move forward with leveraging technology to enhance learning initiatives, it will become increasingly important for them to address issues related to digital literacy and digital competencies. For the past several decades we've generally taken what I refer to as an LIY, or Learn It Yourself, approach to digital knowledge and skills. Although organizations may invest in teaching someone how to use a specific application related to their job, they make virtually no investment in helping individuals learn how to use general digital tools like Microsoft Office and even email. Left to their own devices, most people - and I include myself in this group- are much less efficient and effective at using these tools than they could or should be. As our tools get even more sophisticated, we need the foundational knowledge and skills to be able to use them well - and this foundation should probably be provided via more formal training. In other words, many people need to be "taught how to learn" in the Digital Era. If organizations aren't going to provide the formal training workers need to do that, it's probably in an individual's best interests to pursue those kinds of development opportunities on their own.

- What are social influences on human behavior when talent human number increases?

Social Influences on Human Behavior Because human beings are social and learn from observation rather than depending entirely on instinct, almost all aspects of human psychology and behavior are socially influenced. Languages, modes of dress, gender roles and avoided taboos are all agreed upon at a group level and form the basis of culture. What are the characteristics of social change? Small-scale and short-term changes are characteristic of human societies, because customs and norms change, new techniques and technologies are invented, environmental changes spur new adaptations, and conflicts result in redistributions of power. This universal human potential for social change has a biological basis.

This universal human potential for social change has a biological basis. It is rooted in the flexibility and adaptability of the human species—the near absence of biologically fixed action patterns (instincts) on the one hand and the enormous capacity for learning, symbolizing, and creating on the other hand. Because human beings are social and learn from observation rather than depending entirely on instinct, almost all aspects of human psychology and behavior are socially influenced. Languages, modes of dress, gender roles and avoided taboos are all agreed upon at a group level and form the basis of culture.

On conclusion, when one country can create many talent human, e.g. students, workers. Then they can bring more positive attribution to help or assist themselve country to develop rapidly. Consequently, the country's economic growth speed will be rapid. So, I believe that it has close relationship between economy growth and talent human number to any countries in nowadays societies.

Amazon ecommerce founder successful factors

Nowadays, we are encountering digital age period. Many customers choose to apply websites and mobile apps to buy their products. So,many merchants also choose online e-commerce channel to build online purchase platform to raise its competitive ability in online e-commerce market.

So, customers can apply mobile apps or merchants themselves websites to buy any products in any time and any places conveniently.

However, in electronic (ecommerce) industry, Amazon is the global largest online retail delivery provider. It sells different kinds of products from internet, e.g. books, electronic products, music, movie Cd, DVD, magazine, garden and homw useful tools, children toys, computer,
software, even, cars from online channel to global online shoppers. So, there ate many online buyers choose to buy any products from Amazon web services middle channel. In fact, its products prices can be low, a wide selection, ease website use and convenience to meet all of its customers‘ needs in one virtual store. So, it can still own the high share market in online retail delivery service industry. I shall indicate that Amazon successful factors as below:

It has a clear aim or mission. It's mission is to be Earth's most customer-centric company , where people can find and discover anything , they want to buy online. So, it will gather data ro analyze whether why and how customers will select to buy the kinds of products from internet. Why do its customers forget to choose to buy any products from shops and they choose Amazon to buy their preferable products from online? I believe that it has these characteristics to attract them such as:

It can provide return after sale services within the reasonable time when the customer feels that he does not need to use the product or feels unsatisfactory to the product, then he can return the product to Amazon and Amazon must refund money to him as well as it can provide free charge of grocery delivery service to every customer home.

Instead of these attractive service, it also began to enter publishing market. In July 2002, Amazon started offering services to website developers, marketings its kindle

product, aimed at capturing the publishing market for digital books, then it can sell paper books from online channel. It aims to let readers can choose to either download to read ebooks from its website or borrow ebooks to read from its electronic library or paid visa to print paper books to deliver their paper books to their homes conveniently. So, readers feel that they can enter Amazon publish website to choose any interesting books to buy or borrow to read , they do not need to go to book stores or libraries.It is Amazon's competitive and attractive and unique strengths to build its customers on this online retail market.

On its organization mamagement aspect, it has one effective and efficient management strategy. It has a good CEO manages his e-commerce business. Bezos has been chairman of the board of Amazon , since he founded the compnay in 1994. Amazon has a limitless stock on hand at all time, it enables Amazon to collect high margins when providing low prices, and lets customers to feel consideration every second. So, when the customers feel any enquiries, his customer service team members can apply its intra website email message channel to send email to answer his enquiries when they enter Amazon intra-website email message channel to send email to ask them any enquiries and they can reponse their enquiries immediately in any time or they can phone to Amazon customer service hotline to enquiry them directly. So, its customer service staffs can answer their enquiries either by phone or email communication in short time rapidly. They

won't delay to response their enquiries to avoid they feel worry or unhappy or complain. So, efficient customer service performance can help it to satisy its customer service needs and build good customer service relationship and repeat purchase chance will increase also.

However, global online retail marketplace is expanding rapidly. So, Amazon will have many new or potential online retail competitors, if it neglected to improve its strategy to adapt every online customer individual need or purchase taste, due to customers' purchase need will often change, such as price demand, product delivery time demand, customer service demand etc. spects. So, Amazon needs have different market strategies in different time in order to attract customers' choices in different economic environment, if it hoped to keep online retail leader position.

For example, how to encourage or raise customers' online purchase desires when economy is poor environment. When many people loss jobs, due to many businesses liquidate and loss many clients. So, they need to dismiss many staffs. Then, in society, many families will reduce their consumption desires because their parents loss jobs. So, Amazon needs improve its strategies on above different aspects in order to attract or persuade them to spend much time on internet shopping activities.

Instead of organization management aspect and customer service aspect, the other critical success factors for developing an e-business strategy to Amazon, they may include: How to apply network technology to keep long term close relationship between Amazon its e-commerce organization, online customers, partners, stakeholders and product suppliers. It is very important to influence Amazon's success, because Amazon , such as the e-business delivery service provider will loss the kinds of product sale chance, if the product providers dislike its sale delivery service or feel satisfactory to

its sale strategy or promotion methods or when its online sale delivery service can not let its customers feel its online sale delivery to be satisfactory. Hence, online sale delivery service performance is very important to influence Amazon's success.

Moreover, in its business model, Amazon.com also needs have these key succes factors. They may include: Building strong brand name location, because when online shoppers can remember its brand or loyalty easily when it is famous. Then they won't choose any online retail delivery providers to replace its delivery service easily. So, building one famous and confident online retail delivery service provider loyalty or brand , it can help Amazon to influence many online shoppers have confidence to choose its online retail delivery service in the first time. When they can often remember Amazon and feel it is only one online retail delivery serivce provider, the repeat online purchase chance will also increase, due to they only choose to click on its website to choose any kinds of products to buy more easily.

So, Amazon.com's marketing strategy is needed to design to strengthen the Amazon brand name, increases customer traffic to the Amazon.com web sites, builds customer loyalty, encourages repeat purchases or attracts them to clicks on its websites again to develop incremental products and retail delivery service revenue opportunities. Also, how to design its efficient products delivery value to let product buyers to feel. This factor is important to influence Amazon's products delviery service in success in online retail delivery service market. Moreover, Amazon publish service also needs to build attractive reading feeling to let readers to satisfy its reading provision needs to replace book stores or libraries.

On conclusion, Amazon ought need to continue to change its marketing strategies in order to adapt to its online retail product delivery service changes as well as lets they believe that it is one online customer care product delviery service provider to comapre other online retail delivery service providers, if it hopes to keep its online retail relviery provider top leader position in this e-commece market.

CHAPTER FOUR

Skills technological improvement strategy

Skills shortages on developing country market

Nowadays , future global job market competition will be trended serious. Any employers will expert their employees own different skills to know how to do their jobs efficiently and effectively and easily. So, future any organization employees ought considerate how to learn different kinds of skills or knowledges in order to prepare to satisfy their future employers' different new tasks needs. However, if future any new skillful needs or demands will be raised to future employers' demands. It brings these questions: what skills do global any organization employees need own in general? How to improve or raise employees themselves skills more easily and efficiently? What will happen if future employees do not learn new knowledge to improve or raise themselves skills? Why is learning any new skillful knowledge important ? What will be the possible negative and /or positive consequence if future the organizations do not need their employees to learn any new kinds of skillful knowledge?

Future developing countries need to develop their economy, so they need to employ many employees who own technical skills and /or soft skills. What kind of technical skills and/or soft skills , the developing countries' employees who will need to order to raise competiton in local job market ? I shall indicate the developing country China example. China is one developing country, employers will need different kinds of skillful labors to assist them to develop their businesses. However, China employers will face skillful labour shortage challenge. Although Chinese young age population is high, but many of them do not to be encouraged to learn enough skillful knowledge to fill future new skillful positions. So, the fast speed of training will be important to influence China supply and demand labour market to be more accurately as well as future China's the quality of labour demand number will be influenced to be raised after they have enough training to learn new skills.

How to solve future China skillful shortage of labour? Firstly, nowadays, China employers need to teach their employees to learn how to use and how to operate robotic skills in China's factories. AI robotic has been early developing, so they need to prepare to learn robotic management and operating technical and soft skills in order to satisfy future China factory automation industry development.

China is one world's factory for low-end products to high quality information products, high end technology and services. So, China will need many high skilled workers to assist manufacturers to manufacture many different kinds of products to export or local sale. Moreover, robotic manufacturing skillful workers will also need because robotic will be accepted to assist manual workers to work in China's any factories. This has led to greater demand for labour wirh upgraded skills and competence. So, it seems that China's orkers need to lern any high technological manufacturing knowledge, e.g. learning how to co-operate with robotics to raise productive efficiencies, which will be future many China's manufacturers' skills need intention.

So, when any one of China manufacturer invests robotics to work in its factory . Then, the China manufacturer's labours ought need to know how to co-operate with th robotics to raise productivities and efficiencies. Moreover, these China service industries, e.g. IT, software, accounting, finance, marketing and customer service management, e.g. waiter, property security, shopping center customer service etc. service occupations. In the future, robotics can also used to participate any one of these service industries' part of tasks in order to raise service performance. So, any one of these service industries' employees need to learn how to operate with robotics in order to achieve the most excellent servvice performances to satisfy consumers' needs. So, China service industries labours ought need to learn how to co-operate or manage service natural robotics to work together more efficiently because future China manufacturers will prefer to employ the labours who know how to co-operate and manage and control any service natural robotics more easily and efficiently in order to achieve the most excellent service performance to satisfy customers needs.

Hence, it seems that China manufacturing and service workers need to spend time and effort to learn how to co-operate with manufacturing natural robotics to manufacture any products in factories efficiently or deliver any cargos in warehouses more efficiently or serve customers to let them to feel excellent service performance in restaurants or shopping centers or properties or offices receiption counters. Then, when their China employers apply robotics to participate to work in factories, restaurants, shopping centers, cinemas, offices or properties reception etc. different working places . These low skillful labours will be dismissed easily, due to robotics can replace them to manufacture any products or provide services to satisfy clients' needs in order to let them to fell robotics' performances are more excellent to compare human service labours or their productive efficiencies are more effort to compare workers. So, future China workers need to learn how to cooperate or manage or contol with robotics to work more efficiently, if they do not expect to be dismissed easily.

Future global skillful labor

soft knowledge skill need

In the future several occupations have been identified as the most frequent movers between all labour market states. The elementary occupations include: waiters, bar staffs, clearners, catering assistants, construction and security service workers, care workers, sales assistants and general clerks etc. So, the low educational level workers can learn these soft wkills to raise whose professional workering level to prepare to do these above positions in global elementary occupation job market.

The changes of employer were most frequent for IT programmers, doctors, electricians, carpenters, skilled workers in global labour market. These skilled occupations will have manpower shortage supply challenge, due to either people feel the educatonal level is under low. So, there has no many people have interest to know these knowledg to prepare their elementary careers. So, these kinds of low skilled occupations will have not enough human power supply to global labour job market also, the high skilled or educational job support.

Moreover, the high skilled occupations also encounter labour shortage issue. The skills in short supply related to experienced canadidates e.g. five years or more. For example, pharmaceutical , biogharma and food innovation industries. The occupational shortage roles include: Chemists, analytical scientists, product formulation, analytical development for roles in biopharma, quality control analyst includes pharmaco-vigilance, i.e. drug safety roles. The demand for engineering industry aspect which will aos increase the labour shortage includes process and design (research and development, quality control, automation, lean processes) are skillful labours need to help employers to achieve these intentions. They may include raising competitiveness, boosting productivity and skills availability. So, if future these above any one of occupation labours can not achieve these benefits to satisfy their employers' needs. Then, his/her average weekly or hourly wages will be reduced. It means that the unskilled labour under skilled labour wage can not increased more easily, even they own many year working experiences in any one of above these occupations. If the employer feels the labour is unskilled or below skilled level for any one of these occupations in these any one industry aspect, e.g. wholesale and retal , human health, education, accomodaton and food , construction, professional activities, financial service , public administration, and defence, transportation etc. occupations. Then, these industries' unskilled or below skilled level workers' salaries will be lower level to compare the higher skilled workers who work in any one of these industries.

The reason why future employers need to employ skilled labours. One explanation for slow recovery in demand in negative impact on investment is a prolonged period of high unemployment. This is led to job weekers left labour market or became unemployable due. So, future low skillful level will be one important factor to cause unemployment in society as well as nowadays labours ought need consider whether their skills are needed to improve in order to avoid future competition in job market.

2.1 Why do future labours need to learn worldwide readiness skills

Future employers need employees own worldwide readiness skills, such as reading , writing and arithmatic. Why do employees need worldwide readiness skills? In the future, high economic growth countries need high wage positions, high opportunity jobs which need a large number of skills required of job candidates of these positions " job readinss" and not " job training" , which support developments of these importance and widely desired skills won't only support the success to high-opportunity positions, but also be developed for future success in the competitive global economy. Because real-time business intelligence is needed for the talent marketplace to employ talent employees. So, it explains that it will have many future employers hope to employ owning readiness skillful employees to help them to develop their businesse intelligently. Hence, present employees ought need to hard to train readiness skills to prepare whose future employers' job requirements in the future competitive global job market.

2.2 Why these occupations need readiness skills

In the future these occupations will need to raise readiness skills. For example, mathematical science, teachers (post-secondary), management analysts, computer and information systems, managers, first-line supervisors of construction traders, solar photovoltaic installers. All of these occupations , employers need staffs to own good readiness analytic ability to help them to do more accurate real-time business intelligent decisions. The representative occupations include oral and written communication skills, project management, teamwork, marketing and creativity . Moreover, they need to own specific technology skill, deep science and math or even most business skills as well as these skills are "soft" skills more than hard skills. These kinds of occupation employees need own cooperative effort, creativity, problem solving, detail orientation and integrity personal characteristics, which are relevant across all knowledge and domains.

Therefore, in the future, science, technology,engineering and mathematics relevant occupations need to own more readniness and analytic skills more than othe kinds of occupations. Because these organizations need those professionals on knowledge acquisition, literacy analysis, synthesis and critical thinking skills that will impact their organizations to bring more critical thinking beneficial team culture. These occupational top skills will include oral and written communication skills, project management skill, team oriented skill, marketing and creativity skills, problem solving skill, detail oriented skill, self-motivated skills, management and analytical skills, coaching skill, business process modeling skills, work independent skill, strong leadership skills, management experience and business requirements gathering. All of these skills which will be future employers who need to employ these kinds employees who own these skills in preference. Also, all of these skills concentrate on soft skills more than hard skills. It seems that when above occupational applicants who own any one of thes skills, evn more than one skills. Then, he/ she will have more chance to be selected to employ. Also occupation specific skills requirements are more needed to compare cross-functional skills for above of any one occupation. Because the high concentraton of cross-functional skills require " job readiness" and not " job training" for success, e.g. communicaton, integraton and presentation skills, entrepreneurialism and related skills, microsoft office software skills.

Of particular interest is communication, integration and presentation skills. These skills include ability to seek, evaluate and examine information and data create a reasoned position, present findings and make a case for or advocate for position. So, these skills are very important and they can help future applicants who expect to win any kinds of these positions easily. However, the hard skills can help these applicants to be more successful to win any kinds of these positions when they own these hard skills, e.g. microsoft offic, powerpoint, excel , word, microsoft project etc. softwares.

In conclusion, the global economy is dynamic and many of the skills required for positons in the future will need good technologies and work practices to be developed. The number of skills required t be successful in the jobs forecast to be most in demand in the future is growing. So, it explains that why future any one of these occupations which will need soft skills more than hard skills, due to organizations like to employ the employees who own managerial and analytical effort more than hard skills productive effort to assist their organizations to develop more easily.

2.3 Data -analysis skill needs

In the future, most organizations will have a number of jobs that include data analysis. Economists and labor market forecasters predict occupations need data analytical skill will need much. In addition, fast technological development means th types of technologies and applications workers in this field will need to be familiar with data analytical skill rapidly. It seems that data analytical jobs will have new job opportunity to employees with in-demand skills in future global labor market.

Why and how do employers demand for data analysis skills? Data analysis skills mean the ability to gather, analyze and draw practical conclusions from data as well as communicate data findings to others. The occupations include: data analyst, data scientist, statistician, market research analyst, financial analyst,research manager. In business career, many employers expect to employ statisticans, operations researh analysts, market research analysts and marketing specialists to assist their organizations to gather useful data from market in order to analyze and draw practical conclusions and finding the best solutions or methods to win their competitors.

Therefore, these data analysis jobs will have much need. Large size organizations with 500 or more employees were more likely than small or medium size organizations with 25 to 499 employees to plan hired data analysis positons in the future. For example, human source department will use big data to help make strategic decisions. How HR uses big data . HR will use big data for sourcing, recruitment, or selection, identifying causes of turnover and/or employee retention strategies or trends, managing talent and performance. Why organizations do not use big data. It is possible that they lack of knowledg expertise, the majority of organizatons will have data analysis positions within accounting and finance department, human resources department, business and administration department, information technology department, marketing, advertising and sales department, supply chain and operations department, research and development department, customer service department and other departments. So, future data analysis skill will need to used in different organizational departments.

However, publicly and privately owned for-profit organizations were more likely than government organizations to have data analysis positions in the marketing, advertising and sales function. Also, data analysis skills are required to different levels in any organizations , such as entry level, non-management / individual contributor level, mid-level management level, seniot management or executive level. The analyst, research analyst, market research analyst, scientist-based titles include: data scientists , research scientist, scientist, other descriptive titles include researcher, statistician, mathematician and other . So, data analysis positions will have many different skills to be selected to any one data analysis professional. For example, the data analysis professional can select either to learn the ability to interpret and communicate data analysis results skill or to learn how gathering or analyzing data skill. So, data analysis skill is not onlyone skill, it is more than one skill to let any one employee to select to learn.

Why do organizations need data analysis professionals? On workforce planning aspect, organizatons expect to let strategic direction and content of workforce needed for future business objectives easier, analyzing workforce: supply analysis, demand analsis and gap analysis more earier, developing action plan : recruiting and training plans to deal with gaps more easier, implementing action plan, monitoring, evaluating and revising plan more easier. So, organizations expect the data analysis professionsla can help them to solve these challenges, such as using of advanced technology solutons to integrate disparate planning sources; data availability and format; accessing to and understanding of the organization's data and analytics, developing business case to gain support from senior management and collaboration among HR staff, managers and executive easier. Future industries need data analysis professionals may include manufacturing health care and social assistance, scientific and technical service, finance and insurance, educational services , government agencies, retail trade, transportation and warehousing, construction, utilities, accomodation, and food services, waste management and remediation services, entetainment, and creation, real estate and rental and leasing , repair and maintenance, agriculture, forestry, fishing and hunting, personal and laundry services etc.

In conclusion, data analysis job need explains why future readiness and data analytical skills will be popular needed in globl labour market , due to these both skills are labour shortage and employers will need employees own big data readiness and data analytical both skills in order to win whose competitors more easier.

2.4 What are regional dynamic skills
of global labour market demand

Businessmen expect to improve better economic environment, they will prefer to recruit the most sought after skills of intelligent employees to bring positive beneficial impact to organizations. However, technology and digisation has had a significant influence on workers. Future globalization will trend digital economic development. Hence, it will influence workers' skills to be changed also. In fact, not all changes are positive because some workers will possible lose jobs, either due to new technology replaces their jobs or they lack enough effort to improve their skills in global digital economic labour market environment.

It brings this question: What are regional dynamic skills need whn digital busines environment is growing. In fact, organizations will continue to deal with skills shortages, labour markets across the global are continually changing. so, more employers and workers will need to adopt innovate working pattern, e.g. on call jobs, freelance jobs will grow popularly. The greater flexibility afforded to employ regardly.

Finally, digitalisation includes artificial intelligence, big data , online platforms. All these new technology will influence future employees how to worker. For example, they can apply online platform to work at home conveniently. So, they do not need to go to offices. They can finish their jobs and send to their employers by email easily. This kinds of job pattern can raise efficiencies and employers do not need go to offices often.

An important implication of innovating working which needs the employees who own digital skills in order to serve organizations more efficiently. So, employers are increasingly able to access demographics that were hitherto less active in labour markets. For example, future more women are joining the labour market because part time and self employment opportunities make it easier. This kinds of job pattern can raise efficiencies and employees do not need go to offices often.

An important implication of innovating working which needs the employees who own digital skills in order to serve organizations more efficiently. So, employers are increasingly able to access demographic that were hitherto less active in labour markets. For example, future more women are joining the labour market because part time and self employment opportunities make it easier to manage family with work life. So, digital skilling needs will cause many women lose jobs in possible. If the women lack digital job skills. Because high digital skill occupations need, like those requiring research, medical treatment and architectural design occupational digital skills are more common in the services sector, more women who own digital skill who can compete to win.

High digital skill occupations more easier than men because employers usually select female to do high skill occupations easier than make. However, if those professional service female employees can not learn how to apply digital skills to do these researchs medical treatmentm architectural design professional service jobs. Then, it is also different for these professional service femal employees to raise competition in global labour professional service market. So, these professional service female employees need to learn how to apply digital to do themselves jobs in future global professional service labour market. Otherwise, if the male professional service employees can attempt to learn how to apply digital skill to do themselves jobs in order to improve efficiencies and service performance to satisfy patients, such as medical service needs, school search service needs, construction firms' building needs. Then, the owning high digital technology skillful female employees will be more easier to find the professional service jobs which need digital skill more easier than the lacking digital skill female service professionals in future global digital service professional labour market.

On the other robotic communication skill need aspect, future employers expect workers to know how to communicate with robots to work efficiently in any working environment if the employers need robotc to serve their organizations. For example, communication between the robots on factory floors, and between people and robots could allow robots to start and stopr processes based on real-time conditions around them and alert people when there is a problem, so robots could increase their own efficiency if the workers could monitor themselves and determine when they needed maintenance; efficiency would also be improved if machines and robots could make production decisions on their own by. For example, ordering new suppliers when existing inputs into a production process run low. The increase in productivity of industrial robots will likely reduce the number of manual jobs on the shop floor.

At the same time, the increased output made possible by such robots will mean that manufacturers need more people in accounting, finance, sales, advertising and other roles. The increase in putput may also drive increased employment on manufacturers' supply chains. Hence, future employers expect to employ the workers who can know how to communicate with robots to work efficiently in order to raise productivity in any working environment. It means that it the worker can know how to control and communicate with the robots to work together in the team. Then, his/her communication and controlling robotic skill will help the organization's team to work efficiently and raise productivity in order to reduce time waste and human waste and resource waste considerately. So, future shortage of communication and controlling robotic skillful workers number will increase. It has much beneficial to workers who choose to attempt to learn how to communicate and control robots to work together in any working environment team efficiently. Because future employers will like to use robots to assist manual workers to attempt to raise productive efficiency in any working environment. So, the need of employees who know how to cooperate or communicate with robots whose talent skills will be useful to any future employers.

Future global business leaders will need human machine cooperation skill. This technological skill includes artificial intelligence (AI and internet of things (IOT), will reshape our working change. These machines will participate to our daily working environment. For instance, many business leaders agree that automated systems will free-up their time as well as they also believe they'll have more job satisfaction by offloading the tasks that they don't want to do to intelligent machines.

Therefore, future leaders will expect humans and machines can work as integrated teams within their organizaton in order to their workforce and machines are already successfully working this way. So, they need to expect future employees can know or learn how to work with automated systems more easily, because many jobs will be participated by automated systems, e..g simple accounting tasks, legal administration tasks etc. clerical tasks. They will be participated with (AI) technology, it learns how to cooperate with (AI) technology to finish simplt clerical tasks efficiently.

Future workers will need have autrmated system operational skills: They include that how to operate automated systems to free -up workers' time. Workers will need to learn how to operate automated system to better with healthcare tracking devices workers will need to learn how to operate automated systems to absord and manage information in completely different ways. Workers will need to learn how to operate automated systems of smart machines to work as admin. in any orking environments. Workers need be needed to learn how to operate (AI) automated machines to mak more accurate clerical tasks or efficiencies. So, the automated system (robotic) operational skillful workers' demand and number will increase.

In the future, employers need automated machine manufacturing and service with workers cooperation reasons include that clear protocols, will need to be established if autonomous machines fail. So, they need their workers to learn how to control and manage and communicate with autonomous machines skillfully. They believe move they depend upon technology, the more they'll have to lose in the event of a cyber attack. So, skillful workers are real required to let them to know how to cooperate with autonomous machines more efficiently and easily. Computers will need to be able to decipher between good and bad commands, so future employers have much chance to need the owning automated machines operating workers to assist any robots to make more accurate good or bad decision when robots and workers have need to make immediate judgement in their any related job responsibilites aspect.

Therefore, future owning automated machines operating workers' skillful level will be high. It bases on automated machine manufacturing environment trend factor. Finally, future technology will connect the right employee to the high task at the right time. It implies that when future global employers began to accept to apply robots to help them to raise any productivities efficiently. It will influence many manufacturing positions which need to employ any proficient skillful workers who own automated machines operational skills to know how to communicate or manage or control , even supervise any robots to work in teams in any organizational manufacturing environment efficiently.

In the future, employers also expect employees to own sufficient digital vision and strategic skills, manifest among other things. They can know how to apply data to demonstrate any senior support and sponsorship digital technological skill. They expect to reduce a skill gap and avoid a lack of employee buying and a workforce culture to change in their digital technologicl manufacturing organizations. Future employers also believe outdated technology that can't work fast enough, data overload, privary and security concerns. So, it explains why it is possible that future employers also need digital working environment and automated robots machines to attempt to achieve raising productive efficient aim.

Moreover, it also explains why digital transformation need will be raised. The reasons include: They feel digital technology can gain employees' buying in , making customer experience a boardroom concern, achieving fair compensation , training and goals and strategy achievement more easily, tasking senior leaders with digital working environment change putting policies and technology to support a fully remote, flexible workforce , empowering lines of team work more efficient, teaching all employees how to code/understanding how to adopt to work with automatic machines or rots in any team efficiently. So, automate machine can raise efficiency in manufacturing society.

In conclusion, in the future business society, employees need to be stronger human machine partnerships. So , future manufacturing or service industries will have digital technology and automated machine robotic technology to assist workers to work in any working environment efficiently. They expect digital technology and automated machine robotic technology anticipation to workers' daily jobs in order to bring positive impacting to the customer experience from business owners to decision makers in marketing, customer service, research and developmnt and finance etc. They also expect technological productivity can bring positive relationship between technology and workers emerging technologies' impact on business and the way workers and automated machine work together.

Future organizational skillful
needs how to influence workforce
change to what kinds of employees

In the future whether in general organizations need what kinds of employees' skills, they expect employee individual own. It is one interesting question. The common skills that employees need to own in order to any duties to any organizational departments efficiently, e.g. human resource, marketing, administrative, logistic etc. different departments. For hospital, school, business, professional occupations etc. different organizations. Whether future school ought implement one system educational method to teach different common skills to students in order to let them to leave schools to jobs more easier.

Future employers need to create new technologies including automation and algorithms, in order to create new high quality jobs and improve the job quality and productivity of the existing work of human employees in any organizations, e.g. accounting department will need intelligence (AI) to assist account clerks to do simple repeating accounting job tasks in order to share their work load and raise performance efficiency or legal organizations will need (AI) to assist law clerks to do simple repeating legal draft or legal document revising job tasks . All future general clerical jobs will apply (AI) technological tools to assist human to job, it will produce a comprehensive platform for managing workforce change.

Hence, human manual(employees) need to learn how to adopt (AI) job participation to assist them to do different kinds of simple clerical jobs in any organizational administrative departments . They , clerical employees or white color workers need to learn how manage or dominate (AI) tool to improve job performance to be better. However, (AI) administrative workforce change, it is not only one kind of job automation change role in any physical offices. It influences future administrative clerks need change a more flexible manner, utilizing remote staffing beyond physical offices and decentralization of operations organizational workforce change.

Instead of (AI) participation to administrative job aspect, (AI) will also participate to manufacturing industry environment aspect, a new human-machine manufacturing workforce change will exist to any factories, warehouses working environment. Scientists predict that in present an average of 71% of total task hours across the industries are performed by humans, compared a 29% by machines. In this average is expected to have shifted to 58% task hours performed by humans and 42% by machines. In fact, nowadays, in terms of total working hours, no work task was yet estimated to be predominantly performed by a machine or an algorithm (AI). But, this picture is predicted to have somewhat changed with machines and algorithms (AI) on average increasing their contribution to specific tasks by 57% . For example, in the future, 62% of organization's information and data processing and information search and transmission tasks will be performed by machines compared to 46% today.

Therefore, these high technological skillful job change will bring negative influence to some demotive-skillful or low skillful labors to be dismissed, if they can not upgrade or raise or reskillgul their skill level to improve their analytical thinking , technology design and programming skills to cooperate with (AI) tools to work efficiently together in any organizational manufacturing or offie work environment. Because it will have many employers apply (AI) automation tools to participate with blue -color or whiate -color workers' tasks in order to raise efficiencies or improve performance in any working environment. So, it is right time to young or mid age employees need to upskill and/or reskill their rihgt type of skills to prepare future technology risch work environment changeing needs.

Future technological advances will permit an increasing number of tasks traditionally performed by humans to become automated. It seems that , such automation focused primarily on routine tasks, e.g. clerical work, bookkeeping, basic paralegal work and reporting etc. However, with the advent of big data, artificial intelligence (AI), the internet of things and ever-increasing computing power , i.e. the digital revolutions, non-routine tasks are also increasingly likely to become automated. For example, the recent development in robotics and 3D printing allow firms in advanced economies to locate production closer to domestic markets in fully aumomated factories. As a result, the future strongest incentive to automate because of their relatively higher labour costs will be reduced, when production automated will bring the negative influence to dismiss some foolish or low produtive or low skill workers , the owning high automated productive skillful workers will replace the low productive skillful workers in any factories‘ manufacturing environments. So, technological progress participates to raise quantity of jobs will cause result in significant job losses to low skillful workers. Because future employers will need many high automated productive employees to help them to cooperate with (AI) automated machine to work together efficiently. For example, many proportion of occupations at high risk is greatest in Germany and lowest in Korea, these countries organizations will accept to spend technology investments and education of workers to prepare future automatability manufacturing development successfully.

However, future automatability manufacturing development will bring technological unemployment in possible, due to workers need to adjust to the challenge of automation by switching tasks. Thus, preventing technological unemployment, also technological change does not just destroy jobs, but also generates new roles through its effect on productivity and the demand for new technologies. For example, it has been estimated that, for each high tech-job created in the industries , such as computing equipment or electrical machinery, some 4.9 % additional jobs are created for lawyers, taxi, drivers and waites in the local economy (Moretti, 2011).

Therefore, automated will also influence service industries' job nature change, e.g. taxi drivers need to apply (AI) automated machines to assist them to drive their taxis. When the passenger tells the taxi driver where he/she wants to go. Then, the (AI automated machine will follow the GPS road direction map to be indicated how to drive the taxi to go to the destination automatically . So, future taxi driver is one assistance role to assist the (AI) automated driving tool to dominate the (AI) tool to drive the taxi to catch the passenger to arrive the destination safety in the short time in possible. For another example, future restaurant waiters will need (AI) automated machines's assistance to help them to deliver or dispatch any foods and soft drinks to send to the identified eater's table carefully in accurate and efficient service performance way from the kitchen, in especially in the busy time and many people are sitting in the large size restaurant environment. So, future, waiter roles will be the leader , they need to manage or control or supervise the (AI) robotics how to make decisions to arrange to dispatch which foods or soft drinks to the different tables in preference immediately. Also, future law clerks need to supervise or manage the law robotics how to help them to make decisions to do revision or draft or filing legal tasks in preference in order to avoid any typing words are mistaken to type on computers or revised draft in wrong way to assist manual legal clerks‘ mistaken words are appearanced on any legal documents. So, the law clerk future role will be the trainer role , he/she eeds to teacher the robots how to check any words, e.g. grammers to correct them to be right grammers, or giving the accurate revision legal documents' instruction to let the legal robots to know how to revise each legal draft to prove whether which part of the legal draft will have wrong to be needed to revise.

In conclusion, future many manual workers‘ service or manfacturing job natures will become automated assistance to robotics. So, employees need to upgrade their skills in order to adopt new technological work nature change. So future CEO needs to prepare to learn how to apply robotic technological skills to train workers to raise efficiencies and improve performance because there are many future organizations start to apply robotic manufacturing tools to assist workers to work in any departments. Hence, future excellent CEOs must need to own AI knowledge to satisfy their organizational performance improvement need.

Skill training talent human method

Skill is an ability or effort that you need to put time to develop. Talent refers to an inborn and special ability you own it. So, when one person can attempt to learn ths kind of skill. It is possible that he can be trained to be talent person. How to Create Effective Skills Training with Career Pathing ? Your company's ability to address the skills gap is going to be the most significant issue facing HR in the next decade. Relying on the recruitment of new hires will no longer be a viable solution. Digital transformation of the workplace means that AI and automation are continually rendering skills obsolete while creating new jobs in the process. As those new roles emerge, the existing talent pool will be insufficient to meet demand. Employers will no longer be able to fall back on their default strategy of hiring new workers.

● How to improve staff skill to be talent labour ?

As the 'future of work' begins to assume a more defined shape, the majority of employers are placing more emphasis on training of their existing talent, but skills development is not moving fast enough to keep up with demand. Ongoing upskilling and reskilling can help to offset the impact on your workforce from these fundamental changes.

Creating personalized development opportunities

When it comes to developing your talent, there is no 'one size fits all' approach. To succeed in today's workplace the following steps are recommended. Your approach must become more personal, placing development at the center of your overall business strategy.

Personalized development opportunities should be offered to enhance skills acquisition. This approach enables you to provide your employees with the tools they need to acquire new skills.

As well as being targeted to the individual, employees should be able to learn in their own time. Technology can help to support this. A further, critical point to note is that learning and development is not exclusively for the C Suite but should be offered to all of your employees.

● Career pathing strategy improve employee individual skill ?

Career pathing provides a clear route into all of these options, enables you to create individual learning programs for all of your employees and offers the following benefits.

Employees create their own career paths, which are aligned with your organization's business goals. All employees are guided to understand their own strengths and weaknesses and are empowered to identify key areas for development. They are inspired to work towards vertical or lateral moves within your organization, for example, through job rotation (ie, where employees assume new tasks in a different role for a specified period before they 'rotate' back to their original post). Career pathing enables HR and management to understand and analyze employee aspirations through internal mobility programs and aligns well with your succession planning program. So, career pathing strategy is one kind of good skill to raise staff efficiency or improve performance.

Skills shortages on developing country market

Future developing countries need to develop their economy, so they need to employ many employees who own technical skills and /or soft skills. What kind of technical skills and/or soft skills , the developing countries' employees who will need to order to raise competiton in local job market ? I shall indicate the developing country China example. China is one developing country, employers will need different kinds of skillful labors to assist them to develop their businesses. However, China employers will face skillful labour shortage challenge. Although Chinese young age population is high, but many of them do not to be encouraged to learn enough skillful knowledge to fill future new skillful positions. So, the fast speed of training will be important to influence China supply and demand labour market to be more accurately as well as future China's the quality of labour demand number will be influenced to be raised after they have enough training to learn new skills.

How to solve future China skillful shortage of labour? Firstly, nowadays, China employers need to teach their employees to learn how to use and how to operate robotic skills in China's factories. AI robotic has been early developing, so they need to prepare to learn robotic management and operating technical and soft skills in order to satisfy future China factory automation industry development.

China is one world's factory for low-end products to high quality information products, high end technology and services. So, China will need many high skilled workers to assist manufacturers to manufacture many different kinds of products to export or local sale. Moreover, robotic manufacturing skillful workers will also need because robotic will be accepted to assist manual workers to work in China's any factories. This has led to greater demand for labour wirh upgraded skills and competence. So, it seems that China's orkers need to lern any high technological manufacturing knowledge, e.g. learning how to co-operate with robotics to raise productive efficiencies, which will be future many China's manufacturers' skills need intention.

So, when any one of China manufacturer invests robotics to work in its factory . Then, the China manufacturer's labours ought need to know how to co-operate with th robotics to raise productivities and efficiencies. Moreover, these China service industries, e.g. IT, software, accounting, finance, marketing and customer service management, e.g. waiter, property security, shopping center customer service etc. service occupations. In the future, robotics can also used to participate any one of these service industries' part of tasks in order to raise service performance. So, any one of these service industries' employees need to learn how to operate with robotics in order to achieve the most excellent servvice performances to satisfy consumers' needs. So, China service industries labours ought need to learn how to co-operate or manage service natural robotics to work together more efficiently because future China manufacturers will prefer to employ the labours who know how to co-operate and manage and control any service natural robotics more easily and efficiently in order to achieve the most excellent service performance to satisfy customers needs.

Hence, it seems that China manufacturing and service workers need to spend time and effort to learn how to co-operate with manufacturing natural robotics to manufacture any products in factories efficiently or deliver any cargos in warehouses more efficiently or serve customers to let them to feel excellent service performance in restaurants or shopping centers or properties or offices receiption counters. Then, when their China employers apply robotics to participate to work in factories, restaurants, shopping centers, cinemas, offices or properties reception etc. different working places . These low skillful labours will be dismissed easily, due to robotics can replace them to manufacture any products or provide services to satisfy clients' needs in order to let them to fell robotics' performances are more excellent to compare human service labours or their productive efficiencies are more effort to compare workers. So, future China workers need to learn how to cooperate or manage or contol with robotics to work more efficiently, if they do not expect to be dismissed easily.

In the future several occupations have been identified as the most frequent movers between all labour market states. The elementary occupations include: waiters, bar staffs, clearners, catering assistants, construction and security service workers, care workers, sales assistants and general clerks etc. So, the low educational level workers can learn these soft wkills to raise whose professional workering level to prepare to do these above positions in global elementary occupation job market.

The changes of employer were most frequent for IT programmers, doctors, electricians, carpenters, skilled workers in global labour market. These skilled occupations will have manpower shortage supply challenge, due to either people feel the educatonal level is under low. So, there has no many people have interest to know these knowledg to prepare their elementary careers. So, these kinds of low skilled occupations will have not enough human power supply to global labour job market also, the high skilled or educational job support.

Moreover, the high skilled occupations also encounter labour shortage issue. The skills in short supply related to experienced canadidates e.g. five years or more. For example, pharmaceutical , biogharma and food innovation industries. The occupational shortage roles include: Chemists, analytical scientists, product formulation, analytical development for roles in biopharma, quality control analyst includes pharmaco-vigilance, i.e. drug safety roles. The demand for engineering industry aspect which will aos increase the labour shortage includes process and design (research and development, quality control, automation, lean processes) are skillful labours need to help employers to achieve these intentions. They may include raising competitiveness, boosting productivity and skills availability. So, if future these above any one of occupation labours can not achieve these benefits to satisfy their employers' needs. Then, his/her average weekly or hourly wages will be reduced. It means that the unskilled labour under skilled labour wage can not increased more easily, even they own many year working experiences in any one of above these occupations. If the employer feels the labour is unskilled or below skilled level for any one of these occupations in these any one industry aspect, e.g. wholesale and retal , human health, education, accomodaton and food , construction, professional activities, financial service , public administration, and defence, transportation etc. occupations. Then, these industries' unskilled or below skilled level workers' salaries will be lower level to compare the higher skilled workers who work in any one of these industries.

The reason why future employers need to employ skilled labours. One explanation for slow recovery in demand in negative impact on investment is a prolonged period of high unemployment. This is led to job weekers left labour market or became unemployable due. So, future low skillful level will be one important factor to cause unemployment in society as well as nowadays labours ought need consider whether their skills are needed to improve in order to avoid future competition in job market.

2.1 Why do future labours need to learn worldwide readiness skills

Future employers need employees own worldwide readiness skills, such as reading , writing and arithmatic. Why do employees need worldwide readiness skills? In the future, high economic growth countries need high wage positions, high opportunity jobs which need a large number of skills required of job candidates of these positions " job readinss" and not " job training" , which support developments of these importance and widely desired skills won't only support the success to high-opportunity positions, but also be developed for future success in the competitive global economy. Because real-time business intelligence is needed for the talent marketplace to employ talent employees. So, it explains that it will have many future employers hope to employ owning readiness skillful employees to help them to develop their businesse intelligently. Hence, present employees ought need to hard to train readiness skills to prepare whose future employers' job requirements in the future competitive global job market.

2.2 Why these occupations need readiness skills

In the future these occupations will need to raise readiness skills. For example, mathematical science, teachers (post-secondary), management analysts, computer and information systems, managers, first-line supervisors of construction traders, solar photovoltaic installers. All of these occupations , employers need staffs to own good readiness analytic ability to help them to do more accurate real-time business intelligent decisions. The representative occupations include oral and written communication skills, project management, teamwork, marketing and creativity . Moreover, they need to own specific technology skill, deep science and math or even most business skills as well as these skills are "soft" skills more than hard skills. These kinds of occupation employees need own cooperative effort, creativity, problem solving, detail orientation and integrity personal characteristics, which are relevant across all knowledge and domains.

Therefore, in the future, science, technology,engineering and mathematics relevant occupations need to own more readniness and analytic skills more than othe kinds of occupations. Because these organizations need those professionals on knowledge acquisition, literacy analysis, synthesis and critical thinking skills that will impact their organizations to bring more critical thinking beneficial team culture. These occupational top skills will include oral and written communication skills, project management skill, team oriented skill, marketing and creativity skills, problem solving skill, detail oriented skill, self-motivated skills, management and analytical skills, coaching skill, business process modeling skills, work independent skill, strong leadership skills, management experience and business requirements gathering. All of these skills which will be future employers who need to employ these kinds employees who own these skills in preference. Also, all of these skills concentrate on soft skills more than hard skills. It seems that when above occupational applicants who own any one of thes skills, evn more than one skills. Then, he/she will have more chance to be selected to employ. Also occupation specific skills requirements are more needed to compare cross-functional skills for above of any one occupation. Because the high concentraton of cross-functional skills require " job readiness" and not " job training" for success, e.g. communicaton, integraton and presentation skills, entrepreneurialism and related skills, microsoft office software skills.

Of particular interest is communication, integration and presentation skills. These skills include ability to seek, evaluate and examine information and data create a reasoned position, present findings and make a case for or advocate for position. So, these skills are very important and they can help future applicants who expect to win any kinds of these positions easily. However, the hard skills can help these applicants to be more successful to win any kinds of these positions when they own these hard skills, e.g. microsoft offic, powerpoint, excel , word, microsoft project etc. softwares.

In conclusion, the global economy is dynamic and many of the skills required for positons in the future will need good technologies and work practices to be developed. The number of skills required t be successful in the jobs forecast to be most in demand in the future is growing. So, it explains that why future any one of these occupations which will need soft skills more than hard skills, due to organizations like to employ the employees who own managerial and analytical effort more than hard skills productive effort to assist their organizations to develop more easily.

2.3 Data -analysis skill needs

In the future, most organizations will have a number of jobs that include data analysis. Economists and labor market forecasters predict occupations need data analytical skill will need much. In addition, fast technological development means th types of technologies and applications workers in this field will need to be familiar with data analytical skill rapidly. It seems that data analytical jobs will have new job opportunity to employees with in-demand skills in future global labor market.

Why and how do employers demand for data analysis skills? Data analysis skills mean the ability to gather, analyze and draw practical conclusions from data as well as communicate data findings to others. The occupations include: data analyst, data scientist, statistician, market research analyst, financial analyst,research manager. In business career, many employers expect to employ statisticans, operations researh analysts, market research analysts and marketing specialists to assist their organizations to gather useful data from market in order to analyze and draw practical conclusions and finding the best solutions or methods to win their competitors.

Therefore, these data analysis jobs will have much need. Large size organizations with 500 or more employees were more likely than small or medium size organizations with 25 to 499 employees to plan hired data analysis positons in the future. For example, human source department will use big data to help make strategic decisions. How HR uses big data . HR will use big data for sourcing, recruitment, or selection, identifying causes of turnover and/or employee retention strategies or trends, managing talent and performance. Why organizations do not use big data. It is possible that they lack of knowledg expertise, the majority of organizatons will have data analysis positions within accounting and finance department, human resources department, business and administration department, information technology department, marketing, advertising and sales department, supply chain and operations department, research and development department, customer service department and other departments. So, future data analysis skill will need to used in different organizational departments.

However, publicly and privately owned for-profit organizations were more likely than government organizations to have data analysis positions in the marketing, advertising and sales function. Also, data analysis skills are required to different levels in any organizations , such as entry level, non-management / individual contributor level, mid-level management level, seniot management or executive level. The analyst, research analyst, market research analyst, scientist-based titles include: data scientists , research scientist, scientist, other descriptive titles include researcher, statistician, mathematician and other . So, data analysis positions will have many different skills to be selected to any one data analysis professional. For example, the data analysis professional can select either to learn the ability to interpret and communicate data analysis results skill or to learn how gathering or analyzing data skill. So, data analysis skill is not onlyone skill, it is more than one skill to let any one employee to select to learn.

Why do organizations need data analysis professionals? On workforce planning aspect, organizatons expect to let strategic direction and content of workforce needed for future business objectives easier, analyzing workforce:

supply analysis, demand analsis and gap analysis more earier, developing action plan : recruiting and training plans to deal with gaps more easier, implementing action plan, monitoring, evaluating and revising plan more easier. So, organizations expect the data analysis professionsla can help them to solve these challenges, such as using of advanced technology solutons to integrate disparate planning sources; data availability and format; accessing to and understanding of the organization's data and analytics, developing business case to gain support from senior management and collaboration among HR staff, managers and executive easier. Future industries need data analysis professionals may include manufacturing health care and social assistance, scientific and technical service, finance and insurance, educational services , government agencies, retail trade, transportation and warehousing, construction, utilities, accomodation, and food services, waste management and remediation services, entetainment, and creation, real estate and rental and leasing , repair and maintenance, agriculture, forestry, fishing and hunting, personal and laundry services etc.

In conclusion, data analysis job need explains why future readiness and data analytical skills will be popular needed in globl labour market , due to these both skills are labour shortage and employers will need employees own big data readiness and data analytical both skills in order to win whose competitors more easier.

2.4 What are regional dynamic skills
of global labour market demand

Businessmen expect to improve better economic environment, they will prefer to recruit the most sought after skills of intelligent employees to bring positive beneficial impact to organizations. However, technology and digisation has had a significant influence on workers. Future globalization will trend digital economic development. Hence, it will influence workers' skills to be changed also. In fact, not all changes are positive because some workers will possible lose jobs, either due to new technology replaces their jobs or they lack enough effort to improve their skills in global digital economic labour market environment.

It brings this question: What are regional dynamic skills need whn digital busines environment is growing. In fact, organizations will continue to deal with skills shortages, labour markets across the global are continually changing. so, more employers and workers will need to adopt innovate working pattern, e.g. on call jobs, freelance jobs will grow popularly. The greater flexibility afforded to employ regardly.

Finally, digitalisation includes artificial intelligence, big data , online platforms. All these new technology will influence future employees how to worker. For example, they can apply online platform to work at home conveniently. So, they do not need to go to offices. They can finish their jobs and send to their employers by email easily. This kinds of job pattern can raise efficiencies and employers do not need go to offices often.

An important implication of innovating working which needs the employees who own digital skills in order to serve organizations more efficiently. So, employers are increasingly able to access demographics that were hitherto less active in labour markets. For example, future more women are joining the labour market because part time and self employment opportunities make it easier. This kinds of job pattern can raise efficiencies and employees do not need go to offices often.

An important implication of innovating working which needs the employees who own digital skills in order to serve organizations more efficiently. So, employers are increasingly able to access demographic that were hitherto less active in labour markets. For example, future more women are joining the labour market because part time and self employment opportunities make it easier to manage family with work life. So, digital skilling needs will cause many women lose jobs in possible. If the women lack digital job skills. Because high digital skill occupations need, like those requiring research, medical treatment and architectural design occupational digital skills are more common in the services sector, more women who own digital skill who can compete to win.

High digital skill occupations more easier than men because employers usually select female to do high skill occupations easier than make. However, if those professional service female employees can not learn how to apply digital skills to do these researchs medical treatmentm architectural design professional service jobs. Then, it is also different for these professional service femal employees to raise competition in global labour professional service market. So, these professional service female employees need to learn how to apply digital to do themselves jobs in future global professional service labour market. Otherwise, if the male professional service employees can attempt to learn how to apply digital skill to do themselves jobs in order to improve efficiencies and service performance to satisfy patients, such as medical service needs, school search service needs, construction firms' building needs. Then, the owning high digital technology skillful female employees will be more easier to find the professional service jobs which need digital skill more easier than the lacking digital skill female service professionals in future global digital service professional labour market.

On the other robotic communication skill need aspect, future employers expect workers to know how to communicate with robots to work efficiently in any working environment if the employers need robotc to serve their organizations. For example, communication between the robots on factory floors, and between people and robots could allow robots to start and stopr processes based on real-time conditions around them and alert people when there is a problem, so robots could increase their own efficiency if the workers could monitor themselves and determine when they needed maintenance; efficiency would also be improved if machines and robots could make production decisions on their own by. For example, ordering new suppliers when existing inputs into a production process run low. The increase in productivity of industrial robots will likely reduce the number of manual jobs on the shop floor.

At the same time, the increased output made possible by such robots will mean that manufacturers need more people in accounting, finance, sales, advertising and other roles. The increase in putput may also drive increased employment on manufacturers' supply chains. Hence, future employers expect to employ the workers who can know how to communicate with robots to work efficiently in order to raise productivity in any working environment. It means that it the worker can know how to control and communicate with the robots to work together in the team. Then, his/her communication and controlling robotic skill will help the organization's team to work efficiently and raise productivity in order to reduce time waste and human waste and resource waste considerately. So, future shortage of communication and controlling robotic skillful workers number will increase. It has much beneficial to workers who choose to attempt to learn how to communicate and control robots to work together in any working environment team efficiently. Because future employers will like to use robots to assist manual workers to attempt to raise productive efficiency in any working environment. So, the need of employees who know how to cooperate or communicate with robots whose talent skills will be useful to any future employers.

Future global business leaders will need human machine cooperation skill. This technological skill includes artificial intelligence (AI and internet of things (IOT), will reshape our working change. These machines will participate to our daily working environment. For instance, many business leaders agree that automated systems will free-up their time as well as they also believe they'll have more job satisfaction by offloading the tasks that they don't want to do to intelligent machines.

Therefore, future leaders will expect humans and machines can work as integrated teams within their organizaton in order to their workforce and machines are already successfully working this way. So, they need to expect future employees can know or learn how to work with automated systems more easily, because many jobs will be participated by automated systems, e..g simple accounting tasks, legal administration tasks etc. clerical tasks. They will be participated with (AI) technology, it learns how to cooperate with (AI) technology to finish simplt clerical tasks efficiently.

Future workers will need have autrmated system operational skills: They include that how to operate automated systems to free -up workers' time. Workers will need to learn how to operate automated system to better with healthcare tracking devices workers will need to learn how to operate automated systems to absord and manage information in completely different ways. Workers will need to learn how to operate automated systems of smart machines to work as admin. in any orking environments. Workers need be needed to learn how to operate (AI) automated machines to mak more accurate clerical tasks or efficiencies. So, the automated system (robotic) operational skillful workers' demand and number will increase.

In the future, employers need automated machine manufacturing and service with workers cooperation reasons include that clear protocols, will need to be established if autonomous machines fail. So, they need their workers to learn how to control and manage and communicate with autonomous machines skillfully. They believe move they

depend upon technology, the more they'll have to lose in the event of a cyber attack. So, skillful workers are real required to let them to know how to cooperate with autonomous machines more efficiently and easily. Computers will need to be able to decipher between good and bad commands, so future employers have much chance to need the owning automated machines operating workers to assist any robots to make more accurate good or bad decision when robots and workers have need to make immediate judgement in their any related job responsibilites aspect.
Therefore, future owning automated machines operating workers' skillful level will be high. It bases on automated machine manufacturing environment trend factor. Finally, future technology will connect the right employee to the high task at the right time. It implies that when future global employers began to accept to apply robots to help them to raise any productivities efficiently. It will influence many manufacturing positions which need to employ any proficient skillful workers who own automated machines operational skills to know how to communicate or manage or control , even supervise any robots to work in teams in any organizational manufacturing environment efficiently.
In the future, employers also expect employees to own sufficient digital vision and strategic skills, manifest among other things. They can know how to apply data to demonstrate any senior support and sponsorship digital technological skill. They expect to reduce a skill gap and avoid a lack of employee buying and a workforce culture to change in their digital technologicl manufacturing organizations. Future employers also believe outdated technology that can't work fast enough, data overload, privary and security concerns. So, it explains why it is possible that future employers also need digital working environment and automated robots machines to attempt to achieve raising productive efficient aim.
Moreover, it also explains why digital transformation need will be raised. The reasons include: They feel digital technology can gain employees‘ buying in , making customer experience a boardroom concern, achieving fair compensation , training and goals and strategy achievement more easily, tasking senior leaders with digital working environment change putting policies and technology to support a fully remote, flexible workforce , empowering lines of team work more efficient, teaching all employees how to code/understanding how to adopt to work with automatic machines or rots in any team efficiently. So, automate machine can raise efficiency in manufacturing society.
In conclusion, in the future business society, employees need to be stronger human machine partnerships. So , future manufacturing or service industries will have digital technology and automated machine robotic technology to assist workers to work in any working environment efficiently. They expect digital technology and automated machine robotic technology anticipation to workers' daily jobs in order to bring positive impacting to the customer experience from business owners to decision makers in marketing, customer service, research and developmnt and finance etc. They also expect technological productivity can bring positive relationship between technology and workers emerging technologies‘ impact on business and the way workers and automated machine work together.

In the future whether in general organizations need what kinds of employees' skills, they expect employee individual own. It is one interesting question. The common skills that employees need to own in order to any duties to any organizational departments efficiently, e.g. human resource, marketing, administrative, logistic etc. different departments. For hospital, school, business, professional occupations etc. different organizations. Whether future school ought implement one system educational method to teach different common skills to students in order to let them to leave schools to jobs more easier.
Future employers need to create new technologies including automation and algorithms, in order to create new high quality jobs and improve the job quality and productivity of the existing work of human employees in any organizations, e.g. accounting department will need intelligence (AI) to assist account clerks to do simple repeating accounting job tasks in order to share their work load and raise performance efficiency or legal organizations will need (AI) to assist law clerks to do simple repeating legal draft or legal document revising job tasks . All future general clerical jobs will apply (AI) technological tools to assist human to job, it will produce a comprehensive platform for managing workforce change.
Hence, human manual(employees) need to learn how to adopt (AI) job participation to assist them to do different kinds of simple clerical jobs in any organizational administrative departments . They , clerical employees or white color workers need to learn how manage or dominate (AI) tool to improve job performance to be better. However,

(AI) administrative workforce change, it is not only one kind of job automation change role in any physical offices. It influences future administrative clerks need change a more flexible manner, utilizing remote staffing beyond physical offices and decentralization of operations organizational workforce change.
Instead of (AI) participation to administrative job aspect, (AI) will also participate to manufacturing industry environment aspect, a new human-machine manufacturing workforce change will exist to any factories, warehouses working environment. Scientists predict that in present an average of 71% of total task hours across the industries are performed by humans, compared a 29% by machines. In this average is expected to have shifted to 58% task hours performed by humans and 42% by machines. In fact, nowadays, in terms of total working hours, no work task was yet estimated to be predominantly performed by a machine or an algorithm (AI). But, this picture is predicted to have somewhat changed with machines and algorithms (AI) on average increasing their contribution to specific tasks by 57% . For example, in the future, 62% of organization's information and data processing and information search and transmission tasks will be performed by machines compared to 46% today.
Therefore, these high technological skillful job change will bring negative influence to some demotive-skillful or low skillful labors to be dismissed, if they can not upgrade or raise or reskillgul their skill level to improve their analytical thinking , technology design and programming skills to cooperate with (AI) tools to work efficiently together in any organizational manufacturing or offie work environment. Because it will have many employers apply (AI) automation tools to participate with blue -color or whiate -color workers' tasks in order to raise efficiencies or improve performance in any working environment. So, it is right time to young or mid age employees need to upskill and/or reskill their rihgt type of skills to prepare future technology risch work environment changeing needs.
Future technological advances will permit an increasing number of tasks traditionally performed by humans to become automated. It seems that , such automation focused primarily on routine tasks, e.g. clerical work, bookkeeping, basic paralegal work and reporting etc. However, with the advent of big data, artificial intelligence (AI), the internet of things and ever-increasing computing power , i.e. the digital revolutions, non-routine tasks are also increasingly likely to become automated. For example, the recent development in robotics and 3D printing allow firms in advanced economies to locate production closer to domestic markets in fully aumomated factories. As a result, the future strongest incentive to automate because of their relatively higher labour costs will be reduced, when production automated will bring the negative influence to dismiss some foolish or low produtive or low skill workers , the owning high automated productive skillful workers will replace the low productive skillful workers in any factories' manufacturing environments. So, technological progress participates to raise quantity of jobs will cause result in significant job losses to low skillful workers. Because future employers will need many high automated productive employees to help them to cooperate with (AI) automated machine to work together efficiently. For example, many proportion of occupations at high risk is greatest in Germany and lowest in Korea, these countries organizations will accept to spend technology investments and education of workers to prepare future automatability manufacturing development successfully.
However, future automatability manufacturing development will bring technological unemployment in possible, due to workers need to adjust to the challenge of automation by switching tasks. Thus, preventing technological unemployment, also technological change does not just destroy jobs, but also generates new roles through its effect on productivity and the demand for new technologies. For example, it has been estimated that, for each high tech-job created in the industries , such as computing equipment or electrical machinery, some 4.9 % additional jobs are created for lawyers, taxi, drivers and waites in the local economy (Moretti, 2011).
Therefore, automated will also influence service industries' job nature change, e.g. taxi drivers need to apply (AI) automated machines to assist them to drive their taxis. When the passenger tells the taxi driver where he/she wants to go. Then, the (AI automated machine will follow the GPS road direction map to be indicated how to drive the taxi to go to the destination automatically . So, future taxi driver is one assistance role to assist the (AI) automated driving tool to dominate the (AI) tool to drive the taxi to catch the passenger to arrive the destination safety in the short time in possible. For another example, future restaurant waiters will need (AI) automated machines's assistance to help them to deliver or dispatch any foods and soft drinks to send to the identified eater's table carefully in accurate and efficient service performance way from the kitchen, in especially in the busy time and many people are sitting in

the large size restaurant environment. So, future, waiter roles will be the leader , they need to manage or control or supervise the (AI) robotics how to make decisions to arrange to dispatch which foods or soft drinks to the different tables in preference immediately. Also, future law clerks need to supervise or manage the law robotics how to help them to make decisions to do revision or draft or filing legal tasks in preference in order to avoid any typing words are mistaken to type on computers or revised draft in wrong way to assist manual legal clerks' mistaken words are appearanced on any legal documents. So, the law clerk future role will be the trainer role , he/she eeds to teacher the robots how to check any words, e.g. grammers to correct them to be right grammers, or giving the accurate revision legal documents' instruction to let the legal robots to know how to revise each legal draft to prove whether which part of the legal draft will have wrong to be needed to revise.

In conclusion, future many manual workers' service or manfacturing job natures will become automated assistance to robotics. So, employees need to upgrade their skills in order to adopt new technological work nature change.Such as Amazon is one super ecommerce organization, it ought need all different departments staffs prepare to ungrade their different kinds of skills, e.g. reading skills for KDP publish review book tasks in order to let authors can have more attractive topics to let readers can buy any Amazon ebooks to read. So, reading skills may be the essential element to Amazon any one book review staff in itself online publish business. Even ebook ecommerce platform design whether Amazon KDP publish online platform can attract to let global readers to feel enjoyment to read its ebooks , it is one essential element to help Amazon to increase e-readers number every day, so Amazon publish platform needs to improve itself ebook reading platform design improve to attract many e-readers like to choose Amazon e-reading platform to read Amazon any authors ebooks. So, E-reading platform design staffs need to upgrade themselves e-reading platform design skills. So, Amazon knolwedge workers number must need to increase in order to continue to improve its e-platform design to attract global e-reading customers or e-shoppers choose to buy Amazon any kinds of products.

Reference

Moretti, E. (2011) local labor market in O, Ashentelter and D. Card (eds.) handbook of labor economics, Elsevier, North Halland.

CHAPTER FIVE

Amazon organization resource management strategy

Organization tangible and intangible resources function

Any organizations must have tangible and intangible resources. Tangible resources may include: Staffs, lands, equipment, producing machines, factory etc. They may help organizations to produce products or provide services to earn profit, e.g. one shop may be the firm's tangible assets if it can be designed to be the best and provide soft music to let customers to listen and provide clourful light design , they may influence they to bring happy consumption emotion in order to attract many customers to stay long time in the shop and increases shopping chance, the salespeople (staffs) to attract more customers , they may be influenced to feel enjoy to stay long long time by their services. Although, any customers visit any shops , it must not represent that they quarantee to buy any things before they leave the shop. However, I beleive that any business , their products functions and prices is one influential factor to persuade consumers to do shopping activities, their shop design attraction feeling may be also another main factor to persuade them to do shopping decision because when the consumer feels the shop is comfortable , it will cause he/she feels enjoyable to stay long time in the shop. Consequently, shop design attraction may be another influential intangible resource factor to encourage consumers to buy any things easily, if they can be influenced to stay long time in the shop by the ship design attraction. It is one kind of feeling factor to excite consumers to do shopping decision. SO, shop may be one important organization fixed asset resource to influence consumer individual purchase desire in any business environment. It is one good exmaple organizational tangible fixed asset redsource to help any organizations to create income.

The another kind of intangible resources, they are not seen by any customers and they can not be toughed by any customers. BUt they are organizational resources, they also may help any organizations to earn income. Why can intangible resource help organizations to earn income? I shall explain as below:

Customer services and staff skills, they may be organiztional intangible resources and they may help any organizations to create income. For example, when one shop has one kindly and friendly salespeople, when any one customer enters this shop, he will say" Good morning", " Good afternoon", "Good night" and when the customer leaves this shop, he will say " Goodby". Even, when the customer has not bought any thing till to leave this shop, this salesperson also speaks " Goodby". So, all of shop visitors, when the salesperson sees them, he must speaks above words, so any one must feel he is polite person and he can represents this shop's polite image also. Although, some shop visitors do not buy anything when they are staying in this shop, but they must feel that this salesperson's attitude is polite to let them to feel. THis salesperson can bring happy feeling to let all shop visitors feel. So, he must not be complainted easily, because when this salesperson discovers any one person is staying to close to any one producg shelf location in the shop, he will walk to the person to enquire him" DO you need I help you?" politely. Although, it is possible that this person won't need this salesperson to help him, but this salesperson can let this shop visitor to feel that he does not need find any one salesperson to enquire when he feels that he needs purchase help, e.g. whether the shirt has small size stock, or the shoe has organge colour etc. product information enquiries. SO, this salesperson can let this shop visitor feels he can take care to his purchase choice behavior and he can do and purchase help in this shop any time. So, this salesperson , his excellent service performance can let any one shop visitor feels service satisfaction, instead of his essential sale customer service performance. IN fact, this salesperson may let many shop visitors to feel that he does not only considerate whether whom is his real customer in order to enquire any purchase help. The non purchase plan shop visitors may also feel his kindly customer service help during they are staying in shop any time. So, this salesperson's polite and kindly customer service attitude may influence many non purchase planning shop visitors feel happy to see him in this shop. Consequently, it explains why salespeople excellent customer service performance which may help any businesses to increase customers number. It may be one kind of intangible organization resource to any organizations. I mean that when the shop can train many salespeople to raise customer service sale performance improvement.

Overall, these excellent customer service salespeople mus thelp this business to increase customer number easily, because this shop's all salespeople thier positive emotion may influence any one shop visitor feels enjoyment when they can feel they are taking care to their purchase choice need when they are staying in this shop any time. So, the minute, that the shop visitor does not plan to choose to buy any kinds of products, it does not represent that he does not plan to choose to buy any kinds of products next minute. So, any salespeople their excellent customer service performance may influence any one shop visitor to do purchase planning decision any minute. It seems that " salespeople customer service performance feeling" may be one kind of long time intangible resource to help any businesses to earn income in possible. Hence, it explains that any organizations must have tangible and intangible organizational resources to assist them to develop their businesses in long time success. They are essential elelments to influence whether the business's customers number can increase or decrease.

For computer sale business example, its tangible resource may be computer shop and intangible resource may be computer salespeople skills, because if any visitors feel this computer shop's computer desktop or laptop products can be putted in the right and easy seeking locations on any shelves, e.g. the low range price of laptops or desktops are putted on the lowest shelf position as well as the high range price of laptops or desktops are putted on the highest shelf position. So, when the planning purchase of desktop or laptop shop visitors may compare the different design of laptops or desktops their low range price or their high and low shelves locations easily. So, laptops and desktops putting on shelves position, they may influence any one desktop or laptop buyer individual final purchase choice decision. If the laptop planning purchase visitor, he plans to buy one low price of laptop, when he discovers there are all low range price of laptops are putting on the shelf loe position. Then , he may feel convenience to choose any one kind of low price of laptop design products from the lowest range shelf location easily. So, computer shops' computer putting shelves positions may be one kind tangible resource factor to influence any one computer buyer to choose any one kind of design of laptop or desktop priduct convenience. Their computer product choice time whether it is long or short may influence their final computer purchase decision. Hence, the shop's computers ' putting on shelves positions may be one essential tangible resources to influence any one computer visitor to do purchase decision.

The computer shop salespeople computer knowledge may be another intangible factor to influence any one computer buyer decision. For example, when one planning laptop purchaser wants to know whether the laptop's any function, if he enquiries to the computer salesperson, he ften let him to feel that his explanation can not satisfy his any enquiries about the design of laptop product function knowledge, e.g. how to set up password for this computer privacy. If the computer salesperson lets the planning computer buyer to feel that he is difficult to teach him how to set up the passwrod for the computer to use. Then, the computer salesperson's innocence of computer password set up knowledge which may influence the planning computer buyers makes final non purchase decision to this computer, because his innocence can let him to feel this computer is difficult to set up password , if he is one foolish computer user.

Hence, this computer shop's all computer salespeople their computer knowledge, they may influence any one computer buyer final purchase decision. They must need to be trained to learn how to use any one new design of desktop or latop computer products before they are employed to be salespeople in this computer shop 。 SO, their computer knowledge may be this computer shop's intangible resource to influence this computer shop's customers number to increase or decrease every day. Hence, decision on any organizational tangible and intangible resources to the organization, they depend on whether what kind of the business needs to sell what kinds of products.

The organization is where resources come together . Organizations use different resources to accompolish goals, e.g. human resources, financial resources, physical resources, and information resources. SO, managers are responsible

for managing the resources to accomplish goals. Organizational resources are all assets that are available to a firm for use during the production process. The four basic types of organizational resources are human, monetary, raw material and capital. Managing organizational resources is the ability to understand and effectively manage organizational resources (e.e. people, materials assets , budget). This is demonstrated through measurement, planning and control of resources to maximize resources.
Company resources include tangible assets , such as its plant, equipment, finances, and location, human assets , in terms of the number of empllyees, their skills and motivation and intangible assets (such as technology, patents and copyrights, culture and reputation).

It brings this question: What makes organizational resource unique, in resource based view? Resources are available when they allow a firm to take advantage of opportunities or threats in its external environment. Many resources can either be immitated or substituted over time to any organizations. Hence, effectively managing resources helps companies more consistently deliver projects and services on time. This is because better resource management helps to improve insight into resources availability as well as improves timeline projections. Hence, the types of resources in management they may include: Human resource, natural resource, project resource, financial management, facility management, entertrise asset, public asset management.ON conclusion, I believe that a company's most important resources may be human captial, such as talent employees, their technical knowledge may be intangible resource asset to help the organization to develop its business in longf term success.

Internet will be intangible technology knowledge resource to e-commerce organization

New economy brings new way of resource management. The old loyalty and job security -based organization changes, organizations know that the assets are largely made up employees (HRM), but many new organizations begin to believe technology is important assets, such as Amazon is global ecommerce delivery service organization. It seems internet high technology is its important intangible resource to help it earn global e-buyers number increases . So , many organizations began to believe that technology will be important resource, such as internet can provide online business chance. With all the businesses are taking full advantage of internet, for example, the US department estimates that the value of retail e-commerce in 2000 year was about $25 billion, which represents less than 1% of US retail sales. Despite this, interest in e-business remains high.

- Why internet may be main technology resource to organizations?

E-commere needs strategy in order to win competitors, questions include: What criteria do customers use to choose between our firms and competitors? How do the best employees decision whether to join? What business environment attracts and keeps the best suppliers making with our firms? What characteristics draw the most royal invesdtors to our firms? e.g. Amazon . com's web site and Wal-mart's can apply internet technology resource to create each e-store to let e-buyers to choose any kinds of products to buy athome conveniently. Hence, internet technology, even future other kinds of new technology may be main technology resources to organizations, when they can help organizations to raise sale competitive effort.
I mean that digital economy will be one kind new digital resource to future any organizations. The essential piece is the knowledge, it is what give it life and what makes it an interesting and fulifulling purchase and sale channel for people to spend their time , such as e-commerce virtual organization may be leaded to let purchase and ale transactions carry on easily from online websites. Hence, internet may be main knowledge management (intellectual capital) resource to any e-commerce organizations. It is about the storage, transfer knowledge.
For Amazon publish example, e-books will be knowledge as an object, like a book in library. Amazon can apply internet technology to help it to sell any author's ebooks from its book estores. So, ebooks are Amazon's knowledge resources to help it to create readers incomes. E-books is intangible knowledge resource to Amazon . Any authors' paper and ebooks will be sold cheap price to help Amazon to attract global readers to choose to buy its ebooks from its different countries e-webstores at home conveniently.
Hence, any e-commerce organizations also need HRM (emanagers) to help them to deliver a superior value (world class capabilities) in both te virtual and physical world. E-management will be another main human resources to e-commerce organizations. Why does e-management will be future main HRM resource to e-commerce organization?

The reasons may include:
E-management demands in sort of managerial/e-commerce sale strategy effort, skills at positioning the firm within a networm of industries, e-management also demands the ability to see how the firm fits into a value creation-e-management is different because doing it work requires the e-engineering of business eco-systems, e-management demands the ability to be connected to thousands of inputs about specific changes among many industry participants , such as suppliers , customers, employees, competitors, media and shareholders.
Effective e-management requires the ability to monitor developments that can change with unusually high frequency. However, it is also essential that e-managers distinguish between the few meaningful inputs and the many inputs that have limited significance, ability to sustain organizational change, effectie e-managers monitor changes in their markets. So, instead of e-commerce organizations need to employ talent e-managment staffs to help them to manage overall e-commerce organizations. E-leading staffs (HRM) is another main HRM need. E-leaders need to know how to design online brochures, e.g. online brochures simply involved putting a company's market materials on the web. in order to attract or persuade online buyers visit its websites and choose the most right price of product to buy easily. E-leaders need to lead front-office transactions which involved putting customer facing customers , such as placing on order on the web when leaving back-office activities, such as order fulfillment unchanged.
E-leaders also need to integrate online online purchase transactions in which a firm actually linked its front -office and back -office systems and processes in a fashion, e.g. most companies have developed online brochures , in order to let online advertisement tool to attract e-buyer individual purchase choice from its webstores. Hence, future any e-commerce organizations must need (HRM (e-leaders and e-managers) to help them to bring innovation in order to achieve maximize profit aim. So, internet webstores, e-leaders , e-managers may be future e-commerce organization main resources. So, e-commerce organizations, manages are actors at three levels: In the front line , as entrepreneurs, in the middle , as facilitators, and integrators, at the top as institution builders.
Hence, future new economical society, it creates e-commerce organizations number increases, when consumers began to accept online purchase transaction activities. Hence, it causes e-commerce began to feel internet (e-webstores, e-leaders, e-managers), they will be the most influential resources (intangible knowledge managment and tangible URM both resourcees to influence their success or failure.

- Why does e-commerce organization believe (e-webstore design, e-leaders and e-managers) will be main organizational resources?

The most important question: It asks when e-buyers visit their webstores, wo are their target customers and shich needs of theirs are their trying to satisfy? For exap,e many airlines , e.g. American airlines, China airlines began to feel online e-tickets sale channel is more easily than paper ticket shop sale channel, because many air passengers began to accept e-ticket/online ticket purchase choice more than visiting airline shops . They feel that they do not want to waste time to visit airline shops. They like to pre-book to buy e-ticket to pay from the airline e-websote conveniently. Hence, e-webstore design knowledge management , e-leaders and e-management webstore management skill will be future any one e-commerce organizations their main tangible and intangible resources (assets) to help their e-commerce businesses development.
On conclusion, I believe that the current economy is not a high-tech economy or an internet economy, not an m-commerce economy , but instead customer econoomy. Customers need to gather with information and access, they are demanding, fair, global price, they are demanding that compares deal with them using the distribution channel , they choose manufacturing direct and through dealers and retailers. Base on those factors, they encourage future many e-commerce organizations cause organization change traditional resouce concept, such as land, capital equipment, tangible resource began to change to e-commerce organization's intangibel and tangible resource, such as knowledge management to e-online web store design skills, e-leaders and e-managers e-stores sale management strategy and e-buyer product research and brochure online advertisement design skill. All of these knowledge management skill will be future organizations' main resources to help them to create new economic competition effort.

Organization resources defination

What are organizational resources ? What do organizational resources mean? What kinds of organizational resources

are needed? What negative impact may be influenced if organizations lack enough resources to influence organizational development? Does working time belong to organizational time resources to influence employee individual efficiency e.g. how arranging enough employee to do the identified task in the most short time in order to achieve the most efficient performane? I shall attempt to identify examples to explain above questions as below:
In general, organizational resources are all assets, that are available to a firm for use during the production process. The four basic types of organizational resources are human, monetary , raw materials and capital. Organizational resources are combined, used and transofrmed to finished products during the production process. For organizational human resource example, human resource activities full under the following five core functions: staffing, development, compensation, safety and health core functions.

● HR resource

HR conducts a wide variety of activities. However, in any organizations, the major resources used by organizations are often described as follow (1) human resources (2) financial respirces (3) physical resources and (4) information resources. Managers are responsible for acquring and managing the resources to accomplosh goals. Hence, in organizational HR aspect, it may include these function, such as retirement and selection, performance management , learning and development, succession planning, compensation and benefits, human resource information systems. Because considering that for many organizations employees themselves represent a significant cost to the business, if the organization can use its employees in efficiency.

Then, it can avoid human resource in excess or in surplus on wasting challenge. Then , its employee cost or salary can be reduced. I t means that it does not need to employ in excess employees number, but the organization can still achieve itself the most efficient performance. Hence, any organizations must need to learn how to avoid " in excess employees number supply or wasting employee working behaviors" challenge . Because if some tasks do not need many employees to work together, it can still be achieved efficiency . Then , the organization ought not employee too many or excess employees to finish the kind of task. Thus, learning how to use efficient human resources, it can help organizations to avoid wasting working time to any departments employees. For example, when one factory has limited land to be supplied to become warehouse in order to help it to keep sticks. If it has excess logistic or factory workers number. Then, they are wasting working time to do not important tasks in warehouse, it means that if the factory has only one warehouse, but its area is small, it can allow maximum 50 workers to stay in the warehouse , but the warehouse has above 100 workers are staying to deliver goods in the small warehouse . Then, they must not actieve the most efficiency , even their delivery or transport goods performance will be influenced to worse by noise and crowd warehouse working environment. Hence, excess employees number in any working environment, which can not improve organizational performance or riase efficiency any organizations can not neglect " excess employees number" organizatinal HR resource arranging issue.

The solution concerns arranging the most right or the most exact empllyees number in order to supply to any organizational departments. Then, the organization can avoid wasting employee individual talent, reducing employing cost, improvig performance, achieving the most efficiency. Resource capacity means resource pool who are available in the organization to take up to appropriate human resource arrangement to assist any departmental development in long term efficiency. Hence, organizational human rsources may become talent tangible assets or foolish tangible assets. It depends on how the organization's resource capacity tasks arrangement to every employee in different departments. If the organization neglects how to arrange every employee task in the most exact or the most appropriate employees number in the department.

The department's efficiency must be caused worse, because excess employees number, it can not help it to achieve the most efficiency aim, even it may influence the excess employees , themselves feel waste working hours to do the not essential or not important tasks. Then, the organization may cause talent employee to become foolish employee. Otherwise, the organization's efficiency to be worse, because when the department has not enough employees to work. Then , any one employee may feel hard to work, his/her emotion may be influenced to negative, then his/ her workig behavior may b inefficiency or lazy working. On consequence, the organization may bring economic loss, due to employee individual lasy working behavior, negative working emotion, even high working pressure may be caused, when one employee needs to do more , then the employee's task, but his/her salary can not increase. He/she will feel unfair to compare the another department employee, he /she does not need to spend long working hours or overtime to work per day. SO, any organization needs to avoid shortage employee supply or excess employee supply issue to any departments. Appropriare employees number is the best strategy in order to raise overall organizational efficiency.

● Time resource

Instead of human resource, land, raw material, earth natural resource, electricity, gas may be organization resources . Whether time may be organizational resources, organizational time management vires time as a scarce resource that must be invested as effectivity. Time is an infinite resource . If not properly managed on in an organization. It can have a negative impact on both employer's and employee's productivity. So, organizations should ensure that workers are well equipped to manage time in their duties.So, in management view, any organization managers must need to consider how to manage time, eg . how to arrange employees to work in different departments in order to achieve the most efficiency. They need to understand which resources are in short supply and focus on the prioritizing work across shared resources, they need agree on a common approach, they also need to realize resource management is an ongoing process. Thus, time is an often ignored but invaluable resource in any organization. All activities be it procurement.

An organization's time, in contrast, goes largely unmanaged. Although, phone calls, email, instant messages , meetings, they are general daily tasks to any organizations managers, but mangers need to know how to arrange the most urgent tasks in prior. For example, if the manager can not arrange a meeting to the discuss client tomorroe, as well as the manager needs to spend two hours to meeting with overall 200 employees to discuss how to solve improving efficiency challenge tomorroe. So, this manager needs to make choice whether he ought spend two hours meeting to the business client, or two hours meeting to 200 employees. If he chooses to meet the business client tomorrow, he will help his firm to win the important business chance, but he can not discuss how to improve efficiency in order to find the best method to let 200 employees to know tomorrow. Thus, tomorrow time management will be one importat time resource to the manager. The manager needs to arrange tomorrow two hours time how to plan business meting or efficiency imporvement meerting either to his 200 employees or the one business client. Because if the manager decided to meet the client, he must need to spend today time to aplan or organize how to arrange either business proposal content for the business client or organizational operational challenge questions and solutions for his 200 employees . So, today time management is also important time resource to influence tomorrow either the success business meeting or the organizational 200 employees meeting. So, it seems that time management may be one important resource to any managers more than general employees in any organizations. So, Amazon is one big organization, it employees global many staffs, it ought need to manage its different kinds intangible and tangible resources in order to achieve the most efficient departments operational aim.

Organization efficient using resources economic method

In behavioral economic view , any organizations can attempt to apply behavioral economy method to use resources efficiently. Organizational excellence framework performance measurement takes a systematic approach . One of the most effective ways of using resources and minimizing that use of work. Calculating task cost in the most efficient economic method to help organizations to reduce cost and avoid resources waste, e.g. using resource management software, technology, planning and taking a systematic approach , which aims to manage the most efficient steps to follow to finish or implement each task in the most shor time as well as avoiding excess employees number.

Organizational resource efficiency means using the organization's limited resources in a sustainable manner when minimising impacts on the organization performance. It allows the organization to create more with less and to deliver greater value with less money. HR, raw material, technology input to carry on any organizational resources efficiently ? Management is the process of using organizational resources to achieve organizational goals of using organizational resources to achieve organizational goals effectively and efficiently through planning , organizing , leading and controlling. An efficient organization makes the most productive use of its resource in the most short time and the most eficiency and the least cost aspects.

● What is efficient use of resources to any organizations in economics?

Economic efficiency implies an economic state in which every resource is optimially allocated to serve each individual or entity in the best way when minimizing waste and inefficiency. whan an economy is economically efficient, any changes made to assist one entity would harm another . Hence, budget how much spending on resources, e.g. employee saley, office and/or plant technological equipment facilities , before making resource expenditure spending decision. Budget is essnetial to help the organization to deduce resource using and excess purchase waste since budget and resource of organizations have interlock or interconnet relationship. If the organization can make exact udget, then it can avoid excess expenditure or waste resource to use. So, organizations need to acquire a talented resource pool , that can lead projects to success, when any kinds of resources are achieved to be supplied to use inn enough . For example, using an effective enterprise resource management system that delivers capabilities. Regardless of the approach and tools used, organizations must determine how to balance to use any kinds of resources efficiently. Thus, in organizational efficient resource using behavioral economy view, the organizational efficiency factor means that influences the efficiency of the organization's use if its resources can be both internal and external, e.g. how implementing strategic plans, they may include selecting what methods and resources to use, and leadning employees on guideline, working in coalitions with organizations around to deliver those needs in the most resource efficient way.

In organizational studies, resource managemetn is the efficient and one resource management technique of resource leveling, of finding the answers to the question, how to use available resource efficiently, effectively and economically ot organization resource expense. SO , resource management is the process of allocating resources and allocating.

- What is meant by economic using of resource to organizations?

Economic resources are the factors used in producing goods or providing services. Economic resources can be divied into human resources, such as labors and management, and non humann resource, such as land, capital , goods, finished resources and technology , for example, natural resource is a key input in the production process that stimulates economic growth. Natural resources have limited direct economic use in satisfying human need, but transforming them into goods and services enhances their economic value to the socirty. So, if the country has many organizations know how to use their natural resources input in that production processes. Then, they can create themselves economic benefits directly and attribute economic benefit to society indirectly.

Thus, the types of economic organizations can be identified, there are subsistence recipreocal exchange with subsistence, peasant with primary reliance on self-produced food, but containing some exhange elements, market-commercial , redistribution or state socialist. Thus organizations need to learn hoe to use themselves organizational resources efficiently. Organizational resources are all assets that are to a firm for use during the production process. The four basic types of organizational resources are human, monetary, raw material and capital. Organizational resources are combined , used and transformed into finished products during the production process. So, a business that understands how to use resources efficiently. resource management is the process of allocating resources in order for a company to grow easily.

Organizational economic is used to study transactions within individual firms and determine management approach to managing resources. It is broken down into thee major subjects: agency theory, transaction cost economic and property rights theory. Agency theory is a priinciple that is used to explain and resolve issues in the relationship between business principles and their agents. Most commonly, that relationship is the one between shareholders as principles, and company executives as agents. Agency theory is used to understand the relationship between agents and principals. The agent represents the principal in a particular business transaction and is expected to represent the best interests of the principal without regard for seld interest. So, when the relationship between shreholders and company executives is kept the best.

Transaction cost economic is understood as alternative modes of organizing transactions (governance structure, such as markets, firms and bureaus) that mininize transactions costs. This, cost is the primary determinant of such as firm's decision whether it is the most right (the best) or the worst decision. It will influence the firm ho to spend resource behavior. The cost other than the money price that are incurred in trading good and service. SO, if the organization can often make the best decision to carry on any activites. It will avoid to waste resources efficiently.

For example, if transaction cost influces the commission, paid to a stockbroker for completing a share deal and booking fee charges when purchase concert tickets. The cost of travel and time to complete an exhange , it means that transaction cost. So if the organization can make the best or the most reasonable decision to carry on any business activities. Then, its transaction cost can be influenced to reduce the most level in order to bring resources economic benefit. e.g. sunk costs are indpeendent of any event and should not resulting from economic trade in a market.
Property right theory means contracted choice, through ownership, property rights theour clarifies the firm's boundary choice. The maon egal property rights are the right of possession, the righ tof excession. So, for the efficiency of property rights al scarce resources are owned by someone. IN the right property rights approsed to the theory of the firm, I assume that in the case of sale ownership by party-property rights define the theoretical and legal ownership of resources and how resources can be used by organizatin. So, above three major organizational theories can assist organizations to know how to spend resources efficiently.

The relationship between organization resources using and social resources

Resources needers may include societies needers ,e.g. government house material householders , electricity , water , natural resources needers, schools, public houses , land number and area needs etc. as well as business organiztions , office building material, office, plant, land area, number need, equipment facilities limited number . So, when global office and plant business users need to buy more land, equipment materials etc. and electricity , water. Social resources number reduces to bring resourcee shortage challenge causes. Have they have shortage relationship (resource demand number is more than supply number) between social resources need and business resource need? I shall attempt to explain this question as below:
I assume global business organization number increases, they will need many natural resources, e.g. water, electricity, gas, land to supply for office, plant building , material and staff office electricity, gas, plant , office daily essential power need. So, when global business organizations number increases, they may need to use much raw material and natural resources for equipment facility, office plant building material, even day office, plant electricity , gas power, staff drinking water etc. basic office operational needs, when global business organizations number increase.
The question concerns whether they will cause natural resources shortage to supply to social need , when global business organizatins number increases. First, I shall explains what social resources needers mean as below:

● Social resource are defined as any concrete or symbolic term that

can be used as an object of exchange among people (Foa & Foa, 1980), money, information, goods and services both tangible items , such as are ususally defined the assessment of social need is of central allocation between organization needers and social citizen needers both stakeholders. So, when global human birth rate and life time increases, population number will increase, then their social resources need are also increasing, if global organizaions and population number are increasing in the same time, due to earth natural resources has limit number to supply in order to satisfy organizations and families daily resources need, e.g. building material resources are used to build either to build offices, plants or private houses , public house, lands resources are used either to build private or public houses or offices , plants , water is supplied to either office staffs drinking or families drinking, electricity , gas resources are limited to supply either offices plants use or families private or public houses use. Hence, due to all of earth, but in the same time, global offices , plants, government organizations and families numbers both stakeholders number is continue increasing. They have possible to encounter natural resources shortage issue when natural resources are using much, but they can nt manufacturers to increase by human easily.

● Can responding to resource scarcity help some kinds business grow?

Foe example, the food and agricultural business organizations, e.g. supermarkets, restaurants, they must send plactic material to manufacture plactic bags to supply to supermarket buyers to carry fruits, breads, mil, etc. foods when consumers need to buy the kinds of foods in any supermarkets, if plactic material supply number is decreasing, then a lot plactic bags can not supply to let buyers to carry their foods, due to plactic bags number is shortage , it will cause any supermarket buyers feel inconvenient when they need plactic bags to carry their foods, they choose to buy the kind of foods from supermarket to themselves homes.
So, if plactic bags manufacture material i shortage, it can not be manufactured to plactic bags to supply to global supermarket organizations. Then, the one supermarket can provide enough plactic bags to let them to carry their

foods from supermarkets to themselves homes conveniently. The focus on plactic bag resource scareity is not impossible to occur to supermarket organization case. If families are often using plactic bag to carry rubbish daily at home. Then, plactic bags number can not increase to satisfy global supermarkets food plactic bags and families themselves homes rubbish plactic bags both stakeholders need. Plastic bags can not be manufactured to supply to manufacture lot plactic bags supply to satisfy global families rubbish plactic bags home users and supermarkets food plactic bas users needs. Consequently, plactic bags prices may be influenced to increases, when plactic bags demand increases, but supply decreases. It is one good exaple to explain why plactic bag manufacturered material supply decreases, it may influence plactic bags number decreases and price increases, because families home rubbish plactic bags and supermarket food plastic bags need both increase.

Consequence, supermarket cost may be influenced , due to plastic bags number also increase much, if one day shortage of plactic manufacturing material supply number is shortage. So, it seems that food plastis bags using number, they have close relationship to impact supermarket food plastic bags price, if supermarkets lack enough plastic bag number supplies, then they need to increase food price, even the supermarket may lose customers , if it can not supply plastic bags to let them to use the supermarket itself plastic bags to carry fruits, ,ilk, soft drinks conveniently. Hence, plastic bag material may be one kind of important natureal resource for supermarkets, because any one consumer may be influenced to choose another supermarket when he/she feels the another supermarket can supply plastic bags to let him/her to carry on fruits, milks, soft drinks conveniently.

Another kind of natureal resource , such as steel material for restaurants , steel material can help global restaurants to manufacture kniefs, glass sups for restaurants customers to eat food or drink , if much steels are used to manufactured cars product to satisfy car drivers' driving lesiure need , then it may also influence restaurants s' knieves, glass cups price increases, due to cost increase, restaurants need to increase food price to compensate its knief, glass cups price. even, many families feel need to buy many gloass cups to drink water, then it may also influence global glass cups price increase. If one day steel material is shortage , this kind of natural resource must influence restaurants glass cups , knief cost increases. So, their general food price may be influenced to increase. It is not fair to global restaurants food consumers.

Hence, it explains resource shortage may influence some kinds of business cost increases, as well as consumer foods, products services price increases. It means that " resource shortage may influence some kinds of businesses cost increases".

In fact, in our societies, natural resource shortage may influence any kinds of business cost increases, w.g. car manufacturing industry, if one day stell manufacturing material is shortage. it will cause many car manufacturers can not buy enough steels to manufacture cars. When, global car buyers number increases, but global cars number can not increase rapidly, due to steel material can not supply enough. Then, cars prices may be influenced to raise. SO, it seems that steel resource shortage may bring reasonable chance to let global car manufacturers to raise cars prices. When , global car buyes ' new car purchase needs are increasing, hence, natural resource shortage may influence some kinds of business produce prices increase in possible, when the kind of product , such as many people begin to chose to buy new cars, more than second hand cars. The, when steel material supplies shortage, it may influence new car price increases in global can market.It means that any organizations ought not waste natural resource. Otherwise, it may influence their cost increases.

Environmental resource scarcity would likely have been adaptivve in the human evolitionary parst, resources in the environment and organization resource shortage problem might alsoo effect how satisfied they were. Hence, organizations in virtually every industry face the challenge of new managing resources effectively. The influence would run the other way instability as rival, such as big data platforms for e-commerce organizations, e.g. e-book publishers, online sellers. Big data platforms lift limitations on the size of computing resources that can be applied for data, in other words, data storage and e-commerce organizations can significantly influence computing efficiency.

Hence, organizational resources may also influence computer industry information gathering intangible resources, if the electronic books publish, or online electronic commerce product sellers can gather the most up-date consumer individual purchase behavioral data in short time daily rapidly. Then, they collect the most accurate electronic books readers or the kind of online product buyers past purchase choice in order to judge whther which topics of books are the most popular or which kinds of product to the most popular to let them to implement sale strategy, e.g. whether which topic of e-books prices need to be increased ot decreased, whether which kinds of products prices need to be increases or decreased. So, the big data gathering speed is the technology resource to e-commerce market organizations.

Amazon Organizational Intangible Management Resource Strategy

Management science how applies to Amazon ecommerce organization

Management accounting concept can help organizations to do management budget strategies, e.g. margin analysis, capital budget, inventory valuation and product cost budget, trend analysis and forecast . Management accounting also called managerial accounting or cost accounting, is the process of analysis business costs and operations to prepare internal financial report, records and managers decision making process in achieving business goals.

However, management accountants depend on standard financial statements containing the earning statement, cash flow statement and balance sheet. In addition , it also makes use of additional finds reports in analysizing the information of the organization including budget performance and cost reports. I shall attempt to explain how management account science can help organizations to analyze cost , why and how changes in order to avoid expense increases or excess cost cases or loss increases.

For Amazon e-commerce publish organization example, Amazon publish is a famous publish organization. It applies internet (online) channel to help authors to sell electronic books and paper books to different countries readers. It also cooperate to other publishers to deliver any its anthors books to their webstores, so when one reader chooses its publish partner webstores to buy Amazon any author books, then Amazon publish will share royalty income between them. Hence, Amazon publish may be book distribution partner to its other e-publish partners.

● How resource management can help Amazon publish to manage its cost effectively in order to increase its profit or e-books or paper books sale ability.

Amazon publish is a e-comerce organization. It depends high internet speed to help global authors to register Amazon publish's individual author account , then any global authors may download their book files to produce any ebooks and papers to sell from Amazon publisher webstores as wellas global any readers can apply Amazon publish webstores to buy any author individual paper or ebooks from its web-publish stores rapidly. So, Amazon publish must need have fast speed internet technology to support its books sale ability,

It brings this question: How much does Amazon publish internet expenditure need? Does it need to pay shops rent per month? Because Amazon publish has none any actual book shops to locate in any countries. So, Amazon publish must not pay rent to any countries for its shops. Although Amazon publish does not need to pay rent for any book shops, but Amazon publish needs to pay extra internet expenditure to US internet service provider to support its electronic webstores daily electronic books and paper books every purchase transaction, any countries author individual book electronic files download per day 24 hours . So, Amazon publish must need to pay more expenditure for internet service to support its authors and readers their electronic books and paper books purchase and sale transaction per day 24 hours.

As Amazon publish case, in its financial report indicates , it does not pay any book stores rent expenditure or book stores (shops) building building expediture on its profit and loss account, but Amazon publish must need to pay internet service expenditure to US internet service provider. Moreover, this internet service expenditure must be more amount, due to it needs to provide its webstores online book (electronic books and paper books) to sell and electronic library e-book lending service to global readers, 24 hours. Thus, internet service expenditure must be Amazon publish long-term influential transaction expenditure because, any electronic books and paper books, even e-library books borrow service and readers must need to pay visa card for borrowing book month service fee and purchase books from amazon publish e-publish webstores in any time every day.

Hence, Amazon publish must need have good management account strategy in order to predict whether different countries will have how many readers click to its different countries e-publish webstores to spend time to choose different authors books to buy or borrow to read from intenet channel. So, any countries readers budgeting number, readers reading habit behavior, e.g. US has about one million online readers click Amazon e-publish webstores , but it has only three thousands readers pay visa card to buy its ebooks and paper books from its Amazon electronic publish webstores, in this week , but next week, US has about seven thousands online readers click Amazon e-publish webstores, but it has three thousands readers pay visa card to buy its ebooks and paper books. Hence, it seems tha although this week has one million online readers click to Amazon publish electonic webstores to seek any books, but the book buyer number has only three thousands. Otherwise, although next week, it reduces three thousands e-readers click to visit Amazon e-publish webstores e-readers number , but it still keep same three thousand e-readers to choose to buy Amazon publish's books to read.

I assume that Amazon publish needs to pay a fixed internet service expenditure, e.g. US $500,000, but it design this e-publish webstores can help it to do its different countries e-publish webstores, their daily e-readers visiting number, daily electronic book and paper book sale number and daily e-readers visiting time statistics. It's electronic publish webstores can help it to record any countries' reading habits and reading taste , e.g. how many fiction , story books have sold in the week, how many non fiction books have sold in the week , e.g. business topic books have sold next week.

So, Amazon publish can use its e-publish webstores to gather above data in order to make author book topic sale choice, e.g. whether this week, US market ought sell how many consumer psychological topic book, US market ought sell how many management topic book next week. If this week US market can only sell one thousand consumer psychological topic book to compare its budget is less than one thousand consumer psychological topic books budget sale number reduces, e.g. in the week, there are two thousands readers choose to buy consumer psychological topic books from European market in this week. It implies that there are many European readers who like to read consumer behavior books recently. Hence, Amazon can attempt to concentrate on encouraging authors to write more consumer psychological books to let European readers to read within next several months.

Basic on above effects, Amazon needs to provide rapid internet service to European libraries, schools ,e-book partners to help them to promote Amazon consumer psychology topic books in order to let the European consumer psychological students, consumer psychology lecturers, consumer psychologists to know Amazon publish can provide more different topics concern consumer psychology research in order to increase Amazon 's consumer psychology book European market book buyers bumber.

As above case, I assume Amazon publish needs to pay a fixed internet service expenditure , e.g. US$500,000 per month. Amazon needs webstores to evaluate whether it is value, if it helps European schools, libraries organizations to pay internet fee, in order to let they can let many consumer psychology students and teachers and consumer psychologists to know that Amazon publish may have enough different consumer psychology books to be provided to European publish libraries, schools readers to read. For example, I assume next several month, Amazon publish needs to pay US two million internet service expenditure to global different European countries to help Amazon publish itself to promote its al different authors' consumer psychology topic books as well as it evaluates that it will sell different European countries; students , teachers and consumer psychologists readers, they have about three million readers at least choose to buy its one million consumer psychology topic authors; paper books and electronic books next several months as well as it also needs to evaluate whether it can earn more than US ten million at least royalty income after reducing author royalty from all European countries book markets.

Thus, if Amazon publish makes decision to help European countries schools, public libraries to pay internet expenditure to help it to advertise its one million consumer psychology topic authors electronic and paper books to sell. It must needs to pay fixed US$500,000 internet expenditure for Amazon publish its all e-bpublish webstores and it also needs to pay extra two million internet service expenditure for global all European countries libraries and schools per month. If next month, Amazon publish can earn more than US tem million at least royalty income after reducing author royalty from all European countries book market. Then, Amaozn publish ought attempt to make this internet service expenditure for all European schools, libraries organizations, if it had confidence to earn this royalty amount from European consumer psychology book readers, such as this Amazon publish.

On conclusion, , this Amazon publish organization case, it may attempt to apply management accounting science method to make book sale number budget, royalty income budget, even analysis to reader individual reading habit, book topic choices, book sale price evaluation in order to judge whether the kind or topic book ought concentrates on selling to which countries marekts, such as Amazin publish case, it also may choose different consumer psychology topic books to concentrate on selling to different European countries in next several months, if it can earn all European royalty income more than its internet service expenditure to European schools, libraries, then Amazon may attempt to make this decision. Otherwise, it won't be good decision.

Hence, it implies that management accounting is one kind of business management science, it can apply number to help any organizations to do right or reasonable reason more accurate as well as it is different to traditional financial acounting, it only helps organizations to record and income and expenditure, earn or loss record function. Hence, management accounting may help any organizations to attempt implement useful or effective strategies in order to improve themselves performance.

How resource management helps Amazon makes the most reasonable choice to invest different market ?

Can we apply management accounting concept to investment decision aspect? An organization's investment decision may make risk, so they need risk evaluation to decide whether the project can bring ehat benefit before they want any decisions. Risk management is the process of assessing, managing and mitigating losses . This applies to both business and investing risk management exists in many forms throughout the financial world, such as one individual investor decides to buy low risk government securities, instead of high yield corporate bonds in an example of risk managment companies and investors frequently use financial managment method like options, and future and strategies, like portfolio and investment diversification, in order to effectively manage risk.

For investment management strategy example, it is professional asset management of various securities, including shareholdings, bonds and other assets, such as real estate, in order to meet specified investment goals for the benefits of investors. Investors may be insurance companies, pension funds, corporations, charities, educational organizations or private invetors.

The term asset management is often used to refer to the management of investment funds. So managerial accounting is the process of identifications, measurement , analysis and interpretation of accounting information that helps business leaders make financial decisions and efficiently manage their day operation . The main objective of managerial accounting is to maximize profit and minimize losses . It is concerned with the presentation of data to predict inconsistencies in finances that help managers make important decisions, such as investment decision for Amazon publish book sale country market choice for which topic of books which are the most popular, in order to concentrate on selling the topic of books to the country market. So, Amazon publish needs to gather past different kinds for any one country, number data may include each author ebook and paper books sale prices, each author different book topic books sale number , in order t make which topic of book sale to which countries investment decision aims to increase readers number t o the country book sale market. So, Amazon publish may be apply these tools of management accounting to gather datas to concern book sale record. They may include: Financial accounting, financial statement analysis, book cost accounting, fund flow analysis , cash flow analysis, standard costing, marginal cost, budgetary control , management accounting tools.

● How intangible resource management skill helps Amazon publish to make investment decision?

The main aim of management accounting to investment includes planning, controlling and evaluating. Thus, the advatanges to investment may include; better decision making, increase business efficiency, simplify financial statement, raises profitability, motivates employees, cost control, reliability. Hence, management accounting means " mental accouting", it is a concept in the field of behavioral economies. Mental accouting refers to the different values of person places on the same amount of money, based on subjective criteria, often with detrimental results. Mental accouting is a concept in the field of behavioral economies. Developed by economist Richard H, it contends that individuals classify funds differently and therefore are prone to irrational decision making in their spending and investment behavior. It refers to the different values people value on money, based on subjective criteria, that often has detrimental results, mental (managerial)accounting decisions and behave in financially counterproductive or detrimental ways, such as funding a low interest savings account when carrying learge credit card balances, to avoid the mental (managerial) accounting bias, individuals should treat money as perfectly used tools when they allocate among different accounts, be it a budget account (everyday living expenses), a spending account or a wealth account (saving and investment). Also abother author indicates that managerial accounting means mental accounting, which appeared in the Journal of behavioral decision making, the begins with this definition, " mental accounting" is the set of lognitive operations used key individuals and households to organize, evaluate , and keep tracks of financial activities. He considers of how mental accounting leads to irrational spending and investment behavior.

I believe that Amazon publish may apply mental accounting concept to help it to predict whether which topic of books will be the most popular to sell to the country market more accurately. The reason concerns that it can apply all data gathering to analyze whether past has how many readers paid visa to buy the topic of electronic or paper books to prepare to the country , e.g. in this year, Jan. it had 40,000 readers buy fiction electronic books and paper books from Amazon publish US market website to read , it had 100,000 readers buy fiction electronic and paper books to read in European market website and the year Feb. It had 70,000 readers paper books from Amazon publish US market website, it had 200,000 and paper books from Amazon publish European market website. Now, it is Mar. So, Amazon publish may make assumption that fiction (story) topic book is accepted to read by American and European readers, due to US fiction readers had increased 30,000 number in past one month and European fiction readers had increased 100,000 number in past one month.

However, US and European readers number data is not enough to evaluate whether US and European fiction readers number may still keep to increase. It depends on other factors, e.g. fiction e-book and fiction paper book sale price, if one author's ficton's ebooks and paper books rising prices whether it will influence US and European fiction book buyers make book purchas decision to the author's any fictions. So, Amazon publish need s to make the author's past different kinds of fiction books sale prices record in order to judge whether his fiction book's variable price (changing price) will bring negative or positive impact to his readers' fiction book purchase decision. For exmaple, if the author (A)'s one fiction price increased 10% to ebook and paper book sale price between Jan and Feb. His fiction readers number won't be influenced to reduce, even his fiction readers number can still increase 10%. So, it implies that this author's fiction is attract or popular to US and Eurpopean fiction reader market. Amazon publish ought concentrate on helping this author (A) to advertise his fiction to let many US and European readers to know.Hence, it explains that Amazon publish may attempt to gather past every author individual writing book topic book sale proce whether it is increased or decreased how much %, book sale number in order to make book sale investment decision to concentrate on helping whom to advertise to sell to which book sale country market.

So, it seems that mental accounting concept can be applied to Amazon publish to help it to do any author individual book sale country market advertisement investment decision. For example, if Amazon publish can only spend US$10,000 advertieing expenditure to help author (A) to sell fictions to US and European both markets in Mar. , then it can help author (A) to increase 20% more fiction sale number to US and European both markets. This advertisement expenditure is worth to spend for this author (A) in fiction market.

Hence, it implies that mental accounting concept can be applied to publish investment market, such as choosing which country to sell which topic of books, e.g. US sells more which fiction or European sells more fiction or Japan sells more management business topic books or UK sells more consumer psychology business topic books. All of these issues will be any publisher's important book sale market decision . It may influence their royalty income because if the publisher makes wrong decision to sell not popular topic books to the country market, e.g. in the month, US ought have many business topic readers to choose any business topic books to buy from any publishers, if the publisher makes wrong decision to find many fiction authors to help it to increase fiction stock to prepare to sell to US book market. Then, excess fiction stock may cause low fiction price (fiction book supply or publisher's fiction stock number) is more than fiction book demand (readers). Otherwise, it can not increase business topic books royalty inocme to US book market, because it has not enough different topic, such as management, consumer psychology , accounting, economy , marketing topic business books stock to be putted on book shelves to let US readers to choose when they visit US any book shops in the month.

On conclusion, it explains why mental (managerial) accounting has close relationship to influence customer behavior in behavioral economy view. Mental accounting is a management science or behavioral science tool to help any businessmen to make the most effective or the most reasonable busines decision in nowadays society.

Management science accounting concept how to help Amazon to presict market changing

Accounting aims to help any organizations to record whether the year has what kinds of expenditures, how much of every kind of expenditure finds what factors to cause the kind of expenditure needs to be spent too much in order to avoid excess spending, measurement profict or loss level why what factors cause the year had loss or profit growth in order to achieve long term performance improvement or avoiding loss. Hence, accounting system is not only for bookkeeping record financial performance aim. Accougint may be one kind management science concept to be applied to explain why and how market changes in order to predict whether the company ought implement which strategies to grow up its business groth or increase clients number.

The question concerns why the organization can apply accounting concpet to predict how the market will change in order to avoid profit falls down or loss causes. I shall attempt to explain as below:

For a watch product sale organization example, this watch sale compay own 100 expensive price watch brand products stock to prepare to sell, their sale prices are between US$3,000 to US$5,000 , so the watch brand prices are below than US$3000, they belong to low prices. It has 100 low price watch brand products stock to prepare to sell. Hence, every month, it keeps exact 100 high price of brand watch products stock and exact 100 low price of brand watch products stoc to prepare to sell. I assume this watch company can sell 100 low price watches and 100 high price watches in this month, but next month, it can sell 50 low price watches and 0 high price watches. Hence, it means that next watch , low prices watches sale number falls 50 number and high price watches sale numbe falls 100 number. It ensures that this company's profit may be influenced to fall by the high and low watch price client reducing number factor. However, this company still lacks data to know whether its competitors ; watch price is the main factor to influence its watch buyers number reduces or whether other factors influence its watch buyers number reduces, e.g. whether its high and low watchs are attractive or not attractive to high its watch design buyers number reduces or whether smart phone product invention influences watch users begin feel watchs have not be importnt to help them, because smart phones have time record function, they can replace traditional watch products or this month has higher unemployment rate, so it causes people do not like spend easily , in special, watch is not one kind essential product. Hence, it seems that this watch company can investigate its every month whether its low and high price watch stock sale record in order to attempt tp find whether what are the main factor to cause its watch sale number increases or decreases? I shall follow above every possible points to be investigated by accounting concept in order to explain why its watch low and high price customer number sudden reduces.

I assume that this watch company's last month and this month every high and low price watch brand's sale prices are stable. So, it seems that the influential factor won't be its " increasing sale price" to cause its high and low watch price customers number sudden reduces. If it gathered data concerns its watch competitots similar famous watch brands of general price range. It discovered their general sale prices do not have much difference between itself and their famous brnad of watchs. Also, it discovered that their these famous brand high and low price watch sale number is more than its sale number, e.g. the another similar famous watch brand company can sell 200 high price watchs and 200 low price watchs last month and 400 high price watchs and 400 low prcice watch this month. So, it seems that its high and low price of watch is not main factor to influence its watch sale number, because its high and low price watch's their price level had not changeed within these two months . Moreove, its watchs manufacture material costs had not increased within these two months. So, it ensures that its profit falls must not be influenced by watch manufacture cost increasing factor. Hence, it may depends on its accounting record to conclude the main factors influence its high and low price watch sale number reduces, they may include; poor watch design feeling to watch buyers factor, smart phones increasing need factor, unemploymenr rate rising factor.

The next step concerns how this watch company can apply accounting concept to find whether the main factor is poor watch design feeling factor, or smart phones are popular accepted to replace watch product feeling factor, or rising unemployment rate factor which one influences it s high and low price range watch sale number decreases can apply accounting cencept to investigate which is the main factor to influences its watch sale number decreased in this two months? I shall attempt to confirm this possibility as below:

Firstly, I assume this watch company's accounting record has marketing promotion expenditure, its expenditure includes advertisement fee, exhibition expense only, however, in its expenditure group accounting record, it has none design expenditure with these two months. Hence, it seems that its high and low price range fanous brands watches had not been improved by its improvement design skill method in order to improve their watch style, picture, shape, colour, function , design to satisfy watch buyers'changing watch fashion need in this competitive market. Hence, it seems that poor watch design feeling factor may be one main factor to influence its watch sale number decreases. It implies that accounting record may help it to find lacking new fashion watch design factor may be one main influential factor to cause watch buyers choose to buy other similar famous brands' watch products.

Next, whether accounting concept can help this firm to judge whether smart phones influences its watch sale number? I assume that smart phone products had been selling more than 10 years in this country in this case indicates US country. So, smart phones mus be its long time similar time seeing function competitors in US. I assume that its past 10 years high and low price range famous brand watches sale number must be more than these two months as well as it had not increases high and low price range of watches prices within this 10 years. Hence, it can depend on its past 10 years accounting record to judge whether smart phones product invention may influence watch buyers number decreases within these two months. basic on its past 10 years , accouniting record indicated that its high and lw price range watch sale number had been increasing, and it s watch price had not beedn increased and its markting advertisement promotion expense had been reducing much within 10 years. Thus, its past watching expense and watch price sale amount and profit accounting record may help it to conclude that smart phone product sale to US market is not the main factor to influence its recent high and low price range watchs sale number falls.

Finally, I shall explain whether this watch company may apply accounting concept to explain whether this month's high unmployment rate factor can influence geeral watch buyers' consumption desire as below:

I assume that this watch company employed 20 watch salespeople and their salaries range are between US$2,000 to US $4,000 per month in the first years . It operated till to this month total 20 years . However, its accounting record indicated that its watch salespeople number had been increasing from 20 to 50 number recently and their salaries range had been increading between US$3,000 to US$6,000 permonth. Hence, within these 10 years , this watch company employees number and their salaries range had been continue increasing. . It may depend on its past 10 years accounting record for salespeople salaries and employee number to reflect whether higher unemployment rate is the main factor to influence its watch sale number reduces.

I assume that within these 10 years, its unemployment rare was between 1% to 10%, in US society , although it may had 1% to 10% young people unemployed within 10 years. But, this watch company, I could also increased salespeople employees number and their salaries could also increase more significantly, even their salaries had not decreased in these 10 years. Hence, its accounting record of salsepeople salaries increasing trend , it may reflect this US watch market's local and overseas watch buyer individual buying watch desires ought not be influenced by slight rising unemployment rate factor, it is based on that this watch company will like to increase salespeople employee number, when it discovered there were many potential watch buyers visited its any watch shops every day within past 10 years. Hence, it implies higher unemployment rare won't influence watch potential buyer individual visiting to any one watch shops in US within these 10 years. So, this watch company's past salespeople salaries, employees number, and their salaries rising range record can reflect whether US higher unemployment ratio level can influence its recent high and low price range of watchs sale number decreases in US local watch sale market.

On conclusion, we can depend this watch company past 10 years accounting record to judge whether which one may be the most main fluential factor to influence its recent watch sale number reduces. I make the final conclusion that its poor watch design feeling factor ought be its main factor to influence its recent watch sale number reduces, due to it had not spend any design expenditure to improve its watch style in order to attract many watch buyers' choices within these 10 years. So, I believe that accounting concept can help any companies to revise whether what factos influence their businessess to be better or worse, instead of general booking record function.

Accounting trademark loyalty theory

In accounting theory view, any organizational goodwill or trademark, they are intangible asset because they can not touch, they are the company name. However, when the organization grows up a long time, ususally more than 10 years, if they are famous when consumers choose to buy the kind of product, they will must remember, then the organization's trademark or goodwill, company names will become the company's intangible asset in their balance sheet , financial report, e.g. Cock Coke soft drink, " Coca Coke" may be this soft drink company's trademaek , intangible asset to this soft drink company. Because any country's soft drinkers, they must remember Coca Coke brand soft drink before they make any brands of soft drink purchase choice. The reason may be Coca Coke soft drink . Its brand had been popular to be accept to be the first soft drink choice to any countries people. Hence, Coca Coke soft drink compnay must put is brand name to be intanginle asset in balance sheet, (B/S),

Why does Coca Coke's brand name (intangible asset) value may increase or decrease in B/S. The reason is simple, when general consumers feel Coca Coka drink has better taste to compare other brands soft drinks. Then, they wil choose other brand soft driks to replace Coca Coke soft drink. So, if the year, Coca Coke's any taste of soft drinks sale number decreases, then it will feel its intangible asset of trademark value is devaluation, but if its soft drink sale number increases in this year. Its intangible asset of trademark value will increase in its B/S.

Hence, it explains why Coca Coke 's trade mark value can reflect its soft drink sale number whether it increases or decreases in the year. Thus, any firms mist hope their trademark , goodwill valuation can often increase every year. The question concerns how they can often keep their trademark valuation to increase? Can the firm increase sale number , it can represent that it has long term goodwill valuation increases? Can other factors influence or impact the firm's goodwill valuation changes? I shall attempt to give examples to explain these questions as below:

In fact, goodwill or trademark represents the company's familiity whether how many consumers can remember its brand name , when they choose to buy the kind of product . So, if the firm's products are famous in market, Its products must have many consumers can remember it before they choose to buy the kind of product. So, product's familiar to publish,which ill be one measurement tool to judge whether what may be its goodwill valuation. If there are many consumers remember its brand before they want to buy the kind of products, the firm ought raise its goodwill valuation. It may make market research to enquire whether consumer will choose to buy which brand of product among several similar brands of product. It many people choose to prefer to buy its brand. Then, its brand familiar level to publis will be high grade. It may raise to goodwill valuation inB/S.

So, I think that goodwill fact valuation can not be measured by sale number or sale price or profit or loss amount. It ought be measured by market familiar level. If the product can have many people know its brand exitence in market. Then, its goodwill , intangible asset valuation ought be increased. Otherwise, if there are not may people know or they are familiar its brand existence in market. Then, its probable valuation ought need to decrease . Hence, any firms' goodwill valuation ought reflect their market familiar level for standard.

Do you feel firm goodwill valuation can represent its market value or product sale effort? In accounting principle, goodwill valuation must be measured by money. For example, Coca Coke brand goodwill valuation, in fact, Coca Coke had not pay another in B/S. Its goodwill valuation increases, it is not due to it pays its firm pays cash to buy goodwill. It is due to its capital increase. But, in fact, it does not need to increase cash to capital balance amount in B/S. Because coca Coke has not increase its cash amount, due to goodwill valuation increases. Its goodwill valuation increases, it supposes that is capital amount also be influenced to increase. So, Coca Coke 's goodwill valuation can not represent it has profit growth. Goodwill valuation only represents it has profit growth. Goodwill valuation only represents Coca Coke's present market valuw whether it increases or decreases in soft drink market. It is not actual cash available value. So, why firms need have goodwill valuation. The reason is simple. If one day, the firm hopes to sell its busines to another. When the another potential business buyer feels this firm's goodwill valuation is high. It may persuade b make business purchase decision more easily. because he believes that there are many people are famkliar this product brnad , then they will choose to buy theis product in preference . So, good goodwill valuation can build good business sale image to help the firm can raise business sale price to anyone . Such as Coca Coke soft drink goodwill case, if it can keep high goodwill valuation, then it can persuade any businesses buyers accept to pay high business purchase price. so, B/S goodwill valuation may help any famous business to sell to anyone in the high business sale price more easily.

Can goodwill valuation help the firm to predict market environment changes? For Coca Coke soft drink case example, I assume that it estimated its goodwill valuation is US 3 million , but this year, it estimates its goodwill valuation falls down to US one million. What factors influence Coca Coke feels its goodwill valuation reduces US two million in this year? I believe that is current year goodwill valuatin falls, it has relationship to whole global soft drink taste changes to global soft drinkers. The factors influence global drink makes taste changes , they may include: global soft drinkers begin to dislike to choose to drink any brands of soft drink in preference, if they feel soft drink is one kind of bad health drink. They may choose to buy freash fruits to eat to replace any soft drink. I assume that the other soft drink brand companies' goodwill valuations are decrased. It means that if other soft drink brands‘ goodwill valuation can increase. Then, Coca Coke may believe that there are many soft drinkers prefer to choose other soft drink brands' soft drinks to drink. So, global soft drink markets still have competitive effort. Coco Coke nees to learn how to change its taste and let soft drinkers believe its soft drink can bring health to them to compare other soft drink brands. So, it seems that goodwill valuation also helps any organizations to eveluate how market changes to influence itself product sale effort. It explains why goodwill valuation is one kind of good market changing predictable tool t any businesses in accpunting concept, instead of sale business valuation measurement tool.

On conclusion, accounting principle or accounintg concept is not only be applied to bookkeeping financial record aspect. If the organization hopes to find what factors to influence its customer number or they hope to predict whether market will ought how to change to be netter or worse. It may attempt to investigate its past every year some kinds of expenditure amount record in order to find how any why the firm itself needed to pay more or less to the kind of expenditure. It aims to research what factors may influence its past and present expenditur changes in order to find whether what the most influential factors are influenced itself buyers number increases or decreases . Hence, accounting is one kind of makret research scientific method to any organizations.

Accounting science how predicts e-commerce consumer behavior

Cash e-commerce organizations apply accounting record to predict consumer behaviors? If it is true, how e-commerce organizations can use past accounting record to predict consumer behaviors? In general, e-commerce sale transactions must need any individual e-buyers to register higher address to their e-store in order to deliver products to any one-buyer homes. For Amazon e-commerce organization, when one China client buys a furniture from US Amazon e-commerce organization, when one China client buys a furniture from US Amazon e-store. The furniture is putted to Amazon US itself warehouse. So, when the China e-buyer pays visa to buy the furniture . He needs to register his address to amazon e-store. When amazon confirms that it can receive cash from the China e-buyer visa card, then amazon will deliver the furniture from US amazon warehouse to the China e-buyer home by plane.

So, amazon must have any e-buyer address record and the product sale price record for any one country e-buyer after it comfirms that the e-buye visa card has enough money to buy the product. Thus, amazon can apply past every online transaction to follow these data to do market research, they may include: which country person buys the product, what the product is, how much to the product price, how many of different product number e-buyer purchase within the year. So, amazon can collect all above data to analyze any one country has the highest e-buyer number,e.g. in the year, there ar one million US e-buyers number, there are two million China e-buyer number,which kind of products are the most popular, e.g. soap , computer, furniture, cloth, shoe, shirt, towel, electronic products etc. what the age range is, e.g. young , old, students , workpeople, they choose to buy the kind of product, how many number , the family buys the kind of product to the e-transaction, how many goods return number to the year total e-transaction, how many goods return number to the year total e-transactions.

Hence, amazon can gather all past every e-transaction data to prepare how to predict whether how every country e-transaction will consumer behavior to predict whether how every country e-transaction will influence consumer behavior will change next year in order to let it to prepare how to implement new market strategy,e.g. how to advertise its product, which countries need to spend more advertise to promote its products, evaluate whether amazon needs to spend how much advertisement expenditure to earn more e-sale transactions number to the targe sale country.

Why does amazon's any one e-transaction's accounting record assists it to predict consumer behavior? For china target e-buyers market example, when one Shanghai city e-buyer pays visa to buy one computer from amazon e-store, if the e-transaction can be accepted . Amazon can gather the e-buyer is living in China Shanghai city, which brand of computer , he chooses to buy, how much sale price to the computer, how many of computers number , he buys, how many e-transaction times to the China, Shanghai city buyer within the year. Hence, when amazon needs know where China target market has how many e-buyers number to every city, how many e-transaction return goods and refind number, which kinds of product are the popular to China e-buyers‘ purchase needs, which is the highest price and the lowest price sale level to China, Shanghai city target e-commerce market every e-transaction .

Thus, when amazon collestc all above China, Shanghai past one year any individual e-transaction data, it can compare whether how its China, Shanghai city.

Nest year, e-buyers behavior change in order to analyze whether which kinds of product price ought need to reduce in order to attract many China e-buyers to click amazn webstores to pay visa to buy its products or which kinds of product price may increase, when the kind of product is popular to sell to China target market, or make out of e-stock shelf decision to the kind of product when Amazon discovers the kind of product is not accepted to buy in popular from its e-store. Thus, it seems that Amazon's past any one e-transaction accountning record can help it to analyze whether how every target market its e-buyer behavior is changing in order to change next year sale changing strategy is more reasonable . Hence, it explains why e-commerce organization's accounting record may help it to analyze how future market changes as well as record how every old e-buyer customer whether he/she will choose to buy the kind of old product again or buy new product, even not buy anything from Amazon e-stores this year.

Hence, any e-commerce organization's e-stores can apply online technology skil and accounting concept to help it to learn how to analyze every year post efficient countries' cities different e-buyer individual product behavioral choice in order to judge/revise whether it ought need to change to buy its products from its e-stores conveniently. So, any e-commerce organization explains why it can attempr to apply its post every accounting e-buyer sale transaction record to make every country consumer behavior marketing analysis to compare transaction visiting shop business model more easily, because visiting shop sale model can let the seller to sell its products in its shop, when it locates in the country. But e-commerce sale model can let the product can be sold to different countries more easily.

So, it seems that if the e-commerce organization can have good accounting record system to keep its past all e-transactions record can gather all data concerns any countries e-buyer individual address , how much sale price for the product, how many sold, and refund to the country e-buyers and the e-buyer age is young or old , male or female e-buyer purchase habit.

Can the e-commerce organizatin predict consumer behavior if it implemented inefficiency accounting record system? Firstly, we need to know good or right accounting record system can help the organization to track or find past any transactions more easily. So, if the organization has none good accounting record system , its accounting record system can not be improved efficiently. Then, its accounting record may bring wrong sale price record, wrong profit (over -profit) or less profit or wrong loss (over loss) number record. Then, this wrong sale transaction record may mislead financial performance to publis to know, e.g. current year, its sale performance is improved, but in fact, its current year sale number is less than last year sale number. Consequently, this organization can not predict its consumer behavior. Whether know to change exactly, due to it often has wrong sale number record, e.g. higher or lesser sale price record, and more or less sale number may influence its gross profit earns high amount, even if its any kinds of expense record is more orless, it will influence its net profit is more or less or less is more or less, for example, if the organization earns US one million dollar prodict this year, but due to it smore sale number transaction to cause over profit. So, its financial performance report indicated its earned US two million dollar. So, it believes its buyers number can increase, if its sale prices do not change. This wrong financial performance report many mislead it has good consumer behavior in this year. Then, it will continue implement its old marketing strategy. Consequently, its next year financial performance may be caused worse to compare present. So, it implies that wrong financial record may cause wrong consumer behavior judgement.

Can robots tangible technological resource helps Amazon to do consumer behavior prediction tasks ?

Our future will experience artificial intelligent development stage. Nowadays, we had had some tasks which can be done by robots, e.g. warehouse delivery, restaurnt kitechen dish cleaning tasks, transport tasks, even non drive manual auto driving tasks, shopping center service etc. cleaning or customer service simple jobs duties. If one day, robots cab be applied to do office tasks, e.g. accounting record tasks, they may replace account clersk, even accountants to deal simple accounting record tasks, even complicate management account analysis tasks in office working environment. If future robots can be developed to help accounts clerks as well as accountants to do simple bookkeeping debit and credit every income ot expense transaction record in order to analyze marketing research tasks, then it brings this question: Can future robots replace accounts clerks and accountants to do their accounting tasks in any organizations. I shall attempt to research the relationship between robots and accounting tasks questions as well as whether robots will bring what social influence if robots can replace future human to do any simple and complex accounting tasks for any organizations.

What is need for development of artificial intelligence to accounting tasks aspect? The first computer language used to create artificial intelligence is USP. This language is quite flexible and extensive . Features such rapid prototyping and macro are very useful in creating AI. LISP is a language that makes complex tasks simple. So it seems that it is possible tobots can learn human to do any kinds of accounting tasks, e.g. financial account record, audit check, management account analysis etc. different kinds of acounting tasks for financial , management account, audit check functions in any organizations.

However, scientists believe that artificial intelligence can help accountants be more productive and efficient. Robotic process automation RPA) allows machines or AI workers to complete repetitive, time-consuming tasks in business processed, such as document analysis, handling that are plentiful in accounting . AI can also significantly reduce financial fraud and maintenance accounting errors. Hence, the stages of AI development to accoutning industry, they may include: internet AI, business AI, perception AI, and autonomous AI ., Internet AI is thr simplest stage of AI, business AI has a limted memory, perception AI. This is the first stage in the future of AI. A key feature of this perceptive form of AI is the ability to compile and draw from past experiences, much like human to accounting tasks. The design phase is essentially in literative process comprising all the steps releveant to building the AI or machine learning model, data acquisition, exploration, management and analsis tasks. So, it seems that future robots may be developed to help human to do simple and complex accounting tasks. Combining AI with other technologies, such as robotic, process automation can follow accountants to redirect the time that they used to spend on multiple tasks, toward performing high-value, high -impact taaks. Adding AI to accounting operation can also increase output quality by miniizing human errors. So, AI and automation won't be replacing finance and accounting professionals in the foreseeable futue.

On the contrary, as AI automates many aspects of business, there is a bug opportunity for accounting and finance professsionals to upskill themselves to meet the requirements of the 21 centurey. For AI audit task aspect, AI enables the analysis of a full populatin of data and can identify outliers or expectations. By making it possible for auditors to work better and smarter. AI will help them to optimize their time, enabling them to use their human judgement to analyze a boarder and deeper set of data and documents.

Can AI be used in auditing and accounting ? In the assurance practice, AI is being used to perform auditing and accounting prcedures, such as review of general ledgers, tax compiance, preparing workpapers, data analytic, expense compliance, fraud accounting skills. So, it seems that future AI can replace market research analysists, compensation and benefits managers , instead of financial accountants, management accountants an auditors in any organizations.For bookkeeping clerks position example, these simple account jobs are expected to decrease, by 8% 2024, and it's non surprise because most bookkeeping is getting automated if it has not been as of now, Quickbook, Peachtrss etc. accounting software that does not need any more, because robots do not need any kinds of accounting software to help them to do any simple or complex accounting tasks.

How has teachnology changed the accounting industry? Computers and accounting softeare has changed the industry complexity, with but when robots develop, it will change global accountancy professional more complex. Can robots replace accountants? Automation had brought significant changes the accounting profession over the last decaed. When some tools have made accountants lives easier. However, since robots invention, it developed these tools have also created a false debate about whether automation will overtake the global accounting industry compexity and make accountants irrelvant . The question should not be whether automation will take over accounting, but where its rreal value lives.

In fact, I believe that no any software can match the critical thinkning and trusted counsel that a human advisor offes, as valued accountants, have become business partners, where software is limited to evaluating concrete inputs, accountants can understand clients business goals and observations voice to make decisions. This allows them to serve as advisors to their clients, whether by adjusting business models in real time, or managing emplyer wellbeing . Sok, future AI development ought not replace human accountant's this kind of skill more easily.

- How robotic process automation impact on accouting industry changes?

Searching for methods to efficiently perform accounting tasks can be dated book to the 1950 s, when process mechanisation involved the use of punched cards to store and retrieve transaction data (Keenoy, 1958). Since then IT ad automation have transtormed the way accountants collect, store, process and share data through a variety of tools (Ellis, 1986); Kaye, Nicholson, 1992; Rom, Rohde, 2007). However, robotis process automation is a technology solution that allows end-users to comfigure a software robot to use existing applications to perform accounting transactions manipulate data and communcation with other systems (introduction to robotis, 2015).
Software robots can be easily programmed or trained to perform repetitive, rules-based , high volume operations by replicating human actions when accessing multiple systems, applications, and documents (Embracing robotic automation 2018). Hence, robotic accounting software can bring cost reduction to counting and finance tasks, e.g. one robotic accounting software can replace two to five full time accounting clerks, increased process speed, software robots perform routime tasks faster than employees would manage mamually (Cacity, Willcocks, 2016) . They do not get distracted or tried and thus avoid delays, cycle times decreases significantly improved process control and performance visibility, e.g the collected analytical information is much more detailed and can be used for audit and compliance checks, higher quality data (accuracy, consistency, compliance), e.g. robots can validate the data before reporting or using them future. Assuming that the appropriate rules have been thoroughly tested beforehand, data inaccuracy and quality risk decrease fill tracking and logging robots' action make internal and external audits easier and reduce compliance risks, continuous operation 24 hours a day, or none working day limits. So, robots are applied on accounting task aspect, it can bring positive impact on employees, repetive tasks taken over by robots release employees' times. They can shift their focus on higher value added tasks, solve employee morale proble,. Any accounting department staffs may feel tired when they need over time works, often but robotic accounting staff won't have tired or bored feeling.
However, robotic process, automatin may be applied on these accounting tasks aspect, they may include: internal control period end clising, general ledger, subledgers, closing , validatin of journal entries, low-risk accounts, reconsiliation, consolidation, reporting-monthly , quarterly close, internal performance and management reportng aggregating and analysing financial and operational data, external statutary report, accounts receivable and payable record-maintaining updating customer/supplier data, creating processing, posting payment, collections, billing, matching invoices, aganist sales and purchase orders, cash management, general accoutning, inter-company transactions, inventory accountancye, travel and expenses reimbursement request, audit and document expense report, payroll, stock keeping, fixed asset accouting record, tax accounting. So, the general simple accounting tasks robots will have effort to finish.

● Can robots perform the same management accounting analytical decision making skills to human management accountants tasks?

Although, robots can perform simple bookkeeping audit accounting tasks, but whether complex management accounting analytical and decision making tasks, robots can do the same level of management accounting analytical, decision making tasks to human management accountants?
I shall attempt to answer this question. How robots impact of mental accounting in valuation? No retailers show this price without considering the " 99" in end. This indicates to our mind that the price is cheaper. Its popularity can be verified gas stations all around the world. The difference between robots mental accounting issue and management accountants.
The Anchoring theory was used to verify its possible impacts on capital venture tech finds decisions, during equity trading for an initial investment starting. Management accountants ususally arrange 68% of the finds use-valuation as a basic, when 21% proposed other methods . But still use valuation and only 11% of the investors said they did not consider valuation at allo. the context considered that the human management accountant will consider that the investment would be made in a startup in early stages. That is with little or any real accounting information can image the amount of uncertainty that exists in the type of analysis?
Moreover, why do even experienced fund managers invest based on an impossible calculation> In simplity, it explains that human management accountant in order to do any investment decision. Although robotis will use alaytic mind more than calculating to estimate any investment risk in order to make investment decsion for any

organizations. AI's analytic skill and human management accountant calculation risk skill be their difference on how dealing management accounting investment risk issue aspect. Even, the difference between human management accountant and robotic management accounting automation is their robotic management automation can apply mental accounting theory to judge consumer behavioral choice.

It is a new model of consumer behavior is developed using a hyrod of psychology and microeconomics. The deveopment of the model starts with the mental coding of combinations of risks and losses using the prospect theory value finction. Then, robotic management accounting automatin can attempt to evaluate of consumer purchase for the product is modeled using the new concept of " transaction utility", e.g. one family electronic firm, it is seeling rice cooker, television radio, household electronic products, it can learn how to mental accounting method to help this houseold electronic product firm to predict how any why its different kinds of household electronic products choice may change to its consumer behavior next week, e.g. robots can gather wlectronic product competitors prices data to compare itself company's same kinds of electronic product data e.g. rice cooker prices and its competitors' rice cookers prices, whether its high price , rice cookers price factor or other factors influence its rice cookers sale number decreases in this week. Consequently robotic management accounting software may help this household elecronic product company to analyze whether what are the actual factors to influence its rice cookers prces reduce in this week. It is human management accountants feel difficult to collect past price data in order to make accurate consumer behavior changes, prediction or find whther are the main factors to influence product sale number increases or decreases.

Hence, future robotic management accounting automation can learn the valuation of purchase modeled using the new concept of transactin utulitym such as this houseold electronic product case, robotic management accounting automation many learn the household budget process ,the characterization of mental accounting, in order to find whether household purchase behavior to the company's products whether what the main factors may influence its household producys sale number increases or decreased.

On conclusion, future robots can do simple bookkeeping, audit check , general daily accounting tasks, even robots can also do complex management accounting tasks, they can learn how to apply mental accounting knowledge to gather the company's past all every month different price variable data, sale number, in order to conclude whether what are the main factors to influence the kind of product sale number increases or decreased more accurately to compare human management accountants in any organizations.

Applying HR management accounting learns consumer behavior

Managerial accounting purposes to be used by management in "making by business decision: It includes product caost, budget , forecast and various financial analysis consumer behavior is the series of behaving of patterns that consumers follow before making a purchase through consumer behavior, you can also earn how customers interact with and the year products. So, any organizations may attempt to find any management account past year past per month transaction records to bring consumer behavioral change predictiver knowledge, it can help future decisions about product creation more easily.

Hence , the management accoutning knowledge focuses the process of creating organization goals by identifying, measuring, analyzing, interpreting and communicating informations to managers is call management or manerical accounting. Management accounting focuses on all accounting aimed at informing management about operational business metics. Also, any managers may attempt to gather past product number presentation date to find whether what the main factors can influence consumer buying behavioral change in its any kinds of products, the level of motivation also affects the buying behavior of customers, e.g. whether the products' sale prices sight rise, to influence customer number reduces, or whether the product's traditional old design is not more attractive or popular to accept to compare other linds of competitors' similar product design, or whether the kind of product is not popular to be accpeted to use, the another how invention of similar product ot the market is recession , it need to change another new sale market, if replaces its existence etc. different factors.

Hence, management accounting can help managers to attempt to gather past the product's sale and production past data to carry on analyzing whether what the main factor to influence its customer number reduces or increases in other to improve its sale strategy.

- Computer sale applies management accounting to predict consumer behavior

For computer sale product example, the computer saller may attempt to apply management accounting to analyze why computer buyer behavioral changes, e.g. a study of consumer behavior will reveal what kind of consumers buy computers, could they buy for home and personal use or for office, what features , they look for, what benefit o they seek including post purchase service, huw much they are willing to pay how many they are likely to buy . All of these computer buyer individual purchase behavioral analysis, the computer seller can follow its different models of laptops, desttops, prices, sale number, house or office ise design kind etc. data to research and analyze and predict hether future computer buyer individual need will how changes, in order to prepare and learn how to design new kinds of desktops and laptops to raise competitve effort.

In fact, in computer industry, the factors may influence computer buyer behavioral change, they may include core technical features, past purchase services, price and payment, conditions, physical appearanre, value added features and connectivity and ability are the main seven factors that are influencing consumers' laptop purchases choices.

- How can the laptop computer seller applies management accounting data to analyze whether which is the main factor to influence laptop buyer behavior changes?

for last month, I assume that laptop model (A) laptop computer sale price si per US$1000 and it can sold 1000 number and laptop model (B) laptop computer sale price is per US$1,500 and it can sold 2000 number.SO, it implies that although laptop model (B) computer sale price is more than US$500 to compare laptop model (A) computer, but the model (B) laptop computer can still sell more than 1000 number fo compare model (A) laptop computer last moth. It seems that model (B) laptop's attractive dsign, more fuction, rapid connectivity and mobility and attrative physical appearance main factors may influence laptop (B) model computer products sale number is more than laptop (A) model computer products last month. But, in this month, it has significant change between laptop model (A) and laptop (B). In this month, laptop modle (A) and laptop model (B) prices are not changes, but laptop model (A) can sell 3,000 number and laptop model (B) can sell only 500 number. Consequently, their sale numbers have significantly changes, laptop (A) can increase more 2,000 sale number, but laptop model (B) can decrease 1,500 sale number between these two months. It explains that although it seems that laptop (B) model has possible own attractive physical appearance, and rapid connectivity and mobility, more function to cause it can sell more than laptop (A) model computer produc. But, it ensures that all of anh one these possible factors can not help it to raise sale number in long time. It means that laptop model (B) may have other factors to influence itss sale number, e.g. other brand of laptop computers' physical appearance, more function, connectivity and mobility , features , even they can provide better value added sale service, repair service, product delivery service, feature to compare this brand of laptop seller, or its laptop model (B) buyers had lost confidence to use its laptop model () computer products, because they often need to repair and pay extra repair service fee frequently, e.g. one year has one time to two times at least per year. SO, their past poor frequent repair experience influences they choose to buy other brand of laptops. Otherwise, why laptop model (A) computer products number can sell more 2,000 number , the factor may include non rising price, none frequent past repair experiences to any one model (A) laptop buyer , their individual psychological positive feeling factor . So, it seems that gather these two laptop model (A) and model (B) past sale number, sale price data to conclude whther what main factors may influence its model (A) and model (B) laptop sale number to increase or decrease in long term.

However, this laptop computer seller can not only depend on the gathering these two months short time sale numbers ans sale prices data to model (A) and (B) laptops, in order to make the final conclusion concerns whether what the main factor can influence model (A) and model (B) laptop product sale number changes absolutely. It must need to continue to keep the long time management sale umber and sale prie data record for laptop (A) and (B) in order to conclude whether what the most accurate influential factor is that it can influence laptop model (A) and B() sale number both change in order to implement the improvement strategy for them both.

- Management accounting data can also help this laptop seller to predict future market development or whether which market will have high sale effort, e.g. Japan laptop sale market may have the highest market share ratio, among different Asia countries, or Germany laptop sale market may have highest market share ratio among different

European countries next year. For example, in the last year, this laptop computer seller had sold 50,000 laptops to Japan computer market, it has sold 500,000 laptops to China computer market, it has sold 100,000 laptops to US computer market and 50,000 laptops to Germany computer market, in this year. its these laptop markets sale prices are not changed, it has sold 200,000 laptops to japan computer market, it has sold 400,000 laptops to China computer market, it had sold 200,000 laptops to US computer market and 200,000 laptops to Germany computer market . Hence, it ensures that Germany laptop market has increased 4 times sale number from last year and Japan has increased 4 times sale number from last year. Otherwisem China laptop sale number has decreased 100,000 laptops from last year and US laptop sale number has increased 1 time from last year. So, it can imply that Germany and Japan future laptop sale number may grown rapidly to compare US and CHina laptop sale markets. It also indicates this sale trend also may help this laptop computer to attempt to find whether what factors may influence its US and China laptop sale number fells down,,e.g. whether this local laptop choices increasing factor, it laptop physical appearance is not more attraction, or slow connectivity and mobility speed ,even their model (A) and () laptop prices are higher to compare US and China local other similar brands of laptops prices.

In summary, I believe that management accounting technique can be attempted to apply to help any kinds of products to find whether what main factor(S) to influence their product sale number changes, it is one kind of good data gathering and analytical tool to help any businesses to attempt to predict consumer behavioral changes.

Organization management accounting strategy

What is organization management accounting strategy? As its most basic an organization management accounting strategy is a plan that specifies how your business will allocate resources, e.g. money, labour, and inventory to suppoty production, marketing, inventory and other business activities. IN general, the foure organizational straategy and the culture of the organization categorized into four types: Adhocracy, market and hierarchy.

The purpose of an organization management accounting strategy can be defined as the direction an organization takes with the aim of achieving future business success. Strategy sets out how an organization intends to employ its resources, including the skills and knowledge of its people as well as financial and material assets, in order to achieve its mission or overall targets. So, the key element of an organizational strategy may include: define vision, create mission, set objectives, develop strategy, outline approach, get down to tactics. However, an organizatinal strategy plan is an organizational management activity that is used to set priorities, focus energy and resources, strengthen operations, ensure that employees and other stakeholders are working toward common goals established agreement crowd intended outcomes/ results, and access organizational missions.

Adhocracy strategy is a form of business management accounting that emphasizes individual initiative and self organization in order to accomplish tasks. This is in contrast to bureaucracy which relies on a set of defined rules and set hierarchy in accomplishing organizational goals. The term was popularized by Alvin Toffler in the 1970s. Examples of adhocracy include most project or marix organizations. Among private-sector organizations, high technology firms, particularly young firms facing fierce competition are sometimes organized as adhocracies. However, important examples of adhocracy do exist in government. Hence, adhocracy is a flexible, adoptable and informal form of organization that is defined by a lack of formal structure that employs specialized multidisciplinary trams grouped by functions. Adhocracy is characterized by an adoptive , creative and flexible behavior based on non-performance. Adhocray culture in a business context, is a corpoate culture based on the ability to adapt quickly to changing conditions. Adhocracies ar characterized by flexibility, employee empowerment and an emphasis on individual initiative.

The five basic marketing strategies may include: product, price and promotion and people in management accounting strategy aspect. They are key marketing elements used to position a business strategically. A market strategy refers to a business's overall game plan for reaching prospective consumers and turning them into customers of their products and services. For example, the BSC business 2 customed marketing strategies may include : social networks and viral marekting, paid media advertising, internet marketing, email marketing, direct selling, point-of-purchase marketing, co-branding, cause marketing, conversational marketing. Hence, marketing strategy or management accounting strategy is a long term toeard looing approach and an overall game plan of any organization or any business with the

foundemental goal of achieving a competitive advantage by understanding the needs and wants of customers.
Hierarchy strategy describes a relations of corporate strategy and sub-strategies hierarchically and logically consistent at the level of vision, mission, goals, and metrics , e.g. HR strategy (human resource strategy), to general, the three levels of strategy are: corporate level strategy, this level answers the foundamental question of what you want to achieve, business unit level strategy focuses on how you've going to grow.

The management accounting strategy planning hierarchy is the organization's mission and vision both of ,which should be long-lasting and motivating. At the base of the hierarchy are the shorter term strategies and tactics that unit members will use to achieve the vision. So, the basic levels of management accounting strategy are: corporate, business, functional and operational level strategy. The strategic hierarchy aims to be concept used to understand the different types of strategy decision made in a organization, e.g. michael porter , three generic strategies (cost leadership, differentation, and focus) that can be implemnted at any organizations. So, hierarchical levels of strategy managment accounting may be concerned with selection of which is the right generic strategy to implement, sale method, such as low product sale price, lot differentiation of product choice, and focus an main product feature market sale methods etc.

● The relationship between organizational management accounting strategy and avoiding resource waste

If an organization can implement good managment accounting strategy whether it can assist it to reduce any organizational internal resource waste, e.g. exceed human resource employment cost, facility used cost, using cost, efficient administration or management cost etc. essential organizational cost. Because any organizations must need to use resources in order to achieve efficient providivities, service activities, if the organization can implement effective strategy in order to measure its performance, whether strategy can assist it to judge how to avoid not essential resources spending. Can efficient strategy help organizations to avoid to waste resources? I shall attempt to explain as below:

Whether formal strategy implement can avoid formal technical measurement of scale and concentrates on the loca resource mobilization using aspect os small, medium and large organization? What does resource mobilization strategy mean? Resource mobilization refers to all activities involved in sesuring new and additional resources for your organization. It also involves making better use of and maximizing , existing resources.What are the stepd in resource mobilization?

Firstly, any organizations need to plan od designing a resource moilization strategy and action plan, secondary , finding key elements of a resource mobilization strategy, thirdly,act of practical step to implementatin, fourth identify, fifth step, engagement, sixth step, negotiate, eventh step, manage and report, final step, communicating results.

What are the source of resource mobilization to any organizations? For example includes spreading flyers, holding community meetings, and recruiting volunteers. Material may include financial and physical capital, like office space, money, equipment, and supplies . Human resources, such as labour experience, skills and expertise in a certain field. How does an entrepreneur mobilize resources? To exploit opportunities, entrepreneurs monilize and recombine a variety of resources, such as financial capital (e.g. cash, ot loan from a bank , human capital e.g. skills from a employees, and social capital e.g. information obtained from social contracts. Hence, the overall objectives of the resource mobilization strategy is to securce the necessary funds to deliver on the source mobilization strategic outcomes. To achieve this accurate resource used number and expenditure budget and emergency appeals will need sufficient preditable and contrributions. So, the aim of resource mobilization strategy outlines how secretariat will organize the process of prioritising, plannin, selecting projects, monitoring: broadening the resource channels, as well as coordinating with staffs for mobilising and effectively utilizing resources.

So, the genesis of resource mobilization strategy is a good, solid strategic plan, it should articulate activities that are more routine in nature and can be finded through the organizational internal efficient resource mobilization. Resource mobilization refers to all activities involves in securing . These new directions or new business opportunities are pursued using a distinct resource mobilization strategy .

On conclusion , an efficient resource mobilization plan is a term resource mobilization, it refers to all activities undertaken by an organizations to secure new and additional financial, human and material resources to advance its mission. Inherent in efforts to mobilize resources is the drive for organizational sustainability . So, resource mobilization is about an organization getting the resources that are needed to be able to do the work it has planned. Resource mobilization is more that just fundraising, it is about getting a range or resources from a wide range of resource providers for donors, through a number of different mechanisms. How does an entrepreneur mobile resources? To exploit opportunities, entreprensurs mobilize and combine a variety of resources, such as financial captial , e.g. cash or loans from a bank, human capital e.g. skill from an employee and social capital e.g. information obtained from social contract.

Why do organizations need resource mobilization strategy? The reasons may include: The principles of resource mobilization wih examples, it focuses on forging partnerships built on trust and mutual accountability . So, as to attract adequate and more predictable contributions, with the future goal of sustainability, it refers to all undertaken by an organizatin to secure new and additional financial , human and material resource to advance its mission, in efforts to mobilize resources is the drive for organizational sustainability, community mobilization is the process of bring together as many stakeholders as possible to raise people's awareness of and demand for a particular programme to assist in the delivery of resources and services, and to strengthen community participation for sustainability an dself -reliance, resource mobilization is often referrred t as " new business creaating chance" , the organization has a strong, yet flexible structure , such as writing proposal how to spend the least respurce expenditure in order to achieve the most satisfactory effective result to the organization.

Hence, developing a resource mobilization strategy plan , as the source of new business opportunities to the social and behavioral change considerations must be needed the organization as well as resource mobilization target at a minimum level should be needed to raise at transformational change happen on the ground and advocate for the products and may have to develop new business proposal.

- Can resource mobilization change improve organizational performance?

I believe that resource mobilization can help any organizations to change or improve performance to the better, even the best. I shall explain as below:

What are the sources of organizational change? Change originates in either the external or internal environments of the organization. External sources include political, social, technological or economic environment, externally motivated change may involve government action, technology development, competition , social values and economic variables.

How do organizational resources affect change? Results indicate that organizations possessing greater stocks of historically valuable resources were much less likely to engage in adaptive strategic change, but also that this resoure-driven towards change tended to have a even beneficial effect on performance . Wonder of organizational change management is easier spoken about than achieved by resource mobilization strategic in possible? Can create enterprise level value by effective process for resource allocation?

The key to success involves managing organizational change , so it leads to real and lasting improvements, tailoring to resource allocation how mobilization strategy. So, nowadays, organizational capacty for change: Increasing change capacity and avoiding change overload, organization, today risk is overcommitting resources, resulting in an overload condition wih which it how allocates its resources to tbe used efficiently or inefficiently. For example, on new government regulations, ne products development or growth aspect, organizational change efforts often run into some form of human resistance. First, management staffed its human resource departments with spend most of that time in efficiency. So, whether how organizational change is better, it depends on how it changes its old resources, e.g. human resource, facility, equipment resources, even management time resources to change new improvement resources change to be better . It means providing the resources, budget, authority, credibility and commitment for the effort to truly organizational change on improvement.

- Why does organizational resource budget need?

For example, managing a human resource department involves budget planning and execution . The human resources budger refers to the finds that how HR allocates to all HR processes. Unit should include in an HR budget. It may include: number of employees, projected for next year, benefits cost increases or decreases, salary cost increases or decreases, projected turnover rate, calculation, actual cost incured in the current year, new employee welfare benefits. programs planned, other changes in policy, business strategy , it may impact costs on HR cost aspect. So, an organization needs to budget whether it will have how much on what kinds of resources spending aspect, including human resources, facility, equipment and water , electricity etc. natural resource , it budget is a tool used for planning and controlling financial resources. It is a guideline for future plan of action, espressed in financial terms within a set of period time, knowing organization's priorities, objectives and goals helps it prepare organization resource budget. Effectively leveraging people and budget, resource management is critical for organizations to ensure . They are optimizing and allocating resources to the right initiations, e.g. from a human resource perspective, the data needed to create a new budget include the following number of employees, working arrangement tasks time, management time, employee salary cost, due to costs that only impact the human resource department and impacts the entire organization both aspects. So, efficient HR cost budget can help refine goals that reflect realistic resources and how memebers of the organization to use fund because employee retirement can be expensive and it can b increased or decreased expense in any time, when the month needs increase or decrease employees number to any departments. It depends on whether tasks rate is needed to increase or decrease. So, an organization's HR cost budget can help how it makes the most accurate HR resource expenditure.

Organizational facility, equipment, shop, office, warehouse space resource budget why is important. Office space is as an enabling resource, equipment and furniture to enhance the organization's ability to achieve efficient operations and activities of the best organizational performance. In view of this analysis, facility planning personal would be one important factor to influence whether the organizatin can spend the least expenditure to use its resource. During business growth, any facility equipment, office , shop, warehouse space must increase , moreover staff puts increasing number on existing resources, so be sure to budget in order to make another option is to least equipment instead of buying it, whether you need moving insurance for important equipment and machinery, set budget to help prevent overspending.

All of the tasks that are include in maintaining a facility, such as equipment maintenance and building facilities whether are needed to improve, facility oversight, warehouse and special equipment whether is qpproriate space for customer service and uses resource dynamic of an organization's work patterns with work. It depends partly on the resources an organization is willing to invest or not, when it feels this facility resources are very important to influence its performance.

● What does organization office , shop , warehouse space resource management strategy?

Organization and using space must be land resource, if the organization can manage how to use its space in efficiency, then it can improve service performance or productive efficiency. Space management can be defined as a practice where an organization manages its physical space invnetory which includes tracking , control, supervision and utilization, planning of the space available. So, space management is the mangement of an organization's physical space inventory. Ths involves the tracking of how much space an organization has managing occupancy information and creating spatial plans. So, one efficient space resource using organization, it needs to undertake annual property assessment reviews, leverage individual projects to drive portfolio evoluation applya planning methodology on all project rises, utilize planning to define direction and scope focus on mathematics before graphics, define and collect only the required data on warehouse, shops, office, buildind space using aspect. For example, a space management ffice can give the organizatin an accurate picture of how many employees , it needs to have space for an average day, and show it the trends of demand for this space across weeks and months. This can help the organization to determine how many permanent desks could be converted to hot desks in office, warehouse or shop , saving space. For example, space managementin retail aspect, it is the process of managing the floor space adequately to facilitate the customers and to increase the sale.

Shop space management is very crucial in retail as the sales volume and gross profitability depends on the amount of space used to generate those sales. Space management is a multi-step process that requires data gathering, analysis , forecast and strategizing. In prective, it involes creating a space management system that occupants throughout your organization, so whether the organization realizes it or not, every organization needs to know how to manage its space one way or another , if it hopes to improve its service or productive performance. Make use of these strategic space management and planning techniques, efficient and an unplanned, unmanaged office is not likely to magically transofrm into a well organized of productivity. So, space management is the management of an organization's physical space inventoty , employee working environment, shop product putting sheleves locatin, equipment, desk putting location. All of this tangible space physical factor may influence overall organizational service and/or productive performance and /or sale performance. So, space may be an organization's land usng resource because any organization's land using space must be limited size, they must have land space using shortage challenge if their products stock number increases, but warehouse space can not increase or shop products shelves number can not increase, but product sale number increases.

● The relationship netween organization behavior and resource using management accounting

Has organizational behavior and resource spending, they have close cause and effect direct relationship ? When one organization can perform better, whether it represents that it must spend much resource to use or when it perform poor, it represents that it must not spend much resource to use. Organizational behavior is a field of study that investigates the impact that organizational psychology and human resource management, the cause and effect relationship.

How organizational behavior effects an oganization? Organizational behaviors propose that inventives are motivational factors that are crucial for employees to perform well. It changes the way people make decisions, e.g. decision to increase or decrease resources to use, when the organization feels that it has resource shortage or excess. However, businesse that are able to encourage risks in decision making within the company culture can enhance innovation and creativity.

In fact, organizational behavior has four main elements, people, structure, technology and external environment. So , tangible and intangable resources may influence organization behavior when it is needed to change by management, e.g. human behavior in a work environmen and determines its impacts on job structure, performance, communication, motivation, leadership etc. for example, when the manager has less time to prepare how to organize this meeting process to his client. His short managing meeting plan time , intangible time resource, it can influence his business proposal to be either accepted or rejected to this client. So , time resource whether it is enough or not. It can influence this manager's client proposal meeting whether it is accepted or rejected in possible.

Every employee behavior can determine the importance of group departments in business productivity. So, it seems that resources whether they are enough , they can impact on employee's performance. As a result, managers are able to maintain better relation with their employees by effective utilization of human resource. So, cause and effect relationship plays an important rolw in how an individual is likely to behave in a enough tangible and intangible resource provided or not enough organization.

Modern organizational behavior is characterised by the acceptance of a human resource model, e.g. whether the plant can provide enough productive equipment facility and space shelf for product putting location in order to raise or improve logistic transport efficiency in warehouse. So, plant warehouse space management and shelf putting location productive equipment facility these tangible resource factors may influence warehouse productive performance. It seems that tangible resource provision amount and space management or intangible resource time management resource, they have close relationship to influence organizational behavior. Consequently, it can achieve the result either performance improvement or worse performance. So, resource and performance organizations , they ought have cause and effect relationship in resource management mobilization strategy view.

● How applying artificial intelligent management accounting solution accounting challenges

One of the biggest challenges for management accountants nowadays is the preparation to face globalization in local and global market. Globalization competition is changing government regulation and innovation in technology had to change in the market environment which have greater impact to an organization. The role of managemet accounting to AI, it may help managers to make any management strategy decision, e.g. evaluate sale price is the most reasonable, sale market choice, customer age target evaluation etc. within any organizations. Also known of cost accunting, management account of the process of identifying, analyzing and communicating information to managers to help to achieve business goals. However, the most important job of management accountant is t condoct a relevant cost analysis to determine the existing expenses and give suggestion for the future activities and make better management accounting, when management accountants need to learn how to apply these management accounting data: financial planning, financial statement analysis, cost accounting, find flow and cash flow analysis, standard , marginal cost and budgetary control, they can be made by AI.

In general, the job dutures of management accountant may include: generate sale among client accounts, operates as the point of contact for assigned customers, develops and maintains long term relationships with accounts, makes sure clients receives requested produsts ans services in a timely fashion . So, they need to learn these different management accounting technique: margin analys, capital budget, inventory valuation and product cost, tend analysis and forecasting. Future AI may be taught to learn all of these any one management accounting technique to assist organizations to make more reasonable management account strategy implementation.

The basic principles of management accounting include communication presents insight which is crucial , irrelevance information is valuable, the influence one value is estimated, credibility,recognizing the requirement, good accounting manager, they need to learn how conflict, be open to new ideas: In management accounting tehnology apply, there are three elements of management control system to develop to future Artificial intelligent management accounting technology delegated decison authority , performance evaluation and measurement systems and compensation, reward system.

Hence, accounting technology in AI development has always played a past in making the accountant's job just a played a part in making the accountant's job just a easier. Its own knowledge of technology increased to have the accountant's ability to analyze statistical values. Technology advancements have enhanced the accountant's ability to interpret data efficiently and effectively.

● Future AI management accountant may help human to the honest accounting record

However, any one managment accountant needs have good professional personal quality, honestly and integrity play vital roles in accounting because they allow investors to trust the information they receive about companies in which they invest. Honesty in accounting is the primary characteristics of the profession that allows financial decision-makers to make appropriate judgement . So, the main focus of management accounting is to assist the management of a company in efficiency performing its function-planning, organizaing, divesting and controlling . Management accounting helps with these functions in the following ways: provides data, it serves to a vital source of data for planning, for product costing method example, it is used to cost methods available are process costing, job and different production and decision making. for 3 types of controls may include: internal controls are typically procedures or technical safe guards that are implemented to prevent problems and protect organizations' assets. Future AI technology may help an organizations to do above all management accounting decision jobs ,even replace human in offices to avoid losses. The traditional management accounting technique includes" the use of performance measures, three ROI , budget systems for planning and control, divisional profit reports and cost-profit volume relationship, and breakeven analysis for decisions. The management accounting reports may include order information report, project report, competitor analysis. They are either internally aor outsourced. All of these management accounting methods, future AI can replace human accountants to do .

● Can AI be applied to help Amazon organization to implement management account strategies ?

The two widely used types of accounting are: Financial and management accoutning, for the strategic cost management techniques example, it is the cost management techniques that aims at reducing cost , when strengthening the position of the business. It is a process of combining the decision making structure with the cost information in order to do the strategy as a whole . Hence the role of management account in the organization is to support competitive decision making by collecting, processing and communicating information that helps management plan, control and evaluating business processes and company strategy . So, the strategy management accounting can be defined as the process of identifying, collecting , selecting and analyzing accounting data . So, future AI can be applied to assist accounting teams in strategic decision making and organization effectiveness assessment must be defined.

Future AI can be applied to these management accounting aspect: For methods and techniques of costing management , it may include: Job costing, advestment, salepeople,bonus, contract cost, long periods of time job, batch cost, process cost, one operation (unit or output) , cost service or operating costing, farm cost, multiple cooperation unit. The tools of cost analysis, breakeven analysis, budget cost control marginal cost analysis, cost control , minimum price analysis, standard cost development , target cost. All of these management strategies, AI can do .

The various tools and technique of marginal costing may include: contribution, profit volume ratio, contribution : sale value , p/v ratio, features of profit volume , break even point . Hence, the AI tools can control cost monitoring in execution. For that AI can help organizations to make cost control budget, it is defined as a AI tool that is used by the management of an organization in regulating and controlling of a manufacturing organization. AI can also perform cost budget for material to any manufacturing organizations to help them to reduce the manufacturing cost , e.g. making material choice for the cheapest price.

AI can gather the product material price, e.g. standard cost and normal cost. Then , AI can help the manufacturing organization to choose the best quality of the cheapest material in order to compare whether which kinds of material to produce the kind of product can bring the high economic benefit to let consumers get more satisfactory feeling. Thus, it is future management accounting development direction for AI.

Ecommerce organization resource management strategy

Why does in this e-commerce organization situation, online webstore speed must be the most important factor to influence its sale success. Information technology internet speed, online webstore design, online transation convenience transaction feeling (tangibale and intangible both resource factors) may influence its future clients number ?

In behavioral economic view, any organizations must need to use resources to carry on any business or working activities. Resources may include: management time to managements, working time to employees, information technology etc. office computer to administration, factory equipment to plant workers, plant or warehouse land space to logistic delivery or goods shelves, electricity, gas , water to workplace , even, employees number. HR to any department tasks. So, it seems that before any organization can finish any activities, they must need enough resources supply in order to satisfy any activities need. If the organization overall itself , even overall society. I shall explain as below:

For ecommerce organizatin example, any online trading firms must need to own high speed internet information technology resource to supply to any one technologic staff store to pay visa to buy any product in the most short time rapidly. So, its online store website speeds must need to be very fast in order to avoid to delay any country clients to carry on online transaction. If the ecommerce business organization can not support efficient, high speed internet service to let any countries online buyers to satisfy its online webstore purchase service. Then, any countries' online buyers may choose another online store to replace to buy its similar product easily.

Hence, convenient webstore online purchase service much be very important to influence this online webstore organization. It seems that technologic online internet resource must be the most influential factor to influence this online websore organization clients number. If its online website store can not supply rapid online purchase speed to let any one country to buy its products from its webstores rapidly. Then, its clients number may be influenced to reduce. So, in this e-commerce organization situation, online webstore speed must be the most important factor to influence its sale success. Information technology internet speed, online webstore design, online transation convenience transaction feeling (tangibale and intangible both resource factors) may influence its future clients number . So, judging whether the kind of resource is the most important to influence the organization's success, it depends on whether it needs to use what kind of resource to carry on its daily activities.

In fact, one organizational change has relationship to whether its reponses can have enough supply as well as its behavior can be influenced by the resources variable , the scarcity of any kinds of resources are supplied to be used. So, I believe that whether any kinds of resources are scarcity in the organizational environment, how much they are used, these any kind of resources can bring relationship to influence how organizational perceptions, interpretations and responses.

How an ecommerce organization resource affects society?

Why has online webstore's information technology resource close relationship t influence online buyers number and social job chance?

Organizational impact to the effect on an organization has any reponses to influence how on society chance. However, organizations can also have a positive impact on the economic satisfaction of a town. More oe less jobs supply to the wociety, which can be influenced by whether the organization can have effort to buy how much resources to be used in order to carry on itself any business activities. Hence, it seems that if the organization, such as the above online website sale product organization, if it can have enough money to employ web design professional to help it to design attractive website stores to let attract online buyer purchase choice, as well as paid higher internet service fee to improve its fee to improve its online internet speed in order to let any countries online customers can still click its website rapidly, even in busy online click time. Many people click computer mouse to enter ecommerce website stores in the same time. Then, any one won't choose another websites stores to replace its online sale service easily. Even, if it can buy many advanced computers to let its staffs can use the best quality computers to follow any client's ourchase transaction in short time. When , they confirm that whether the client's visa card payment can accept and what product he has paid to buy from its webstore. Then, the staff can know where the accurate address of the country , the client's product can be delivered rapidly. It will avoid to delay any product delivery. So, if this online store seller can have enough internet information technology source to support its whole computer information department staffs to wrk efficiently. Then, it can increase more online transaction chance in success. Consequently, it can grow up its online sale business, it will create many new potisition, due to its computer information technology department must need to increase employees to help it to deal any countries online buyers online purchase service transactions and online product sale delivery service immediately in order to avoid online product delivery service to global online buyers. So, it can bring more job chance if this online webstore organization can have enough effort to buy high technological computer information products to let its online customer service staffs to use in order to improve online product delivery service store to let global many online buyers' attention . Consequently, it can apply online webstore purchase channel to apply website purchase channel to persuade many global online buyers online purchase choice to its webstore easily. So, it seems that this online webstore's information technology resource has close relationship t influence online buyers number and social job chance.

How do organizational resources affect organizational change?

IN general, resoults indicate that organizations possessing greater stocks of historically valuable resources were much less likely to engage in adaptive strategic change, but also that this resource-driven disinclination towards change tended to have a begin or even beneficial effect on performance . So, in general, if one organization lacks any one of these three important resources. It can influence this organization's performance to worse, they many include: human resource , financial resource, phycial resources and information resource. However, managers are responsible to acquiring and managing the resources to accomplish goals. If the organization can have enough resources to be used. It can bring positive impact to influence its overall organizational performance, even, when it has not any resource scarcity, it can avoid negative impacts on the society, such as increasing jobs chance. Hence, scarcity of capital, human and social resources to be provided to the organization, it will influence the organizational structure changes, even employee individual work attitude is influenced to change worse, when he/she can not have the best resources to be used in order to raise efficiency or improve performance more easily.

How to build organizatonal resource using right psychology

The psychology of management is the branch of psychology studying mental features of the person and its behavior in the course of planning, organization management and the control of joint activity. The human factor is considered as the central point in the psychology of management as its essence and a core. Hence , organizational psychology plays a very important rolw at the time or recruitment very important role at the time of recruitment taking disciplinary action or resolving disputes between employees. HR focus and expertise mainly lies in dealing with people . So , it makes sense that the study of the human mind, how to use organizational resources efficiently.

The organizational side of pschology is more focused on understanding how organizations affect individual behavior, organizational structures , social norms, management styles and role expectations are factors that can influence how people behave within organizations. In general, industrial organizational psychologists use psychological principles and research methods to solve problems in the workplace and improve the quality of life (e.g. avoiding often waste industrial resources in manufacturing process aims). They study workplace workplace productivity and management and employee working styles. They get a feel for the morale and personality of a company or organization, e.g. suggesting to use skills and knowledge relating to psychology how to reduce same productivity level, but the organizational resources can be reduced to use. It is one kind the most efficiency resources using method to any kind of organizations.

On conclusion, industrial and organizational psychologists will often use science to study human behavior organizations and the workplaces. Their aims to help organizations to reduce excess resource using in any manufacturing process in order to reduce cost. Employers who need to attempt to learn how employees use resources to do work activities, it can bring these advanaages : learning how to use neuroscience to attract the right talent, retain high performing employees, because any organizations‘ resources will be used in order to manufacture any products or work activites by any employees in any time.

Employees are the ones who get the job done. They know how the organization and especially ho w their specigif team works best. So any one employee may be the important factor to influence the amount of resource use, any organizational resource use amount, it has close relationship to any employee work behavior. Moreover, resources, that is , group-level resources associated with shared relationship that foster a quality exchange of information and interaction between individuals within the workplace , helping any one employee to learn more about on the job training, use employee training optios to ensure department leader optimizes the employees' motiviation and potential retention. Aim to give opinions to employees to know how to avoid resource using waste method to achieve cost saving aim to the organization.

Can Amazon resource shortage influence consumer behavior changes?

Can bring either positive or negative or both impact to change consumer behavior when the consumer begins to feel resource shrtage occurrence to choose to buy the kind of product or consume the kind of service?

Consumer researchers have suggedsted that chronic resource scaraity, specially, an inproveished early home environment with fewer resources and high levels of instability and uncertainty can lead to chronic differences in choice behavior (Griskevicius et al. 2011). How are consumers affected by scarcity? Scarcity affects producers because they have to make a choice on how to best ise their limited resources. It also affects consumers because they have to make a choice on what services or goods to chooce. Hence, resource shortage may be situational factor influence, situational influences are external circumstances or conditions existing when a consumer makes a purchase decision. Because the kind of product is facing resource shortage issue to influence the product manufacturer can not have enough resource to manufacture the kind og product. SO, number supply is decreasing, such as cars product, if steel number supply is decreasing, it can influence global car manufacture number decreases. When global new car buyers feel that they can not buy any kinds fo new cars easily. Then, even global new car price rises, they won't influence new car buyers purchase desires. So, in new car sale market, if steel supply number reduces, global new car buyer number will not decrease easily.

How does a consumer make choice with scarce resources?

Like producers, consumers also have to make choices, since consumer resources , such as time, attention, and money are limited. They must choose how to best allocate them by making tradeoff. The concept of trade-offs due to scarcity is formalized by concept of opportunity cost. In fact, research in marketing often begins with two assumptions, by scarcity of products and/or a scarcity of resources, dfferent types of scarcity individually and jointly influence.

Consumer behavior , an integrative analysis of research finding remains that scarcity principle in consumer behavior, it refers that scarcity to the condition of resources shortages, it can affect consumer behavior. So, consumer behavior and resource shortage, they seem have close cause and effect relationship between them. For buying behavior example, when one male consumer with high shopping motivations, when he knows a scarcity arrtibute and thus are a vary limited resources, e.g. he allows to buy the product within 5 minutes , when the shop will close soon and thus a very shop time clising time limited. It can persuade the male customer to make purchase decisin immediately. So, it seems that intangible resource , such as shop closing limited time, scarcity may also be a fundamental phenomenon that influences consumer behavior, when the consumer feels that shop will close, it does not allow himw to continue to stay long time in the shop. The shop closing time nay persuade the customer to buy the product immediately.

It explains that why the influence of quantity scarcity and time restriction on consumer, this implies that when consumers‘ cognitive resources are not restricted by external environmental factor influence, such as shop soon closing time or web traffic to media, when the online buyer , he dislikes to spend long time to click on any website stores to choose themselves brands of the kind of product choice to make purchase decision. The online buyer may only click one website store to make purchase decision immediately.

So, it explains why online sellers can sell their products firm online stores easily, because their website stores web traffic is not busy at the moment. There are not many online buyers click themselves webiste stores at the moment. So, when there are many online buyers can click themselves webstores to choose any kinds of products in shor ttime rapidly. Then, their online sale chance may be influenced by " not busy website stores web traffic jam to media time factor".

Hence, it seems that when one consumer feels resource shortage, it may persuade the consumer to choose to buy the kind of product immediately. I suggest that people may not only differ in terms of how they choose to consume, this could include encouraging consumers , such as impact pf resource scarcity on price-quality judgement. It means that the predictable " panic shopping" in response, experiencing resource scarcity can also increase a sense of community by encouraging consumer to share shopping experience. So, product uncertainity , which is able to motivate behaviors, such as urgency to buy.

This, scarcity , also is known as paucity, is an eonomics term used to refer to a gap between the buyer purchase desire and external environmental factor, for exmaple time and money are characteristically scarce resources, to urge consumers to make purchases or else they won't guarantee next day purchase the product.

Howvеer, the cost of using a resource is called the opportunity cost, the value of the next scarcity in economics connotes not that something is nearly impossible to finf. In common, consumers must choose between correct consumption and future consumption, for example, the COVID 19 crisisi may bring positive urgent time to save product, e.g. medical mouth cover protection product, when many medical mouth cover protection product buyers believe the brand of covid 19 medical moth cover protection products supply is shortage, they believe they ought buy the brand of medical mouth cover protection product supply is shortage, they believe thay ought buy the brand of medical mouth cover protection products immediately.

Otherwise, they can not find this kind of covid 19 medical mouth cover protection products to buy later. So, the anticipation to the covid 19 crisis will help some brands of medical mouth cover protection proucts, they can be sold rapidly . So, panic buying may be encouraged when the covid19 mouth cover protection product buyers feel a common brand share covid 19 mouth cover protection products shortage resource through a collection action. Hence, even the brand of covid 19 medical mouth cover protection products prices are raised, the covid 19 mouth cover buyers still choose to buy the brand of covid 19 mouth cover protection products, because they believe that they can not buy the brand of covid 19 medical mouth protection cover products later, when this brand of covid 19 medical mouth cover manufacturers won't continue to manufacture this kind of covid 19 medical mouth cover products again.

So, it explains that crisis and product sale time limited intangible resources can influence consumers to make a lot purchase decision suddenly. On conclusion, resource scarcity is essentially about current brand for a resource exceeding available supply. Resource scarcity occurs when demand for a natural resource is greater than the available supply leading to a decline in the stock of available resources.

However, limited time may be one kind of intangible resource shortage to influence consumers to choose to make the purchase decision to avoid that they lose the final purchase chance. So, the intangible limited time psychological factor may help businessmen to sell their products in short time, when the consumers feel that they have no enough time to choose any kinds of product to buy or they believe that they can not buy the kind of product later. So, resource shortage may bring position impact to influence consumer behavior in behavioral economy view.

Do they have relationship between organizational resource economic behavior and social needs?

In organizational behavioral economy view, economic systems that shape behaviors and constrain access to resource necessary to organizations and society both. People are influenced to organizations as employees, consumers. IN behavioral economy view, economics is the social science that examines how individuals, businesses and overall societies manage scarce resources. Because none resource exist in unlimited quantities, even internet technology resource , societies must establish priorities and decide how best to allocate resources in such a way that meets as many needs and wants as possible . So, organizational behavioral and economics to explain why employees sometimes make irrational business decisions , and why and how the organization employee individual behavior does not follow the predictions of economic models . Because any organizational employees are emotional and easily distracted brings , they make decisions that are not in their self interest when they are working in organization. Hence, how whether it is more or less any organizations use themselves resource. It may influence the social whether it has much or less resources to society. It can use which interact within the organization,

Why have they interaction to influence resource supply between orgaizations and societies?

In sociology, a social organization is a pattern of relationship between and among individuals and social groups. Characteristics of social organization can include qualities, such as division of labour, communication system, leadership , structure of a organization. For hospital example, it is one social organization, whether how it uses its resource , it can inluence whether society has how much resources can use. Hospital is one social resource organization (division of labour), e.g. doctors, nurses teams, cleaner teams, patient customer enquire teams, counter service teams. They are a major influence on social behavior and is the link between human nature reaching to the hospital organizational and social environment. Hoe many actual patients number , social need in the year, if the year , there are not many patients need to feel to go to hospital , then it can influence the hospital feels resource excess, or it won't need to use more hospital resource to serve its patients in the year. S, social patients needs and hospital medicine supply needs, they have close relationship every year. It means that the hospital's medicine manufacture material won't need much, it the year has not many patients or patients number is decreasing. So, shopital organzation hoe to need its resource, it has close relationship to patients number in society (nature, demographic, economic, cultural and social behavior patterns and consciousness). So, it explains why the social organization is the best of all organized human society, such as hospital organization example, its patients number will influence medicine resource need.

Another example is bus public transport service social passengers number choice to catching bus transport tool, it can influence whether how buses use oil nature resources needs. If the year , there are less passengers to choose to catch buses, they choose to catch trams, trains, ferries in preference, then due to every bus reduces passengers numer, it does not often driven , following the fixed timetable. If the bus stations often have no many passengers are waiting buses, then many buses are often staying in bus stations. Consequently, bus oil fuel nature resources need must reduce. Thus, social bus passengers number may have indirect relationship to influence buses oil fuel natural resources needs every year. It means that bus oil fuel nature resource use amount is influened by social passengers public transport tool choice needs. It is one good example bus public transport service organization seems to be one social organization.

- How Amazon e-commerce applies resource management principle to bring avoiding resource waste benefit?

For Amazon e-commerce example, it does not apply scientific management principle, due to it is not one product manaufacturing industry, it is online sale service and foreign delivery service organization. It ignores one of the key of scientific management, its creators genuinely believed that you had to pay higher wages to anyone asked to puch themselves to their physical limits. Under scientific management wages are paid to the workers as per the piece-wage system. Minimum wage is not assured, so every work needs to pay incentive wafe when he can manufacture more piece product, but Amazon believes that pay higher wages to any one can bring incentive productivity , such as it only provide online sale and foreign deli ery service to any one online buyer client, e.g. it can pay higher wage to the warehouse workers, because they need to cooperate with robotics to work hard and the human warehouse workers need to learn how to dominate any one warehouse logistic robotics to know hoe to delive and put goods to the right shelves in order to avoid to put wrong goods to the not right shelves position in warehouse.

So, in Amazon scientific management skill to workers view, its warehouse workers are smart workers, they need to know how to dominate any one warehouse robotics to do the right goods delivery to put on right shelves tasks daily. Their wages ought need to pay higher in order to avoid theig goods wrong delivery to wrong sheleves in careless. SO, Amazon feels that it needs to pay higher salary to the warehouse workers because they need have more smart and robotic control skills. When they and robotic to works together in Amazon warehouses.

So, such as Amazon warehouse workers case, Amazon ecommerce organization can apply scientific management principle to reduce resource waste. I shall explain as below:

Amazon 's warehouses have save diffeent kinds of products to prepare to deliver to different countries buyers, after Amazon had confirmed that it has receive visa card payment from online channel by each online buyer successfully. So, it must have smart warehous workers, they know how to control and dominate any one warehouse robotics to cooperate to send every right shelf position message to every one warehouse robotis to know, when the warehouse robotic receives the right product delivery to the right shelf message from the warehouse warehouse, it will delvier the product to the shelf position carefully. So, avoiding none of any wrong goods putting on the wrong shelves positions occurs easily. When, every one, there has none any wrong goods are putted on wrong sheleves positions occurrence, the spending investigation time to any wrong goods putting on wrong shelves position, it does not need to any one warehouse manager to do every day, So, Amazon does not need to waste time to do any goods putting on wrong warehouse workers number, when it applies many warehouse robotics to assist them to work in order to raise goods delivery efficiency in warehouse, e.g. Amazon warehouse can apply three logistic robotics and one human warehouse worker number to do one goods shelf delivery task. Before, it needs to employ ten human warehouse, logistic workers to reponsible to do one goods shelf delivery task. I assume that the goods shelf can put total 300 pieces of different kinds of products per day. So, Amazon can reduce none warehouse logistic workers number when it increases three logistic robotics to help them to do these 300 goods delivery task per day. Hence, its wage expenditure must decrease. Moreover, logistic robotics do not feel tried , bored, overtime work, these three robotics only follow any one of warehouse worker's message to let them to know whether which kind of product is needed to put on which number of the shelf positiion. Then, these three logistic workers can remember where the product is putted on the shelf position and help any one logisitic worker to get the right product to already deliver to the foreign buyer's home from Amazon's warehouses easily, they must raise efficiency more than only workers , they work in Amazon warehouses.

Hence, Amazon believes higher wage can enourage smart logistic workers can have good performance to dominate how every logistic robot , e.g. avoiding to send wrong message to let any one logistic robotic to put wrong product to the wrong shelf number position. SO, Amazon can apply warehouse scientific management method to avoid warehouse worker individual wrong message delviery to any one logistic robotic occurrence, when they can receive higher wage, and the three logistic robotics and one warehouse worker cooperation relationship is the most suitable workers cooperation number.

Amazon 's warehouse does not need more nine workers to often move in the crowd warehouse space environment to avoid worker accident and wrong goods putting on wrong shelves number position occurrences both. Hence, Amazon can apply scientific management method on warehouse avoiding resource waste aspect, when it decides to apply logistic robotics and workers cooperation in order to avoid wasting time to investigate whether which kinds of goods are put on where the wrong shelves number positions per day tasks occurrence in possible and it can bring delay to deliver goods to the online buyer's home. it is one good example of scientific management avoiding time waste method to Amazon warehouse organization.

Can Robotic Help Warehouses To Avoid Resource Waste On Behavioral Economic View

● Behavioral economy view whether robotic can help
warehouse to avoid time and human resource
waste

IN fact,robts are being used in different types manufacturing to create more efficiency with fewer resource. Robots also reduce errors, to leass waste is produced. Less waste is produced and the robots are able to final and separate the small parts more efficiently than human hands can. For example, on environment recycled aspect, robots can help reduce waste that is incinerated by efficiently sorting materials that can be recycled quickly and more efficiently than humans reducing the input poser and cost control with such processes. So, robots can bring positive affect the environment, because robots use less energy and produce less waste.

As a whole, there are multiple benefits to using robots to fight climate change,e.g. robots can prevent pollution and emissions through careful monitoring optimize the manaufacturing processes to reduce energy consumption. Moreover, robots can help with recycling, the use of robots allows facility operators some new flexibility. Most technologies used in recycling allow to sort materials. The sensing robots (sensoes) allow robots to receive information about a certain measurement of the environment , or internal components. This is essential to robots to perform their tasks, and act upon any changes in the environment to calculate the appropriate response.

- How Amazon warehouse applies logistic robots to help it to waste resource waste

Hence, although robots can take our jobs, because they can help organizations to avoid resource waste, and it can bring negative effect to influence we lose jobs. ON behavorioral economic view, robots can help employers to reduce employees number, but it won't influence organizational overall performance to be worse or inefficiency, such as Amazon warehouse applies logistic robots to assist workers to deliver the right kind of goods to put on every correct shelf number position rapidly every day. Hence, one logistic robot can replace at least 10 store workers to do goods delivery tasks every day, e.g. one store worker needs to spend one minute to find the right kind of good to deliver to prepare to arrange to deliver it to fly to overseas client. Logistic robots only need 10 seconds to find the right kind of goods from the near 200 number shelves in Amazon warehouse as well as they are putting 300 different kinds of goods on these 200 shelves in Amazon warehouse every day.

Because each logistic robot has very good memory. Each logistic robot must remember any kinds of goods , their putting number position on which shelf, e.g. when the worker needs to find the model laptop product from 300 different kinds of products,in Amazon warehouse. They are putting on 200 number shelves number following positions. IN general, human worker will need to spend about one minute to find the model of laptop product from these 200 number shelves in warehouse. For example, when one worker needs to find the brand Apple of one laptop product model: PHZ0123, when the warehouse has total 300 diferent kinds of products are putting on total 200 numbers of different shelves positions. Any one Amazon store worker must need to type this Apple brand laptop" Apple" name and its model number" PHZ0123 on the store computer as well as to search its putting on shelf number position from computer. Then, the Amazon store computer will find this laptop product to find its present putting on the correct shelf number position , e.g. 50 number of the shelf positon, or none stock record of all this model PHZ20123 laptop is sold out. So, Amazon store computer must need time to help this store worker to search this laptop product's putting on shelf number position as well as the worker needs time to walk to the right shelf number position to find this laptop product.

However, logistic robotic does not need to spend time to type this laptop product brand name and model number in order to search where it is putted on the shelf number position. The Amazon store worker only needs to speak this laptop product brand name, e.g. Apple and the kind of product, e.g.laptop and model number, e.g. PHZ0123 and its piece number, e.g. one piece number. Then, the Amazon logistic robot can follow the store worker's sound to find its past this kind of product's shelf number position memory to move to this shelf correct number position and finds it to deliver to the worker immediately. So, if the worker speaks 10 kinds f different products one time, then the logistic robotic can help this worker to find these 10 of different kinds products from their correct shelves numbers rapidly. Hence, it seems that logistic robots can help Amazon store workers to reduce each product search time as well as logistic robots can help workers to do goods delviery tasks. So, in logistic robotic behevioral economic vire, logistic robotics can replace many workers to do product position research and delivery tasks, store workers only need to speak the kind of product name, model, brand name and delivery piece number to let the logistic robotic to know. Then, the logistic robotic can follow the store worke's sending message to find the product's past memmory in order to tell the store worker, whether the product has how many stocks on shelf, or none of stock on shelf and where is putted on . Hence, any one store worker does not need to spend much time to search where any kinds of products shelves number position are. They only need logistic robotics to help them to do any kinds of products deliver to , or 20 or more different kinds between products location and the store worker's location. It means that the store worker only needs to stay on the same location to wait the logistic robotic brings his products comes back after he speaks to let the logistic rotic to know whether which kinds of products and piece number he needs . Then, he checks the logistic robotic's all products where they are correct or not. He may put all of these different kinds of gatherng products to the lorry to prepare to send to airport to fly to another country to deliver to the overseas client's home immediately when he confirms that all goods are his correct.

Hence, such as Amazon warehouse case, logistic robotics can help it to reduce many products searching time tasks and avoiding delivering wrong product to any overseas client's home rick occurence. Also, logistic robotics can reduce store workers number, because logistic robotics can replace 10 to 20 human store workers number absolutely. Otherwise, human store workers may have errors in their product search process, e.g. finding the wrong product from shelf or putting the product to the wrong shelf number position, but logistic robotics can reduce to 0 error to put wrong product on the shelf number position or spends long time to search the kind of product from the shelf number position. So, in logistic robotic behavioral economic view, robotics can help businesses to avoid products putting on wrong shelves number position error risk, reduce store workers number, reduce product shelf number position search economic time.

Can Robotic Help Warehouses To Avoid Resource Waste On Behavioral Economic View

● Behavioral economy view whether robotic can help warehouse to avoid time and human resource waste

IN fact,robts are being used in different types manufacturing to create more efficiency with fewer resource. Robots also reduce errors, to leass waste is produced. Less waste is produced and the robots are able to final and separate the small parts more efficiently than human hands can. For example, on environment recycled aspect, robots can help reduce waste that is incinerated by efficiently sorting materials that can be recycled quickly and more efficiently than humans reducing the input poser and cost control with such processes. So, robots can bring positive affect the environment, because robots use less energy and produce less waste.

As a whole, there are multiple benefits to using robots to fight climate change,e.g. robots can prevent pollution and emissions through careful monitoring optimize the manaufacturing processes to reduce energy consumption. Moreover, robots can help with recycling, the use of robots allows facility operators some new flexibility. Most technologies used in recycling allow to sort materials. The sensing robots (sensoes) allow robots to receive information about a certain measurement of the environment , or internal components. This is essential to robots to perform their tasks, and act upon any changes in the environment to calculate the appropriate response.

● How Amazon warehouse applies logistic robots to help it to waste resource waste

Hence, although robots can take our jobs, because they can help organizations to avoid resource waste, and it can bring negative effect to influence we lose jobs. ON behavorioral economic view, robots can help employers to reduce employees number, but it won't influence organizational overall performance to be worse or inefficiency, such as Amazon warehouse applies logistic robots to assist workers to deliver the right kind of goods to put on every correct shelf number position rapidly every day. Hence, one logistic robot can replace at least 10 store workers to do goods delivery tasks every day, e.g. one store worker needs to spend one minute to find the right kind of good to deliver to prepare to arrange to deliver it to fly to overseas client. Logistic robots only need 10 seconds to find the right kind of goods from the near 200 number shelves in Amazon warehouse as well as they are putting 300 different kinds of goods on these 200 shelves in Amazon warehouse every day.

Because each logistic robot has very good memory. Each logistic robot must remember any kinds of goods , their putting number position on which shelf, e.g. when the worker needs to find the model laptop product from 300 different kinds of products,in Amazon warehouse. They are putting on 200 number shelves number following positions. IN general, human worker will need to spend about one minute to find the model of laptop product from these 200 number shelves in warehouse. For example, when one worker needs to find the brand Apple of one laptop product model: PHZ0123, when the warehouse has total 300 diferent kinds of products are putting on total 200 numbers of different shelves positions. Any one Amazon store worker must need to type this Apple brand laptop" Apple" name and its model number" PHZ0123 on the store computer as well as to search its putting on shelf number position from computer. Then, the Amazon store computer will find this laptop product to find its present putting on the correct shelf number position , e.g. 50 number of the shelf positon, or none stock record of all this model PHZ20123 laptop is sold out. So, Amazon store computer must need time to help this store worker to search this laptop product's putting on shelf number position as well as the worker needs time to walk to the right shelf number

position to find this laptop product.
However, logistic robotic does not need to spend time to type this laptop product brand name and model number in order to search where it is putted on the shelf number position. The Amazon store worker only needs to speak this laptop product brand name, e.g. Apple and the kind of product, e.g.laptop and model number, e.g. PHZ0123 and its piece number, e.g. one piece number. Then, the Amazon logistic robot can follow the store worker's sound to find its past this kind of product's shelf number position memory to move to this shelf correct number position and finds it to deliver to the worker immediately. So, if the worker speaks 10 kinds f different products one time, then the logistic robotic can help this worker to find these 10 of different kinds products from their correct shelves numbers rapidly. Hence, it seems that logistic robots can help Amazon store workers to reduce each product search time as well as logistic robots can help workers to do goods delviery tasks. So, in logistic robotic behevioral economic vire, logistic robotics can replace many workers to do product position research and delivery tasks, store workers only need to speak the kind of product name, model, brand name and delivery piece number to let the logistic robotic to know. Then, the logistic robotic can follow the store worke's sending message to find the product's past memmory in order to tell the store worker, whether the product has how many stocks on shelf, or none of stock on shelf and where is putted on . Hence, any one store worker does not need to spend much time to search where any kinds of products shelves number position are. They only need logistic robotics to help them to do any kinds of products deliver to , or 20 or more different kinds between products location and the store worker's location. It means that the store worker only needs to stay on the same location to wait the logistic robotic brings his products comes back after he speaks to let the logistic rotic to know whether which kinds of products and piece number he needs . Then, he checks the logistic robotic's all products where they are correct or not. He may put all of these different kinds of gatherng products to the lorry to prepare to send to airport to fly to another country to deliver to the overseas client's home immediately when he confirms that all goods are his correct.
Hence, such as Amazon warehouse case, logistic robotics can help it to reduce many products searching time tasks and avoiding delivering wrong product to any overseas client's home rick occurence. Also, logistic robotics can reduce store workers number, because logistic robotics can replace 10 to 20 human store workers number absolutely. Otherwise, human store workers may have errors in their product search process, e.g. finding the wrong product from shelf or putting the product to the wrong shelf number position, but logistic robotics can reduce to 0 error to put wrong product on the shelf number position or spends long time to search the kind of product from the shelf number position. So, in logistic robotic behavioral economic view, robotics can help businesses to avoid products putting on wrong shelves number position error risk, reduce store workers number, reduce product shelf number position search economic time.

Amazon organizational intangible resource management strategy

● How to implement effective intangible resources management strategy to achieve performance improvement to Amazon e-commerce organization? Why does non intangible resources effective negligence management to Amazon organization, it will cause worse performance to Amazon e-commerce organization any one e-buyer?
One efficient organization must need have efficient and effective resources management strategy in order to provide enough resources for its organization overall different departments cooperation effectively and efficiently. How to implement effective resources management strategy to achieve performance improvement? Why does ersources shortage to organization, it will cause worse performance? I shall explain the reasons as below:
For Amazon e-commerce organization example, it is one global the most large goods transport delivery service moddleman role between global online customers and their product salespeople. Amazon owns its webstores, so global any one country buyer clicks to its different countries webstores , then he/she can choose any kinds of products to buy from Amazon any one country webstore. However, the product is owned the another seller. So, any products are not owned by from Amazon any one country webstores. However, the product is owned by the another seller. SO, any products are not owned by Amazon. It only provides webstores to let global any one e-buyer to buy the product after he/she has paid visa payment. So, Amazon's role is one middleman. It needs to provide goods transport service to help the product's seller to deliver the product to whose e-buyer individual hoime in the most short time, e.g. when one China e-buyer clicks to Amazon China webstore , after he chooses any brands of computers product

from Amazon China webstore, he makes purchase of the brand of comouter decision. Then, he needs to pay visa to Amazon 's China webstore . When Amazon confirms that ie can accept payment by the China e-buyer's visa. Then, Amazon will deliver the product to the China e-buyer's home within one week or longer time, the delivery days time depends on how much delivery fee, the China's e-buyer , he can pay. So, Amazon only can receive commision infomr from the computer brand product seller. Because Amazon can build famous loyalty of rapid goods delivery service provider barnad and its different countries websites can provide above one million different kinds of brand products to let global different conuntries e0buyers to choose in order to make the most fair and the most reasonable purchase price decision from its different Amazon different countries webstores per day. So, Amazon can help its different countries sellers to apply Amazon itself unique different countries' websotes design to attract global many different countries e-buyers to click to Amazon's webstores to find any kinds of products to choose to buy conveniently.

So, such as Amazon e-commerce organization case, if it hopes to attract global different countries e-buyers prefer to click to Amazon itself any one webstore more than other firms themselves webstores . Then, it must need have enough resources (tangible and intangible) both in order to provide raoid goods delviery service and many different kinds of goods choice provision service and reasonable price consumption channel to let any one countrye-buyer feels confidence and safe payment transaction and enough product advertisement, photo, price, function information in order to make final purchase decision from Amazon itself different country webstores more easily.

Hence, the tangible and intangible resources are needed to supuply to Amazon e-commerce organization. They may include: Product photos, price information, product advertisement which are shown to Amazon's different countries webstores , enough online customer service enquiry employees number, enough computers number, enough computers number, different countries offices and warehouses number, computers, internnet technology etc. tangible resource as well as customer service enquiries feedbacks, global rapid goods delivery transport service to any one country e-buyer's home, safe e-payment channel, providing to buy global any one country sellers their products in the most reasonable and the most fair purchase transaction. All ot these issues are any one e-buyer individual purchase feeling to Amazon. SO, they are intangibel (non-tangible) resources to Amazon. It means that if Amazon can let global any one e-buyer feels it's e-purchase service provision can let they feel more satisfactory , then they will choose to buy Amazon webstores any kinds of products more than other sellers their webstores products, because Amazon webstores can provide the kind of product of different brands choice, it aims to compare whether which brand's price is unreasonable too high or which brand's product's quality is worse, or design is not very atrraction. So, Amazon's intangibale resource, such as rapid goods delivery service, online or phone customer enquiry service, webstores' products information whether e-buyers can feel satisfactory, e.g. reasonable price, clear product photo many different kinds of brands product choice. All of these intangible resources to Amazon, they may also influence Amazon's future e-buyer number absolutely.

● How can Amazon raise intangible resource number to be effective?

SO, I explain that Amazon hadboth kinds of resources. They may include tangible and intangible resources. Internet speed, whether it is intangible resources. Internet speed, whether it is rapid or slow to satisfy global e-buyers online purchase speed and non online traffic jam accidents feeling. Amazon webstores any brands of products, photos, price information images whether they are clear to let any one global ebuyer to feel when they click to Amazon any one webstores. All of these internet technology resources to Amazon any one webstore will influence Amazon e-commerce organization's e-buyers number will increase or decrease . For example, if Amazon's China webstore can not let Chinese e-buyers to feel that it can not provide different kinds of brand products photos' clear image to let any one Chinese e-buyer to see the product photo clearly. When one Chinese e-buyer clicks to Amazon Chinese webstore to find any brands of laptop products to prepare to choose one to buy. But when he clicks to Amazon China webstore, he can not feel any one brand of laptop's photo is clear to let he feels. Then, theser unclear laptop photos may influence the Chinese e-buyer forgets his laptop purchase decision from Amazon 's China webstore easily. He may clcik to the another brand of laptop seller webstore to buy the brand of laptop from the laptop seller itself webstore. SO, Amazon's webstore design may be the important intangible resource to influence global any one e-buyer's visiting Amazon's any one webstore times or reducing to do to choose to visit Amazon's webstore behavior , due to they do not click to Amazon any one webstore websites again.

I recommend that Amazon ought consider how to design its any countries webstores in order to attract global e-buyers visiting Amazon itself webstores times number increase. So, global e-buyers' visiting Amazon different countries webstores times which will be Amazon's most important intangible resources to cause its future global e-buyers number. This kind of intangible resources may help Amazon e-commerce goods delivery service organization to raise its competitive effort,, because when one country's ebuyer feels Amazon can provide the most attraction and fair purchase channel from its different countries webstores. Then, the country's e-buyer will talk to his friends, families to prefer to choose Amazon if they have online purchase desire. Because Amazon's any one e-buyer , he .she will persduade his/her friends, families to choose Amazon's e-purchase channel., if he feels it can provide excellent e-purchase method to satisfy his online purchase need. Consequently, Amazon's e-buyers number may be influenced to increase.

ON conclusion, such as Amazon case, how to decide its whether which is the most important tangible and/or intangible resources in order to raise competition effort. It depends on whether how the seller sells its product, in order to concentrate on spending to increase the kind of resources number, such as Amazon e-commerce goods sale and delivery service organization case, internet webstores design intangible image dissatisfactory or satisfactory feeling which may be the most influential global e-buyers number increases or decreases. Moreover, Amazon's internet webstores design intangible satisfactory or dissatisfactory feeling resource may also influence e-buyer before or after e-purchase service requiry feedback feeling, safe visa card payment feeling, fair and reasonable brands of products price information and different brands of product photos image seeing satisfactory or dissatisfactory feeling , they are intangible resource asset to Amazon when global any one ebuyer must need to click to its any one webstore to find its any kinds of product to make purchase decision. So, any organizations must need to spend limit money to support its the most influential intangible resource , instead of tangible resources in order to increase clients number. On conclusion, we can increase organizational resources on these several aspects: Organizational resources are all assets that are available to a firm for use during the production process or service process, such as Amazon ecommerce organization case. The four basic types of organization resources are human, monetary, raw materials may be tangible, but internet technology may be another intangible resource to today any organizations. Improving organizational resources aim to improve efficiency, it means as the ability to accomplish something with the least amout of wasted time, money and effort or performance as well as effectiveness, such as improving internet speed, and none online traffic jam accidents occurrence easily. It means as trhe degree to which something is successful in producing a desired result success. However, we can improve resources by these way, they may include : Review who manages resources within the organization, build an-up-to date knowledge raise and company wide resource pool, manage the resource pool in line with the market, focus on education and talent employees growth, keep the customers in mind, work on quality services or products, learn to use technology , such as Amazon needs to learn how to raise high speed internet service for its webstores, and avoid online traffic jam frequent occurrent to its any one country webstore.

To sum up effective resource management strategy can help any organizations to increase resource number. Resource management is acquiring , allocating and managing the reosurces, such as individuals, and their skills, finances, technology , material , machinery, and natural resources required for a project. Hence effective effective resource management strategy ensures that internal and external resources are used effectively on time and budget, resources may be obtained internally from the host organization or procured from external resources. SO, effective resource management can help organizations to save resources being wastes and finances being spend on the wrong things, a significant cost saving factor. Hence, such as Amazon e-commerce organization, it needs to know how to learn how to apply internet technology to improve its different countries webstores design, shorten goods transport delivery time, gathering more different brands of product prices, data and phoducts photos improving safe visa card transaction secret to increase e-buyer individual e-purchase confidence. When Amazon can concentrate on effective allocate limited resource to achiev ethese objectives. Then, its global e-buyer number may increase significantly.

Management accounting science how applies to Amazon ecommerce organization

Management accounting concept can help organizations to do management budget strategies, e.g. margin analysis, capital budget, inventory valuation and product cost budget, trend analysis and forecast . Management accounting also called managerial accounting or cost accounting, is the process of analysis business costs and operations to prepare internal financial report, records and managers decision making process in achieving business goals.

However, management accountants depend on standard financial statements containing the earning statement, cash flow statement and balance sheet. In addition , it also makes use of additional finds reports in analysizing the information of the organization including budget performance and cost reports. I shall attempt to explain how management account science can help organizations to analyze cost , why and how changes in order to avoid expense increases or excess cost cases or loss increases.

For Amazon e-commerce publish organization example, Amazon publish is a famous publish organization. It applies internet (online) channel to help authors to sell electronic books and paper books to different countries readers. It also cooperate to other publishers to deliver any its anthors books to their webstores, so when one reader chooses its publish partner webstores to buy Amazon any author books, then Amazon publish will share royalty income between them. Hence, Amazon publish may be book distribution partner to its other e-publish partners.

- How management accounting cocept can help Amazon publish to manage its cost effectively in order to increase its profit or e-books or paper books sale ability.

Amazon publish is a e-comerce organization. It depends high internet speed to help global authors to register Amazon publish's individual author account , then any global authors may download their book files to produce any ebooks and papers to sell from Amazon publisher webstores as wellas global any readers can apply Amazon publish webstores to buy any author individual paper or ebooks from its web-publish stores rapidly. So, Amazon publish must need have fast speed internet technology to support its books sale ability,

It brings this question: How much does Amazon publish internet expenditure need? Does it need to pay shops rent per month? Because Amazon publish has none any actual book shops to locate in any countries. So, Amazon publish must not pay rent to any countries for its shops. Although Amazon publish does not need to pay rent for any book shops, but Amazon publish needs to pay extra internet expenditure to US internet service provider to support its electronic webstores daily electronic books and paper books every purchase transaction, any countries author individual book electronic files download per day 24 hours . So, Amazon publish must need to pay more expenditure for internet service to support its authors and readers their electronic books and paper books purchase and sale transaction per day 24 hours.

As Amazon publish case, in its financial report indicates , it does not pay any book stores rent expenditure or book stores (shops) building building expediture on its profit and loss account, but Amazon publish must need to pay internet service expenditure to US internet service provider. Moreover, this internet service expenditure must be more amount, due to it needs to provide its webstores online book (electronic books and paper books) to sell and electronic library e-book lending service to global readers, 24 hours. Thus, internet service expenditure must be Amazon publish long-term influential transaction expenditure because, any electronic books and paper books, even e-library books borrow service and readers must need to pay visa card for borrowing book month service fee and purchase books from amazon publish e-publish webstores in any time every day.

Hence, Amazon publish must need have good management account strategy in order to predict whether different countries will have how many readers click to its different countries e-publish webstores to spend time to choose different authors books to buy or borrow to read from intenet channel. So, any countries readers budgeting number, readers reading habit behavior, e.g. US has about one million online readers click Amazon e-publish webstores , but it has only three thousands readers pay visa card to buy its ebooks and paper books from its Amazon electronic publish webstores, in this week , but next week, US has about seven thousands online readers click Amazon e-publish webstores, but it has three thousands readers pay visa card to buy its ebooks and paper books. Hence, it seems tha although this week has one million online readers click to Amazon publish electonic webstores to seek any books, but the book buyer number has only three thousands. Otherwise, although next week, it reduces three thousands e-readers click to visit Amazon e-publish webstores e-readers number , but it still keep same three thousand e-readers to choose to buy Amazon publish's books to read.

I assume that Amazon publish needs to pay a fixed internet service expenditure, e.g. US $500,000, but it design this e-publish webstores can help it to do its different countries e-publish webstores, their daily e-readers visiting number, daily electronic book and paper book sale number and daily e-readers visiting time statistics. It's electronic publish webstores can help it to record any countries' reading habits and reading taste , e.g. how many fiction , story books have sold in the week, how many non fiction books have sold in the week , e.g. business topic books have sold next week.

So, Amazon publish can use its e-publish webstores to gather above data in order to make author book topic sale choice, e.g. whether this week, US market ought sell how many consumer psychological topic book, US market ought sell how many management topic book next week. If this week US market can only sell one thousand consumer psychological topic book to compare its budget is less than one thousand consumer psychological topic books budget sale number reduces, e.g. in the week, there are two thousands readers choose to buy consumer psychological topic books from European market in this week. It implies that there are many European readers who like to read consumer behavior books recently. Hence, Amazon can attempt to concentrate on encouraging authors to write more consumer psychological books to let European readers to read within next several months.

Basic on above effects, Amazon needs to provide rapid internet service to European libraries, schools ,e-book partners to help them to promote Amazon consumer psychology topic books in order to let the European consumer psychological students, consumer psychology lecturers, consumer psychologists to know Amazon publish can provide more different topics concern consumer psychology research in order to increase Amazon 's consumer psychology book European market book buyers bumber.

As above case, I assume Amazon publish needs to pay a fixed internet service expenditure , e.g. US$500,000 per month. Amazon needs webstores to evaluate whether it is value, if it helps European schools, libraries organizations to pay internet fee, in order to let they can let many consumer psychology students and teachers and consumer psychologists to know that Amazon publish may have enough different consumer psychology books to be provided to European publish libraries, schools readers to read. For example, I assume next several month, Amazon publish needs to pay US two million internet service expenditure to global different European countries to help Amazon publish itself to promote its al different authors' consumer psychology topic books as well as it evaluates that it will sell different European countries; students , teachers and consumer psychologists readers, they have about three million readers at least choose to buy its one million consumer psychology topic authors; paper books and electronic books next several months as well as it also needs to evaluate whether it can earn more than US ten million at least royalty income after reducing author royalty from all European countries book markets.

Thus, if Amazon publish makes decision to help European countries schools, public libraries to pay internet expenditure to help it to advertise its one million consumer psychology topic authors electronic and paper books to sell. It must needs to pay fixed US$500,000 internet expenditure for Amazon publish its all e-bpublish webstores and it also needs to pay extra two million internet service expenditure for global all European countries libraries and schools per month. If next month, Amazon publish can earn more than US tem million at least royalty income after reducing author royalty from all European countries book market. Then, Amaozn publish ought attempt to make this internet service expenditure for all European schools, libraries organizations, if it had confidence to earn this royalty amount from European consumer psychology book readers, such as this Amazon publish.

On conclusion, , this Amazon publish organization case, it may attempt to apply management accounting science method to make book sale number budget, royalty income budget, even analysis to reader individual reading habit, book topic choices, book sale price evaluation in order to judge whether the kind or topic book ought concentrates on selling to which countries marekts, such as Amazin publish case, it also may choose different consumer psychology topic books to concentrate on selling to different European countries in next several months, if it can earn all European royalty income more than its internet service expenditure to European schools, libraries, then Amazon may attempt to make this decision. Otherwise, it won't be good decision.

Hence, it implies that management accounting is one kind of business management science, it can apply number to help any organizations to do right or reasonable reason more accurate as well as it is different to traditional financial acounting, it only helps organizations to record and income and expenditure, earn or loss record function. Hence, management accounting may help any organizations to attempt implement useful or effective strategies in order to improve themselves performance.

CHAPTER SIX

How Amazon solves its future marketing challenges

Amazon faces what future marketing competition

Nowadays, any kinds of businessmen may apply internet to do themselves e-commerce sale channel easily and conveniently. So, Amazon needs to find strategies how to persuade any kinds of brands of sellers to choose its e-stores to help themselves to advertise, promote and sell their products to replace themselves online stores from Amazon its e-stores. It will be one long term marketing strategic problem to Amazon needs to consider how to attract global many sellers choose Amazon's e-stores to replace themselves e-stores (online sale channels) easily. How to increase global sellers confidence to choose Amazon e-stores to help them to sell their different kinds of products ? I shall attempt to indicate some useful marketing and management strategies to explain as below:

Firstly, I shall indicate what kinds of challenges Amazon will face in future ecommerce market. Although, Amazon's cloud dominance core online sale marketplace had succeed, but it still faces many challenges.
It needs to implement useful strategies to solve in order to increase its online buyers number and online sellers number both.

` On growth challenge concerning aspect, Amazon needs to learn how to grow investors confidences to let Amazon itself can help them to apply its e-stores to help them to advertise their products from Amazon e-stores to replace Google cloud online advertisement service competitor as well as Microsoft cloud online advertisement service competitor both main online advertisement service providers. It seems that global online sellers may also choose Google and Microsoft cloud advertisement to replace Amazon cloud advertisement service.

So, Amazon's marketplace needs to find itself on the defensive for reasons unrelated to the probe improvements in e-commerce technology on the whole could mean that fewer sellers see Amazon as their primary sales channel, instead of Google , Microsoft cloud advertisement sale channel. Hence, Amazon needs to implement strategy how to help any global sellers to change positive shopping experience on traditional web stores improvement, in order to help they to promote their brands more effectively.

ON online shopping confident challenge aspect, Amazon became the dominant e-commerce marketplace in the world by offering hundreds of million of products at competitive prices. However, Amazon will face third-party sellers participation to cloud market online sale agent competitive challenge. Third-party sellers , such as Google, Microsoft have made up an increasing share of products on Amazon in recent years, roughly 58% of sales on Amazon were key third-party sellers, but that comes with its own host of problems, including fakes, counterfeits and unsafe products that Amazon has not been able to successful compete easily in third party cloud e-commerce sale market. Past surveys have shown that Amazon is among the most trusted technology brands out there, but if it gains a reputation as a sketchy products, some consumers could not to do their shopping at first past sites. Hence, Amazon needs to let global many sellers believe that it is the best third party cloud advertisement service provider to compare its another third part cloud advertisement service providers , such as Google. Microsoft in order to persuade many global sellers choose to use its cloud online advertisement service.

What is Amazon marketing strategy? Amazon uses the high runner strategy to market its products. This strategy was data to uncover which products are in the highest demand in every category . Amazon's pricing strategy and bids heavily on advertisement to pull people to those sellers themselves products. In future, Amazon's marketing strategies include: SEOP, cheap price advertisement, user-generated content, video marketing, dedicated website. Hence, Amazon's future marketing strategy or communication strategy aims to increase customer traffic to Amazon websites, create awareness of products or services, promote repeat purchases, develop incremental product and service revenue opportunities.

However, Amazon can improve marketing strategy to help its sellers to boost their products sale by providing free shipping, reviewing [product sale analytics, testing different advertising methods. So, Amazon has three big market sale channels, the retail marketplace, Amazon Prime, and Amazon web services. Moreover, Amazon needs to build effective growth strategy. It's Amazon's secondary intensive growth strategy. It aims to generate more revenue from markets where the company currently operates because Amazon is depended on its customers, which is why when consumerism grows, the business by default grows. It means that whose global e-commerce online e-stores purchase market grows, the global visiting shops market customers number will be influenced to fall down. So, it implies that they have close customer number relationship between e-stores customers number and visiting shops customers number to different kinds of businesses.

Even, future Amazon business may have this competitive strategy, it can be described as cost leadership taken to the extreme strategy. Cost leadership strategy seems as cheap , bulk products sale, such as " discount stores " sale method. All of Amazon's products are sold by the cheapest sale product method. So, Amazon marketing communication mix integrates print and media advertising, sales promotions , events and experiences, public relation and direct marketing. Amazon places a particular focus on print and media advertising and sales promotions elements of the marketing communication channels. So, Amazon was direct marketing. It is so advanced that they see what their customers are searching for, offer products, that are the same of similar and send their emails for when the price changes for an item, the customers have been eyeing up.

However, Amazon's management principles of leadership in organization, it is also important to influence organizational growth. It can drive Amazon to boost sale, they include: customers obsession, leaders start with the customer and work backwards, leaders are owners, invent and simplify, learning and be curious. Hiring and developing the4 best, insisting on the highest standards. So, Amazon company makes include customers are at the top of the company's interests, Amazon wants to make everything as simple as it is possible. Hence, Amazon applies intensive growth strategy. It is a growth strategy that focuses on cultivating new products or new markets and sometimes both. Amazon aims to help its any kinds of product sellers to bring new online advertisement experience feeling to let online buyers to aware their new products existences.

Hence, Amazon needs to help its sellers to change their e-business model from " direct sales" to sales-and-service model, aggregating many sellers under one virtual roof and receiving commission from the other companies sales, because Amazon needs to make income through its online retail e-stores, subscriptions and web services, among other channels. Retail remains Amazon's primary source of revenue, with online and physical stores accounting for the biggest share. Essentially , Amazon is choosing growth over profits. And, Amazon is able to lose money to help its sellers grow their markets shares from e-business model.

In fact, most Amazon sellers market least US$1,000 per month in sales, and some super-sellers make upward US$250,000 each month in sales. However, Amazon also helps someone without cost to create selling, such as Amazon publishers. So, Amazon publishers do not need to spend any cost to sell e-books or paper books when they download their books on Amazon publish. Hence, Amazon can attract many different countries authors choose to cooperate to sell their books from Amazon publish platform. It means that Amazon's business model , which was initially based on ecommerce had changed and now incorporates entertainment, music, cloud computing, meal delivers etc. e-publishing etc. Although, Amazon sells a lot more through its subsidiaries, the core Amazon busi9ness model is based on an e-commerce market platform . Amazon sells products or the platform but, also allows third-party sellers to sell consumers.

How does Amazon future business model? Amazon future business model ought depend on geographically and terms of products and services offered to help its different kinds of product sellers to sell their products, such as continue expanding on selling music, videos, electronics, video games, software, houseware, toys, games, e-books as well as attracted customers were Amazon its personalized recommendation tools and customers reviews, this developing a community of consumers , which is essential free online service to any one Amazon customer.

So, Amazon will obsession rather than competitor focus, passion excellence, and long=term, thinking. Amazon must continue focus on those operations in order to grow income. They may include: Amazon marketplace business model, Amazon asks for a fee from its sellers to promote and advertise their products, Amazon's subscription business model has been vital to the brand growth. In exchange for a monthly fee. Subscribers have access to the platform's video and music streaming catalog, free two days shopping, unlimited photo storage etc.

Amazon was services business model, it is a low cost complete IT structure platform, whose services are contracted by companies, organizations, and institutions around the world. Amazon kindle, business model, it is Amazon's e-reading service, users can buy, browse, and download books, magazines and newspapers , available at kindle store. Amazon patent business model, it has more than 1,000 patents, several of which are licensed by other campaigns. Amazon advertising business model, it is Amazon ad. Platform offers sponsored ads and video. It is a very efficient marketing channel, since the audience there with the intention of buying. Hence, Amazon 's customer segments may include: sellers, buyers and developers. Sellers are all the companies that use Amazon's e-commerce platform to sell their products to all the community involves with Amazon web-services.

Amazon's cloud computing platform, As its own website states, they are customers and partners, e.g. any public sector or private sector organizations. And the buyers are global people, who acquire products and services through Amazon's channels. So, Amazon can track its custo0mer based on some characteristics, such as interest, engagement, and personnel information (e.g. gender, geographical space, language among other), ion order to predict any countries potential consumer behaviors more accurately.

Hence, Amazon's business model is based on three value propositions: low price, fast delivery, and a wide selection of products in order to let consumers feel these benefits, e.g. convenience to connect to Amazon's any web stores to buy any kinds of products, with an reasonable price, safe and reliable delivery service. Also Amazon can build long term good relationship to its global buyers from its web stores, such as product reviews, and comments on the platform, telephone, online chat and email contact. Aside from Amazon's online resource, other key resources to bring Amazon's benefits, they may include physical spaces of the company, such as offices, warehouses, supply chain structure and automation etc.

In fact, human resources are essential for Amazon , which needs to help it to operate daily online purchase and sale activities effectively, such as Amazon's e-stores designers, engineers, developers. Hence, Amazon key partners may include: world wide different brans of product sellers, affiliates, bloggers who earn a commission for any referrals that need to a sale. In addition to helping with sales, they also promote traffic to the Amazon platform. Amazon's platform independent software vendors, who adapt Amazon's online platform technology to work, content creators , they are independent authors, who can publish their works through kindle direct publishing, subsidiaries, include companies that provide storage spaces, stores and systems, in additions to brands and products, developed by Amazon itself, such as Amazon essentials, Amazon elements, kindle , Alexa etc.

Also, Amazon needs to know how to let its future cost structure to reduce in order to achieve saving cost benefit in long time. Its cost structure includes its complete IT structure, customer service center, software development and maintenance, information security, marketing as well as expenses involved in maintaining its physical spaces, such as fulfillment centers, sortation centers, and delivery stations. Hence, future Amazon will need to implement useful methods to help its any departments to reduce operational cost as well as have to persuade partners, sellers, product buyers to help them to raise sales growth, earn more commissions, bringing advertisement effectiveness, subscription income growth, web service growth and patents income.

Amazon's main competitors may include: online stores, Walmart, Alibaba, Otto, Jingdong, ebay, fliplcart, Newegg, ralcuten. So, if Amazon can persuade these any one online competitors to be its future partners, Then, it may reduce its online competitors number significantly. However, Amazon SWOT analysis indicates its strengths may include: Building famous e-commerce brand valuation, customer orientation, such as reasonable prices, personalized suggestions, and reviews make a loyal consumer community, innovation, it always develops new products and services, when improves its regular business, it does not maintain physical stores and has little inventory. It is able to keep a low- cost structure, large selection , it owns an extensive product mix, allowing customers to buy anything on the same platform, more global third-party sale partners, logistics . Also, Amazon's weaknesses may include: limitable business model, kindle e-book publish faces many e-publish competitors, employee workplace conditions may feel worse , focusing dependence on distributors, that exposed Amazon to a wide range to issues, especially considering renegotiation of terms. But, Amazon also has these opportunities, such as expansion. Amazon can expand its operation in developing countries, increasing physical stores number, it can make some big purchases, such as acquisitions and that can increase market share and reduce competition. But, it also has threats, e.g. some government regulations can threaten Amazon distribution inside some countries, exploitations , labor, cybercrime, it can threaten the security of the platform and its users, it faces strong competitors, A video streaming service, such as Disney Add, HBO,. Netflix.

Moreover, it can not estimate when economic recession , online stores are not adapted to alive to economic recession and uncertainty can impact Amazon's sales, fake reviews, customers rely on reviews to make purchase and Amazon needs to have more positive product review more than negative product review from its online customers.

On conclusion, Amazon is one good case to explain future any kinds of e-businesses will face what challenges in order to decide how to implement effectiv3e strategies to help them to solve any possible not predicted challenges in order to raise competitive effort.

CHAPTER SEVEN

How social change helps Amazon development

What are the relationship between online shopping demand and supply relationship

According to market economy theory, the relationship between supply and demand balances out at a point in the future; this point is called the equilibrium price.

Economists and companies analyze the relationship between supply and demand when making strategic product decisions. Both economists and companies analyze the relationship between supply and demand when making strategic product decisions. The assumption behind a market economy is that supply and demand are the best determinants for an economy's growth and health.

Consumer Behavior Influences Demand

One way that companies or economists might analyze this relationship is to create graphs that chart the equilibrium price of certain goods and services in order to determine product development and their production schedule. Consumer behavior dictates which products are produced and sold because consumers create the demand that companies attempt to meet. As a result, companies may study consumer behavior in an attempt to understand the current demand and predict future demand. It is vital that companies maintain the capacity to produce enough of a good or service that they can satisfy consumer demands.

Supply and demand are two sides of the same market coin. Generally, supply is how much of something is available or will be produced at a certain price. Demand is how much of something people want to purchase or consume at a certain price. One way to develop a more precise relationship between the two is to consider how the price of something affects its supply and its demand. Generally when the price of a good goes up, so does the supply, since firms are willing to create more when they can sell at higher prices. But when the price of a good goes up consumers will, at the same time, generally demand less. It is the interaction of supply and demand that determines how much will be produced and consumed and at what price, converging to a state known as equilibrium.

Human social job change demand and supply relationship

The relationship between social change and human behavior

Human Behavioral network job brings social economic benefits

Whether human social job change it depends on social job demand more or job supply more? What does human network job mean ? Why may human network job be popular? Why human network job behavior may influence economy ?

Nowadays internet is popular to use. We can apply internet to find data , search any new things, even earn money. Why does internet

may become huma network job source. For example, e-publish may be one kind of new human network job. Any authors may apply internet

channel to help them to sell electronic or paper books from e-publisher web store. They may apply facebook, you tub etc. any online

channel to promote themselves new books to let new readers to know whether when they may buy themselves favourable new topic books to read
from electronic publisher web store.

Thus, future electronic publisher industry may help any authors to build internet network platform to help them to sell and promote
ot advertise their any one new electronic or paper book topic to let global any one reader to choose to buy their any new topic books from electronic publisher web store easily and conveniently. However, it implies that electronic network platform author may be one kind of future new human network job in our societies.

How electronic network platform author job may bring economy benefit in macro economy view? A person can have few friends, contacts and still be very influential if these few
friends and contacts are themselves highly influential, e.g. one author must not need to know any one reader in global society. When they like to choose any electronic books from electronic internet network platform. They may become the author's any one topic book buyer, when they feel the author's any one topic book is fun and attract they make decision to buth the strange author whose the topic book from electronic book publisher's platform web store conventiently in short time. Although, they are strangers, they do not know themselves , but the reader can understand what it way that made Google from writing platofrm to create new creative mind and typing network job method to replace traditional hand writing book method for global authors. It will be one kind of new human network writing job.

Hence, global any one reader can apply an innovative search engine , such as google.com to find whether whom author personal new topic books are value to read from internet.
Then, the electroniuc publisher's web store may be new book store platform sale network to help the author to sell many electronic or paper books from electronic network platform
in short time. So, internet may be future new network plaform to help global any one author to create network writing job absolutely. Furthermore, internet may be popular social media
to help any one author to build goold relationship between his/her readers. It is one kind of new network, human network job. New authors do not need to buy many paper books to prepare to put in any one book shop warehouse. Their every book can print on demand to reduce out of book stock in any one book shop. They may choose to sell either electronic books or paper books both from any one book publisher web store. So, electronic network platform may be one kind of good writing channel to help human authors to create income and it can also help authors to bring new creative mind and new topic fun content books to let readers to know and buy to read from electronic publisher network platform.

Why does human behavior may be one kind of new human network job to bring global economic advantages. ALthough, it may be free income or without inocme, but the person does the network behavior, his/her behavior may be bring advantages to influence many other people's health. For this case, when a worker in a coffee shop in an airport gets a vaccination aganinst the flu, it does not only helps him or her stay healthy, but also helps the many travellers who might otherwise have been inflected if that workers caught the flu. So, the externality , the result implies the vaccination of even a part of a community conveys benefits to the whole community. For example, governments pay special attention to the vaccinations of school children, teachers, health mothers, and the elderly, categories of people particularly susceptible not only to catching, but also to transmitting a disease.

It is not accidential that governments are heavily involved with vaccination . When there are externalities, free market, fail to persuade individual incentives with society's
their the worker's decision of whether to get a vaccine ends up attracting whether other people get sick. The workers might not fully take all these other people's potential suffering into account when making her or his vaccination decision.

As Stanford University does many suggestions, understand this and tries to help them make the right decisions and so providers free flu vaccines for its staff and students.
Small pockets of unvaccinated individuals can allow a disease to gain a spread more widely well-being. For example,

parent weighing the costs and benefits of a vaccine for their child is not always thinking of the consequences of that vaccination to other people. THese are markets in which subsidizing or regulating behavior can make everyone better off. Because the reason for requiring that a child be vaccinated before enrolling in school is not just to protect that child, because each child's vaccination affects others via potential contagions.

On conclusion, it seems that many traditional paper book publish business begain to change to electronic book publish business. Due, to online technology existence, it influences many readers choose to buy electronic books to read. Hence, due to readers reading demand change which is from paper book reading habit to electonic book reading habit.Then,it explains that electornic book supply number depends on electronic book reader reading demand in economic view.

Robots take our jobs behavioral and economy influences

Robot job behavior brings economy influences

Whether robot labor needs are depended on employer labor demand more or robot labor number supply more? If one day robots can replace human to do simple, even complex jobs. They will bring what influences to our global societial economy.The popular economic refrain declares that the

global middle class is dying and robots will soon take our jobs, e.g. shopping center customer service jobs, library service jobs, cinema ticket sale jobs, restaurant kitchen cooker jobs,

even, bus drivers, taxi drivers etc. public transport driving jobs, accountant, doctors etc. professional jobs. Whether it is beautiful or petty matter if our future societies have many human jobs can be replaced to do from robots. Businessman must may reduce to employ employees and reduce to pay salary or wage, when robots can be replaced to do their employees tasks. But, societies must bring unemployement rate rises , due to societies will have many people loss jobs when their employers choose to buy robots to serve their clients or do any office tasks or customer service or cleaning etc. tasks.

In micro economy view, employers may save money in long term, but in macro economy view, it will cause unemployment ratio rises , even crime rate rises when there are many people lose

jobs in societies. These models of doom, though, fail to account for the hundreds of businesses riding the waves of change in their industries when robots may be invented to replace human to do many simple , even complex tasks in our future societies.

WE may image that one small factory needs to manufacture fishes canes to sell to supermarket, the small , cheaper stuff and higher margin parts of the fishes manufacture industry. Before, this factory needs to employe many human factory workers need to help every fresh customer makeing the perfect fishing gear, designed for performance, durability, and cost in order to achieve to manufacture every fish cane in whole fished processing manufacturing stages. Every worker needs to spend about 15 to twenty minutes to finish every fish cane , till to delivery to any supermarket to sell. If this fish canes manufacturing factory can apply manufacturing robots to help them to finish any one working tasks , every robot can only spend five minutes to finish whole fresh fish cane manufacturing process. Thus, every robot can

help this factory save 10 to 15 minutes time to finsh every fish cane manufacturing process. IN fact, time is money, because when every robot can help this factory to reduce 10 to 15 minutes time to compare human worker. Then, this factory can finish about 20 fish canes in one hour if it can use robot to help it to manufacture fish canes. Otherwise, if this factory still use human workers to help it to manufacture fish canes, then it can finsh about 3 to 4 fish canes in one hour. SO, the manufacturing efficiency ensures that robots must help this fish manufacturing factory to raise fish canes number more than human workers. So, in robotic behavioral economy view, manufacturing robots must help this fish canes manufacturing factory to raise fish canes manufacturing number and deliver increasing number to supermarkets to prepare to sell every day. Robots can help this fish canes manufacturing factory bring manufacturing time saving, rising manufacturing efficiency, improving performance and reducing wages expenditure long time advantages in micro economy view. However, manufacturing robots can also bring disadvanages to society, e.g. increasing unemployment ratio, increasing crime rate, this factory workers will lose jobs and income, they need earn social welfare from government and increasing government finance pressure in short time, even long time in macro economic view.

Stanford University graduate program in economics, Scott lecturer explained that "in demand and supply economic theory for robots supply and demand case, robots supply number increasing may influence human workers demand number decrease. It sometimes calls " the efficient frontier".

No specific human beings were mentioned in any of economics classes. As robots supply and demand in market case, They (robots) may be purely theoretical " agents" who reached to the most reasonable sale prices in order to persuade any one businessman buyer to make manufacturing robot buying decision whether robots can help him / her to bring how much saving time , saving money, saving cost, improving performance, efficiency economic benefit before he/she plans to reduce workers number when he/she decides to apply robots to replace human workers in his/her factory or office or any service department, e.g. cinema ticket sale service, shopping center customer service, shopping center cleaning , supermarket customer service etc. service or sale tasks. When robots can replace human to do any one of these tasks in any organizations. So, robots may be human worker agents who reached to prices the way robots would react to a software

command. There was nothing that explained why some people thrived and others did n't or why truly brilliant, hardworking people could fail when much lazier folks succeeded." Having been admitted to the Stanford University graduate program in economics, Scott lecturer hoped to get his answers there.

How robots influence our future social changing? Using the right technology can be a boon to your business in this economy. For internet example, it is easier than ever to find well-matched customers all around the world, to stay in contact with them, and to more quickly design the products they want. If you focus solely on being cutting -edge, though you risk letting the technology

take over what should be very robust relationships with your customers , employees, and colleagues. IN nowaddays society, technoligical advances and cutomation, personal

relationships in business are more crucial than ever. I mean that robots can not replace human to serve clients to let them to feel more comfortable and passion more easily. For shoe shop case example, if the shoe shop apply one robot to serve its clients to replace human shoe salesperson to serve its shoe customers. Robots ensure that they can not persuade every shoe potential buyer to make shoe buying decision more easily when robots need to contact every shoe potential buyer. The reason is simple, because robots can not touch any one shoe buyer individual emotion very easier.

If the shoe buyer needs the robots to help him/her to choose any right shoe styles when he/she can not feel himself / herself can make the most right shoe style choice decision. The robots can not replace human shoe salesperson to make shoe style choice judgement more easily. They must need longer time to analyze whether which shoe style may be the most suitable to the shoe buyer. Otherwise, human shoe salesperson may attempt to make the most right shoe style choice decision to help any one shoe buyer to chooce the most right style shoe because he/she owns shoe style sale experience, shoe style knowledge, the most important reason is that they can feel every shoe customer individual emotion to touch whether he/she will feel comfortable or happy when they attempt to help every shoe customer to seek the most right shoe style in every shoe customer whole shoe searching processing. Othwerwise, serving robots are only one machine, they can not touch or feel every shoe customer individual emotion whether he/she feel comfortable or unhappy or happy when they need to contact them in whole shoe searching processing. Hence, I believe that some tasks robots can

not repalce human staff to do very easily. Otherwise, robots may bring disadvanatges to let any one businessman to loss his/her customers, due to robots can not touch every customer

emotion to compare human staff in service tasks more easily. Robots serving customer behaviors may cause money lose and customers number lose to the shop in micro economic view.

On conclusion, in demand and supply economic theory for robots supply and demand case, robots supply number increasing may influence human workers demand number decrease. So, it seems that robots number supply will be depended on global robots supply number more than robots demand number because when human began to accept robots to replace human to do general simple jobs in global labor market. Then, it means that global robots labor number must need to be increased in order to satisfy global businessmen workers number need. If any kinds of robot workers manufacture number is not enough to be supplied to let global future businessmen to buy, then robot supply will be shortage and they can not provide to satisfy global businessmen robots labour purchase need. So, future robot number will be depended on supply more than demand.

Human intellectual demand and supply behavior relationship

Intellectual human economic behaviors

What does intellectual human economic behaviors mean ? Human foolish behavior is depended on social enjoyment need more or material social supply more? I believe that when we choose or decide to do intellectual behaviors, then our societies will be influenced to bring economic growth in consequence.I shall attempt to indicate pollution case to explain how and why eithet our intellectual or foolish behaviors may bring economic growth or recession in consequence as below:

On one hand, for air pollution social case aspect example, if we only consider to buy cars to drive for working aim or holiday leisure aim. Then, our societies air will be polluted. Our health will be influenced to bad. Our car driving behaviors may cause global environment air pollution serously. In long tiem, global air pollution will bring our bodies health to be bad. Although, ourselves car driving behaviors may bring our driving travelling leisure enjoyment and comfortable feeling in short time, also we so not need to pay public transport fare often, but we need to compensate ourselves health economic intangible loss due to air pollution , when cars number increases, dirty air will cause ouselves health to become bad.

In the result, we will need to pay more medical expenditure when we are old age, due to ourselves bodies will become bad, due to we breathe global dirty air every day, due to ourselves cars pollute air in long time, e.g. 10 to 20 years, even 30 more without limited air pollution environment. So, driving cars behavior may be one kind of human foolish behavior and our foolish behavior may bring ourselves future long time medical expenditure absolutely.

One the other hand, water pollution social aspect, if we often keep much rubblish to pollute sea, oil exploration porcessing pollute ocean , ships gas pollute ocaen, then fishes will eat polluted food and drive dirty water, due to global ocean is polluted.

In fact, because human only to conside how to buy boats to carry on leisure enjoyment activities, or catch cruises to travel on the sea. Also, oil manufacturers only consider researching anywhere to find new oil exploration places to manufacture oil product, when their oil exploration processes pollute ocarn . Consequently, global fishes drink polluted warer or eat polluted food. They will have poison. SO, human will have high chance to eat poison polluted fishes, due to fishes are poison or are polluted.

So, human is doing foolish activities, we only hope to find oil exploration places to pollute ocean or we only spend money to buy ticket to catch ships to travel anywhere in global ocean. All of these human foolish behaviors will bring pollution to global ocean. On consequently, we will need to compensate to eat polluted or dirty or poision fishes, ourselves bodies health will be bad. In long time, we need have high chance to pay medical expenditure when we are old. So, pollution case may be one good example to explain how and why human foolish behavior may influence ourselves future need to compensate serious medical loss.

All of these human foolish behavior will bring pollution to global ocean. On consequently, we will need to compensate to eat polluted or dirty or poison fished , ourselves bodies health will be bad. In long time, we will have high chance to pay medical expenditure, when we are old. So, pollution case may be one good example to explain how and why human ourselves intellectual or foolish behaviors may influence future long time economic loss or economic growth or recession in micro and micro economic view.

On another water pollution aspect hand, if we often keep rubbish to sea, oil exploration processing pollutes ocean and ships' gas pollute ocean, then fishes will eat polluted food and drink dirty water, due to fishes will eat polluted food and drink dirty sea water because the global ocean is polluted seriously.

In fact, because human only consider how to buy boats to carry on any leisure water activities, or catches cruises to travel on the sea. Also, oil manufacturers only consider any where to find oil exploratin places to manufacture oil products from ocean, when their pol exploration processes can plooute ocean. Consequently, global fishes drink polluted water or eat direty food. They will have poison. So, human will have high chance to eat poison fishes. Otherwise, such as pollutin case, it can infuence inflation or deflation. Consequently, the reason indicates supply and demand theory. If air pollution is serious, then we will consider health issue, global cars demand number may be influenced to reduce, when global cars number demand will reduce, global car prices and supply number will need to change to fall down in order to attract or persuade global car consumers choose to make car purchase decision. Hence, global car manufacture number and car price will be influenced to reduce, due to global air pollution issue. Consequently, deflation will occur because when the country citizen usually does not spend much extra saving money to buy car expensive goods. Money value will be low. Otherwise, if global cair pollution is not serious, human considers to buy cars to enjoy driving leisure lives. So, global car demand is influenced to increase , also global car price will also influenced to increase.

Consequently, gobal human will choose to buy cars to drive. Due to we accept to spend extra saving to buy expensive car goods. Car sale price and supply may be influenced to rise up. Money value is influenced to reduce. Inflation may be influenced, due to global car consumers number increases, we would not have extra money to spend easily. Car expensive goods expenditure influences our spending habit to avoid to make car purchase decision more easily. So, human intellectual or foolish activities may bring inflation or deflation consequency in possible indirectly in macro economic view.

On conclusion, above pollution case explain that how and why human intellectual or foolish economic behaviors may bring inflation or deflation consequency as wll as economic growth or recession consequency as well as any goods demand and supply increasing or decreasing consequency. It implies that human behavior may have indirect relationship to influence any goods demand and supply number to either increase or decrease result as well as any goods price will be influenced to increase or decrease in micro and macro economic view. Hence, Human foolish behavior is depended on social enjoyment need more or material social supply more because human needs to raise enjoyment feel , so we will choose to do foolish behavior, e.g. air pollution, when many people choose to buy cars to drive to replace catch public transport. So, such as car market, it depends on car demand number more than car supply number absolutely in demand and supply view.

The relationship between social change and human behavior

Why does economic changes may influence human individual behavioral change? I shall attempt to indicate shopping behavior and staying at home behavior to explain their case and effect relationsip as below:

Human behavior can be influenced by economic change or economic change can be influenced by human behavior? Why does recession may influence consumers reduce shopping desire? In social recession suitation, it is possible that many people lose jobs suddenly, due to businessmen lose many customers. They need to make decision to reduce employees number in order to continue to keep businesses. Consequently, many firms (organizations) their employees may lose jobs. When they have much time, due to lose jobs, they will feel to avoid to spend too much time and money to go to shopping often. Many losing jobs people, they will often stay at homes.

So, they will reduce time to go to shopping, then non essential products won't their preferable choice purchase products. Hence, recession will change many losing jobs people their shopping or consumption desires to avoid to buy non essential products often . Usually when economic boom, many people have jobs to do because consumers number must increase when many people have jobs to do. Then, many people can accept to spend money to buy non essential products often. Many people feel spend time to go to shopping can satisfy their purchase of any kinds of new products useful psychology or desire. So, recession is one good example to explain it can influence many people do not like often to leave homes to go to shopping easily. Many people like to stay at homes, becaue they feel worry about spending too much shopping time when they leave homes. Their staying home time is one good negative shopping behavior example. So, economic change may influence human individual behavior changes , they have direct cause and efect relationship in behavioral economic view.

May human behavior influence economic change? Is it possible that human behavior may bring the country social economic change in macro economic or micro behavioral economic view ? I shall indicate publishing industry example. Do you feel that if there are many students feel learning is very important when they read many books or many of students feel interesting to read or they have reading new books in habit, then it is possible that the country will have many students like to spend time to go to any book shops to choose the books, they feel that they can help they learn new knowledge. Then the country will increase students number, they often spend time to visit any one book shop every week. Their visiting book shops behavior which may become their habits. So, the country will increase students number, they often spend time to visit book shops. Also, it implies that visiting book shops behaviors may be their behavioral habits.

So, when the country has many students often spend time to visit book shops , their visiting book shops behaviors may help any one book shop to raise books sale chance. So, the country's student individual often visiting book shop behaviors, their habitual visiting book shops behaviors must may assist help any one book shop to increase books sale number absolutely.

Consequently, any one book shop , its books sale bumber must be influenced to increase to increase because the country will have many students like or feel need visit book shops habit in order to choose any suitable books to buy to read at home in order to raise themselves learning effort. When the country has many bok shops often have many students visit their book shops, then their books sale number may be influenced to increase. It explain why student individual visiting book shop behavior may help any one book shop sale number increases also. So, visiting shops products sale number is depended on online products supply number, if online products supply number increases, then it may cause many customers choose to buy the kind of products from online webstore. So, any shop products sale number will depend on onlint products supply number in supply and demand view.

Technology how encourages online shopping behavior

Human Behavioral network job brings social economic benefits

What does human network job mean ? Why may human network job be popular? Why human network job behavior may influence economy ?

Nowadays internet is popular to use. We can apply internet to find data , search any new things, even earn money. Why does internet

may become huma network job source. For example, e-publish may be one kind of new human network job. Any authors may apply internet

channel to help them to sell electronic or paper books from e-publisher web store. They may apply facebook, you tub etc. any online

channel to promote themselves new books to let new readers to know whether when they may buy themselves favourable new topic books to read

from electronic publisher web store.

Thus, future electronic publisher industry may help any authors to build internet network platform to help them to sell and promote

ot advertise their any one new electronic or paper book topic to let global any one reader to choose to buy their any new topic books from electronic publisher web store easily and conveniently. However, it implies that electronic network platform author may be one kind of future new human network job in our societies.

How electronic network platform author job may bring economy benefit in macro economy view? A person can have few friends, contacts and still be very influential if these few

friends and contacts are themselves highly influential, e.g. one author must not need to know any one reader in global society. When they like to choose any electronic books from electronic internet network platform. They may become the author's any one topic book buyer, when they feel the author's any one topic book is fun and attract they make decision to buth the strange author whose the topic book from electronic book publisher's platform web store conventiently in short time. Although, they are strangers, they do not know themselves , but the reader can understand what it way that made Google from writing platofrm to create new creative mind and typing network job method to replace traditional hand writing book method for global authors. It will be one kind of new human network writing job.

Hence, global any one reader can apply an innovative search engine , such as google.com to find whether whom author personal new topic books are value to read from internet.
Then, the electroniuc publisher's web store may be new book store platform sale network to help the author to sell many electronic or paper books from electronic network platform
in short time. So, internet may be future new network plaform to help global any one author to create network writing job absolutely. Furthermore, internet may be popular social media
to help any one author to build goold relationship between his/her readers. It is one kind of new network, human network job. New authors do not need to buy many paper books to prepare to put in any one book shop warehouse. Their every book can print on demand to reduce out of book stock in any one book shop. They may choose to sell either electronic books or paper books both from any one book publisher web store. So, electronic network platform may be one kind of good writing channel to help human authors to create income and it can also help authors to bring new creative mind and new topic fun content books to let readers to know and buy to read from electronic publisher network platform.

Why does human behavior may be one kind of new human network job to bring global economic advantages. ALthough, it may be free income or without inocme, but the person does the network behavior, his/her behavior may be bring advantages to influence many other people's health. For this case, when a worker in a coffee shop in an airport gets a vaccination aganinst the flu, it does not only helps him or her stay healthy, but also helps the many travellers who might otherwise have been inflected if that workers caught the flu. So, the externality , the result implies the vaccination of even a part of a community conveys benefits to the whole community. For example, governments pay special attention to the vaccinations of school children, teachers, health mothers, and the elderly, categories of people particularly susceptible not only to catching, but also to transmitting a disease.

It is not accidential that governments are heavily involved with vaccination . When there are externalities, free market, fail to persuade individual incentives with society's
their the worker's decision of whether to get a vaccine ends up attracting whether other people get sick. The workers might not fully take all these other people's potential suffering into account when making her or his vaccination decision.

As Stanford University does many suggestions, understand this and tries to help them make the right decisions and so providers free flu vaccines for its staff and students.
Small pockets of unvaccinated individuals can allow a disease to gain a spread more widely well-being. For example, parent weighing the costs and benefits of a vaccine for their child is not always thinking of the consequences of that vaccination to other people. THese are markets in which subsidizing or regulating behavior can make everyone better off. Because the reason for requiring that a child be vaccinated before enrolling in school is not just to protect that child, because each child's vaccination affects others via potential contagions.

Robots take our jobs behavioral and economy influences

Robot job behavior brings economy influences

If one day robots can replace human to do simple, even complex jobs. They will bring what influences to our global societial economy.The popular economic refrain declares that the
global middle class is dying and robots will soon take our jobs, e.g. shopping center customer service jobs, library service jobs, cinema ticket sale jobs, restaurant kitchen cooker jobs,
even, bus drivers, taxi drivers etc. public transport drivinq jobs, accountant, doctors etc. professional jobs. Whether it is beautiful or petty matter if our future societies have many human jobs can be replaced to do from robots. Businessman must may reduce to employ employees and reduce to pay salary or wage, when robots can be replaced to do their employees tasks. But, societies must bring unemployement rate rises , due to societies will have many people loss jobs when their employers choose to buy robots to serve their clients or do any office tasks or customer service or cleaning etc. tasks.

In micro economy view, employers may save money in long term, but in macro economy view, it will cause unemployment ratio rises , even crime rate rises when there are many people lose jobs in societies. These models of doom, though, fail to account for the hundreds of businesses riding the waves of change in their industries when robots may be invented to replace human to do many simple , even complex tasks in our future societies.

WE may image that one small factory needs to manufacture fishes canes to sell to supermarket, the small , cheaper stuff and higher margin parts of the fishes manufacture industry. Before, this factory needs to employe many human factory workers need to help every fresh customer makeing the perfect fishing gear, designed for performance, durability, and cost in order to achieve to manufacture every fish cane in whole fished processing manufacturing stages. Every worker needs to spend about 15 to twenty minutes to finish every fish cane , till to delivery to any supermarket to sell. If this fish canes manufacturing factory can apply manufacturing robots to help them to finish any one working tasks , every robot can only spend five minutes to finish whole fresh fish cane manufacturing process. Thus, every robot can

help this factory save 10 to 15 minutes time to finsh every fish cane manufacturing process. IN fact, time is money, because when every robot can help this factory to reduce 10 to 15 minutes time to compare human worker. Then, this factory can finish about 20 fish canes in one hour if it can use robot to help it to manufacture fish canes. Otherwise, if this factory still use human workers to help it to manufacture fish canes, then it can finsh about 3 to 4 fish canes in one hour. SO, the manufacturing efficiency ensures that robots must help this fish manufacturing factory to raise fish canes number more than human workers. So, in robotic behavioral economy view, manufacturing robots must help this fish canes manufacturing factory to raise fish canes manufacturing number and deliver increasing number to supermarkets to prepare to sell every day. Robots can help this fish canes manufacturing factory bring manufacturing time saving, rising manufacturing efficiency, improving performance and reducing wages expenditure long time advantages in micro economy view. However, manufacturing robots can also bring disadvanages to society, e.g. increasing unemployment ratio, increasing crime rate,

this factory workers will lose jobs and income, they need earn social welfare from government and increasing government finance pressure in short time, even long time in macro economic view.

Stanford University graduate program in economics, Scott lecturer explained that "in demand and supply economic theory for robots supply and demand case, robots supply number increasing may influence human workers demand number decrease. It sometimes calls " the efficient frontier".

No specific human beings were mentioned in any of economics classes. As robots supply and demand in market case, They (robots) may be purely theoretical " agents" who reached to the most reasonable sale prices in order to persuade any one businessman buyer to make manufacturing robot buying decision whether robots can help him / her to bring how much saving time , saving money, saving cost, improving performance, efficiency economic benefit before he/she plans to reduce workers number when he/she decides to apply robots to replace human workers in his/her factory or office or any service department, e.g. cinema ticket sale service, shopping center customer service, shopping center cleaning , supermarket customer service etc. service or sale tasks. When robots can replace human to do any one of these tasks in any organizations. So, robots may be human worker agents who reached to prices the way robots would react to a software

command. There was nothing that explained why some people thrived and others did n't or why truly brilliant, hardworking people could fail when much lazier folks succeeded." Having been admitted to the Stanford University graduate program in economics, Scott lecturer hoped to get his answers there.

How robots influence our future social changing? Using the right technology can be a boon to your business in this economy. For internet example, it is easier than ever to find well-matched customers all around the world, to stay in contact with them, and to more quickly design the products they want. If you focus solely on being cutting -edge, though you risk letting the technology

take over what should be very robust relationships with your customers , employees, and colleagues. IN nowaddays society, technoligical advances and cutomation, personal

relationships in business are more crucial than ever. I mean that robots can not replace human to serve clients to let them to feel more comfortable and passion more easily. For shoe shop case example, if the shoe shop apply one robot to serve its clients to replace human shoe salesperson to serve its shoe customers. Robots ensure that they can not persuade every shoe potential buyer to make shoe buying decision more easily when robots need to contact every shoe potential buyer. The reason is simple, because robots can not touch any one shoe buyer individual emotion very easier.

If the shoe buyer needs the robots to help him/her to choose any right shoe styles when he/she can not feel himself / herself can make the most right shoe style choice decision. The robots can not replace human shoe salesperson to make shoe style choice judgement more easily. They must need longer time to analyze whether which shoe style may be the most suitable to the shoe buyer. Otherwise, human shoe salesperson may attempt to make the most right shoe style choice decision to help any one shoe buyer to chooce the most right style shoe because he/she owns shoe style sale experience, shoe style knowledge, the most important reason is that they can feel every shoe customer individual emotion to touch whether he/she will feel comfortable or happy when they attempt to help every shoe customer to seek the most right shoe style in every shoe customer whole shoe searching processing. Othwerwise, serving robots are only one machine, they can not touch or feel every shoe customer individual emotion whether he/she feel comfortable or unhappy or happy when they need to contact them in whole shoe searching processing. Hence, I believe that some tasks robots can

not repalce human staff to do very easily. Otherwise, robots may bring disadvanatges to let any one businessman to loss his/her customers, due to robots can not touch every customer

emotion to compare human staff in service tasks more easily. Robots serving customer behaviors may cause money lose and customers number lose to the shop in micro economic view.

Intellectual human economic behaviors

What does intellectual human economic behaviors mean ? I believe that when we choose or decide to do intellectual behaviors, then our societies will be influenced to bring economic growth in consequence.I shall attempt to indicate pollution case to explain how and why eithet our intellectual or foolish behaviors may bring economic growth or recession in consequence as below:

On one hand, for air pollution social case aspect example, if we only consider to buy cars to drive for working aimr or holiday leisure aim. Then, our societies air will be polluted. Our health will be influenced to bad. Our car driving behaviors may cause global environment air pollution serously. In long tiem, global air pollution will bring our bodies health to be bad. Although, ourselves car driving behaviors may bring our driving travelling leisure enjoyment and comfortable feeling in short time, also we so not need to pay public transport fare often, but we need to compensate ourselves health economic intangible loss due to air pollution , when cars number increases, dirty air will cause ouselves health to become bad.

In the result, we will need to pay more medical expenditure when we are old age, due to ourselves bodies will become bad, due to we breathe global dirty air every day, due to ourselves cars pollute air in long time, e.g. 10 to 20 years, even 30 more without limited air pollution environment. So, driving cars behavior may be one kind of human foolish behavior and our foolish behavior may bring ourselves future long time medical expenditure absolutely.

One the other hand, water pollution social aspect, if we often keep much rubblish to pollute sea, oil exploration porcessing pollute ocean , ships gas pollute ocaen, then fishes will eat polluted food and drive dirty water, due to global ocean is polluted.

In fact, because human only to conside how to buy boats to carry on leisure enjoyment activities, or catch cruises to travel on the sea. Also, oil manufacturers only consider researching anywhere to find new oil exploration places to manufacture oil product, when their oil exploration processes pollute ocarn . Consequently, global fishes drink polluted warer or eat polluted food. They will have poison. SO, human will have high chance to eat poison polluted fishes, due to fishes are poison or are polluted.

So, human is doing foolish activities, we only hope to find oil exploration places to pollute ocean or we only spend money to buy ticket to catch ships to travel anywhere in global ocean. All of these human foolish behaviors will bring pollution to global ocean. On consequently, we will need to compensate to eat polluted or dirty or poision fishes, ourselves bodies health will be bad. In long time, we need have high chance to pay medical expenditure when we are old. So, pollution case may be one good example to explain how and why human foolish behavior may influence ourselves future need to compensate serious medical loss.

All of these human foolish behavior will bring pollution to global ocean. On consequently, we will need to compensate to eat polluted or dirty or poison fished , ourselves bodies health will be bad. In long time, we will have high chance to pay medical expenditure, when we are old. So, pollution case may be one good example to explain how and why human ourselves intellectual or foolish behaviors may influence future long time economic loss or economic growth or recession in micro and micro economic view.

On another water pollution aspect hand, if we often keep rubbish to sea, oil exploration processing pollutes ocean and ships' gas pollute ocean, then fishes will eat polluted food and drink dirty water, due to fishes will eat polluted food and drink dirty sea water because the global ocean is polluted seriously.

In fact, because human only consider how to buy boats to carry on any leisure water activities, or catches cruises to travel on the sea. Also, oil manufacturers only consider any where to find oil exploratin places to manufacture oil products from ocean, when their pol exploration processes can plooute ocean. Consequently, global fishes drink polluted water or eat direty food. They will have poison. So, human will have high chance to eat poison fishes.

Otherwise, such as pollutin case, it can infuence inflation or deflation. Consequently, the reason indicates supply and demand theory. If air pollution is serious, then we will consider health issue, global cars demand number may be influenced to reduce, when global cars number demand will reduce, global car prices and supply number will need to change to fall down in order to attract or persuade global car consumers choose to make car purchase decision. Hence, global car manufacture number and car price will be influenced to reduce, due to global air pollution issue. Consequently, deflation will occur because when the country citizen usually does not spend much extra saving money to buy car expensive goods. Money value will be low. Otherwise, if global cair pollution is not serious, human considers to buy cars to enjoy driving leisure lives. So, global car demand is influenced to increase , also global car price will also influenced to increase.

Consequently, gobal human will choose to buy cars to drive. Due to we accept to spend extra saving to buy expensive car goods. Car sale price and supply may be influenced to rise up. Money value is influenced to reduce. Inflation may be influenced, due to global car consumers number increases, we would not have extra money to spend easily. Car expensive goods expenditure influences our spending habit to avoid to make car purchase decision more easily. So, human intellectual or foolish activities may bring inflation or deflation consequency in possible indirectly in macro economic view.

On conclusion, above pollution case explain that how and why human intellectual or foolish economic behaviors may bring inflation or deflation consequency as wll as economic growth or recession consequency as well as any goods demand and supply increasing or decreasing consequency. It implies that human behavior may have indirect relationship to influence any goods demand and supply number to either increase or decrease result as well as any goods price will be influenced to increase or decrease in micro and macro economic view.

The relationship between social change and human shopping behavior change

Why does economic changes may influence human individual behavioral change? I shall attempt to indicate shopping behavior and staying at home behavior to explain their case and effect relationsip as below:

Human behavior can be influenced by economic change or economic change can be influenced by human behavior? Why does recession may influence consumers reduce shopping desire? In social recession suitation, it is possible that many people lose jobs suddenly, due to businessmen lose many customers. They need to make decision to reduce employees number in order to continue to keep businesses. Consequently, many firms (organizations) their employees may lose jobs. When they have much time, due to lose jobs, they will feel to avoid to spend too much time and money to go to shopping often. Many losing jobs people, they will often stay at homes.

So, they will reduce time to go to shopping, then non essential products won't their preferable choice purchase products. Hence, recession will change many losing jobs people their shopping or consumption desires to avoid to buy non essential products often . Usually when economic boom, many people have jobs to do because consumers number must increase when many people have jobs to do. Then, many people can accept to spend money to buy non essential products often. Many people feel spend time to go to shopping can satisfy their purchase of any kinds of new products useful psychology or desire. So, recession is one good example to explain it can influence many people do not like often to leave homes to go to shopping easily. Many people like to stay at homes, becaue they feel worry about spending too much shopping time when they leave homes. Their staying home time is one good negative shopping behavior example. So, economic change may influence human individual behavior changes , they have direct cause and efect relationship in behavioral economic view.

May human behavior influence economic change? Is it possible that human behavior may bring the country social economic change in macro economic or micro behavioral economic view ? I shall indicate publishing industry example. Do you feel that if there are many students feel learning is very important when they read many books or many of students feel interesting to read or they have reading new books in habit, then it is possible that the country will have many students like to spend time to go to any book shops to choose the books, they feel that they can help they learn new knowledge. Then the country will increase students number, they often spend time to visit any one book shop every week. Their visiting book shops behavior which may become their habits. So, the country will increase students number, they often spend time to visit book shops. Also, it implies that visiting book shops behaviors may be their behavioral habits.

So, when the country has many students often spend time to visit book shops , their visiting book shops behaviors may help any one book shop to raise books sale chance. So, the country's student individual often visiting book shop behaviors, their habitual visiting book shops behaviors must may assist help any one book shop to increase books sale number absolutely.

Consequently, any one book shop , its books sale bumber must be influenced to increase to increase because the country will have many students like or feel need visit book shops habit in order to choose any suitable books to buy to read at home in order to raise themselves learning effort. When the country has many bok shops often have many students visit their book shops, then their books sale number may be influenced to increase. It explain why student individual visiting book shop behavior may help any one book shop sale number increases also.

How human productive behavior may influence economic development

May any country which citizen behavior assist themselves country development? It is one cause and effect economic question. I mean that if the country itself citicen can not concentrate mind or energy to choose to do one kind of industry in order to let themselves country can bring the most benefit, then whether the counry itself economy can bring the most serious economic benefit. I shall attempt to indicate these countries themselves indistry choice to explain whether these countries themselves citizen productive behavior may help themselves countries to achieve the largest economic benefits. I shall indicate as below:

New Zealand farmer individual wine productive behavior

For New Zealand country example, this country concerns itself effort is foucs on farming agricultural aspect. So, this country has many farmers concentrate on farming agricultural aspect. May New Zealanders choose to spend time to produce different kinds of wines, e.g. wine or red grape wine is for the people are eating meat, or they are eating dinner.

When these New Zealanders their behaviors choose to do farming or agriculture to grow and produce different kinds of taste of white or red grape wine drinking products job. Themselves grape agriculture behavior will influence these New Zealanders themselves, they can learn how to improve different kinds of grape wine drinking products in order to achieve every kinds of white or read grape wines taste improving aim during their white or red grape producing process.

Why can New Zealander every individual white or read grape wine producers improve their white or read grape wine taste more easily? In behavioral economic view, it can explain that why any one New Zealander white or read grape wine producer can be encouraged or excited or persuaded to concentrate nervous and energy and effort to learn how to improve their white or red grape wine products easily.

In fact, New Zealand is one agricultural food export country. It has good natural environment resource , e.g. land, seed to provide any one farmer to produce themselves any kinds of agricultrual food products, e.g. fruit, or wine food products. Because New Zealanders know themselves country has enough natural resource . So, in common, many New Zealanders choose to attempt to do farming agricultural jobs in order to export themselves any kinds of fruit or meat or wine products to overseas or sell to domestic in order to earn profit.

So, when these New Zealand farmers number has been increasing every year. This country farmers will feel themsleves competition between this New Zealand farmers themselves are serious due to they may feel New Zealanders choose to do agriculture businesses in order to export themselves different kinds of farming food to overseas or sell to local to earn profit.

Hence, when many New Zealand farmers feel that farmers number has been increasing every year. They will feel themselves competition is serious. They must need to spend much time and nervous and effort to research what method is the best how to produce the best taste of white or red grape wine products in order to let local or overseas wine buyers to choose to buy his/her producing white or read grpae products to drink.

Hence, in competition psychological view, may influence many New Zealand white or reaad wine producers had been beginning to change their learning behavior on researching what method is the best in order to produce the best quality of taste red or white wine products to sell in order to attract overseas or local white or read grape wine drinkers to choose to buy his/her wine products. Their behavior will focus on learning how to raising or improving white or read grape wine taste method more than only focus on producing a large number white or red grape wine products. They believe wine quality is more important to compare wine producing number. So, New Zealand wine producers themselves wine producers behaviors have been changing on concentrating on researching wine quality method aspect more then wine producing number aspect in behavioral economic view.

America high technological productive behavior

For America example, US is one high technological country, it owns many high technological knowledge talent inventors, e.g. computer science inventors. Hence, US must attract many diferent countries owning high technological computer inventors choose to go to US to develop their computer science profession career. Also, it seems that when many computer science inventors or professions choose to go to US to develop themselves computer science new career. In behavioral economic view, due to their leaving themselves countries choice, which may bring influence themselve country job behaviors need to be changed. They must need to adapt US new live. Because they will forgive their past computer science job. These computer science professionals need to spend time to adapt US new lives. They " past computer science job behaviors" will need to be changed to their new US any computer employer's new computer science job model.

Because their traditional computer science jobs needed to be forgot in their themselves countries. They will feel their old computer science job knowledge and behavior needed to change in order to let their US any one new of computer company employer feels satisfactory to accept their new working behavior in any one US computer organization.

So, on the other hand, many US computer company employer will feel that they must need time to accept any one new overseas computer science professions their working behaviors, their working attitude daily, because these foreign comouter science professional, their past computer working behaviors and working attitude must be different to US domestic computer science professions.

In behavioral economic view, these overseas computer science professions, their working behaviors and attitude must be needed to change in order to adapt any one US new computer company itself domestic or local computer science professional stafs themselves daily working behaviors and attitude because these overseas and local computer science professionals must need to team work together.

In behavioral economic view, it is only one way that foreign computer science professionals must need to change themselves past country traditiona daily working behaviors and attitude in order to cooperate with these US local computer science professionals in teams more easily.

Consequently, if these foreign compute science professionals can change their past working behaviors and attitude to let any one US local computer science professional feels to cooperate with them easily in short time. Then, the US computer company itself whole computer professional teams themselves efficiencies will be influenced to raised or improved by the changing past working attitude and working behaviors of these foreign computer science professionals. So, in behavioral economic view, only if US any one computer company hopes itself computer teams themselves efficiency can be raised or improved when it decides to employ foreign computer science professionals and US domestic computer science professionals. They need to work in teams together. They must need to let these foreign computer science professionals to know how to change their working behaviors and attitude to let their domestic computer science professionals feel easy to work together. Then, the US computer company itself whole team efficiency must be rasied or improved easily in short time.

● Share market investment behavior influences Amazon share price rises

For China share market example, economic development depends on financial market. Because if many Chinese have interest to invest to carry on shares buying and selling activities in orde to learn how to earn shares interest and share profit when the China shareholder can make decision to sell himself/herself shares in the the high price, then he/she can earn money when he/she can sell the China company's shares in the high sale share price position.

If China has many Chinese like to spend time to carry on investing shares activities. Themselves shares buying and selling behaviors will influence China has many companies can increase fund from many Chinese shareholders in order to have enough money to expand or develop themselves businesses in China in long term.

Consequently, when China can have many Chinese like to attempt to carry on buying and selling shares investing behaviors in China share market. Themselves buying and selling shares behaviors can help many Chinese companies have effort to increase enough money or capital in order to continue to do their businesses in long term absolutely. So, it explains why when many Chinese become shareholders , they can assist China will have many companies continue to develop their businesses if many Chinese like to carry on shares buying and selling investing behaviors in long time in China financial investment market nowadays in behavioral economic view.

Why has any individual country have many people invest share behavior which can influence the country's macro consumption desire?

I shall apply shares market buying and selling investment behavior to explaiin why shares investment behavior which may impact the country's overal consumption desire as below:

In behavioral economic view, I assume that when the coutry has many people have interest to attempt to carry on shares buying and selling investment behavior, then their frequent shares buying and selling behaviors which may bring negactive consumption desire or shopping desire of these shares investors their consumer behavior.

The reason is simple, when the country has many share buyers number suddenly been increasing rapidly. Consequently, these large group share investors must need to spend much time to research any kinds of company shares variations, whether when their share prices will rise up of fall down in order to achieve buying the company's shares in the lowest price and selling the company's shares in the highest price level in order to earn profit.

Basic on this reason, they must need to spend much extra time to research share prices changing behavior every day, e.g. one working person will wait to leave his/her job, after he/she can spend time to gather data to research the day's share price changing behavior after dinner. So, the working person's right time may be his/her share price market research behavior. Before he/she may spend his/her night time to go to shopping after dinner, but nowadays, he/she will fogive to do his/her shopping behavior before dinner or after dinner at hight sometime. He/she will make decision to spend much night time to turn on computer to click on share market website to research his/her share purchase choice to investigate whether his/her share price whether it rises up or falls down at the moment in order to make his/her share buying or selling decision at ever night time.

I mean the when the country has many people are share investors, their shares investment behavioral spenging time which will influence many shops lose customers at might often because the country will have many people feel need to spend night time to turn on computer or watch television to investigate share price variation. So, the country will have many people / share investors choose to stay at home in order to carry on share price variation investigation behavior, they need to listen share market update news from radios or watch the share market update news from computer or TV at home every night. Consequenly, they must reduce times to leave themselves homes at night. So, their shopping behavior also will be reduced. Because these share investors feel need to spend time to investigate share price variation news at homes which can bring economic benefits (high opportunity benefits) when they choose to forgive to leave homes to go to shopping times (opportunity cost) every night.

On conclusion, it seems that when the country has many people are share investors, then their share price investigating behavior may bring negative shopping emotion at night. Consequently, the country's any one shop may lose many customers from this share investor consumer group in behavioral economic view. Hence, when the country's share investors number had been increasing rapidly, it will influence any shops lose many customers from this share investing customer group at night frequenly in short time, even long time in behavioral economic view, because their shopping desires or shopping emotion will be brought negative feeling when they make decisions to spend much time to listen radios or watch TV or computers share price update nes at night. Hence, share market will bring negative impact to influence consumer shopping desire or negative shopping emotion in behavioral economic view.

Can technology influence human shopping behavioral change?
Nowadays, technological development has reached mature stage, whether technological mature stage may bring positive or negative shopping emotion influence to global consumers. I shall aplly internet inventin or ecommerce shopping channel tool to explain whether internet technology can bring postive or negative influence to global consumer behavior in behavioral economic view.
Internet is a good technological tool, it brings e-commerce business chance. In fact, commonly, global has have many businessmen choose to use internet channel to carry on their products transactions between global online-buyers and their electronic websites. So, global many shoppers had begun to feel online shopping is more convenient to compare visiting shops shopping. Their shopping behaviors have been changed from internet technological tool. Global has many shoppers choose to buy any products from any overseas or local businessmen their web stores. They only need to spend time to find any businessmen their webstores to choose the most suitable products to pay visa to buy from their webstores. at homes. So, in general, global had have may shoppers had changed their shopping behaviors from visiting shops to visiting webstores at homes often.
So, it seems that internet technological tool had influenced global many shops disappear, but internet webstores will be replaced their actual shops on streets. Some of businessmen either they choose webstores to replace shops or choose websotes and shops both or still keep shops only. Hence, internet tool influences global businessmen have three kinds of products sale channels to let globa local and overseas consumers to choose how to buy their products. However, in fact, many of global shoppers, youngers and olders had begun to accept to buy any products from webstores. They feel to spend time to leave homes to visit shops , their shopping behaviors will be wasted time to not essential part to their daily lives. Hence, since internet technological invention, it had changed many consumers their traditional visiting shops shopping habit to change to buying products from webstores channel.
However, on the one hand, internet creates webstores ecommerce shopping channel to let global many consumers do not need to leave homes to go to shopping. It brings negative visiting shops shopping emotion to global general consumers nowadays. But on the other hand, it also brings positive visiting internet webstores shopping emotion to global general consumer nowadays. So, it seems that global many consumers feel that they often do not need to spend much time to go out shopping. Many global consumers feel convenient and enjoy to choose any products to buy from different internet webstores, when the online buyer chooses the most suitable product, he she only needs to pay visa card to buy the product from the online seller's webstore conveniently at home.
Hence, online shopping can bring economic benefit to online buyers, e.g. avoiding walking time or spending transport fare to visit the shop to go to shopping, shortening or reducing shopping time to do another important matter.
On conclusion, global many consumers began feel online shopping can bring more economic benefits on shortening shopping time, avoiding transport fare spending aspect. So, online shopping will be popular shopping behavior for future long time. It may encourage global many shoppers can make rapid shopping decision in short time in order to carry on any products buying transaction to global any one online shopper in short time easily in behavioral economic view. So, global many businessmen had begun to build themselves one attraction webstore in order to persuade different countries consumers to choose to click themselves webstores from internet channel to buy any kinds of products in short time easily.
So, internet technology had changed consumers traditional shopping behaviors to build positive online shopping emotion as well as raise online sellers' any products sale chance easily in behavioral economic view.

Why and how human behavior may influence the country's economic growth or recession?
When one country has many people choose to do the same matter for one period, whether their behavior may influence the country's pvera; economic growth or recession . I shall attempt to indicate cases toexplain their

relationship as below:
For flowing rubblish behavioral case example, do you feel that when the country has many people often flow rubblish on the streets, instead of their flowing rubblish behavior may bring streets dirty? But, their flowing rubblish behavior may explain that this country has people may have enough money to buy food to ear, or enough cloths to wear, enough bottles of water to drink, even they may have enough money to buy new television, radio, refrigeraters , washing machines, desktops or laptops electronic home products from old to new to use in order to satisfy their living needs. So, when they flow old electronic home products, their flowing old home electronic products behaviors may seem that they have enough money to buy other new home electronic products to replace old home electronic products to use at homes.
However, it seems thaat this country ought have many people have jobs to do. So, many of them, they can easy to make purchase decison to flow any old home electronic products and buy any new home electronic products to use . Because this country has many people have jobs to do. So, they can often not use old home electonic products to become rubblishs to flow on streets after they had bought any kinds of new home electronic homes.
In fact, it also implies that this country's economy grows rapidly. So, many businesses can glow up rapdly. When they expanded their businesses, they must need to increase employees number in order to let they help themselves to raise productivity or serve their clients absolutely. So, when the country has many businesses can grow up, it seems that its economy must be better or it is improved to compare past. Due to many different kinds of home electronic products had been often bought to use by this country people in this period. So, this country's any streets can be observed that expensive electronic home products were flowed on streets anywhere. then, this country will have many electronic home products sellers can sell their home electronic products very easily. When this country has many people can find any kinds of jobs to do easily. So, due to unemploymen rate had been decreasing.
In behavioral economic view, as this many electronic home products rubblish country case, we can observe this country may have many people have jobs to do. So, consumption number has been increased long time. So, cheap food, or expensive home electronic products may be rubblish on any streets. This country's people , their flowing rubblish behaviors may be explained that many of people have enough jobs to do, so they have ability to buy any good taste food to eat or buy any kinds of expensive electronic home products to use. So, this country's economy may be improved for this long period. So, in behavioral economic view, when this country can have many electronic home products rubblishs are flowed on anywherer in streets frequently. It seems that this country will have many people have jobs to do, so it causes they often change old home electronic products or replaced them easily, when they have enough income to spend to buy any kinds of new home electronic products to use at homes easily. Moreover, their flowing old electronic home products behaviors also indicate that this country has many people their salaries may be increased in possible from their emplyers. When this country can have many different kinds of home electornic products are sold. It means that this country's electronic home products needs or demand had been increasing, due to many people have jobs to do and income increases to excite their living of needs also improve. Consequently, this country may seem have better economic improvement. We can observe from this country's electronic home products rubblish increasing income in theis period.
On conclusion, this country ought experience economic growth at this period. So, " flowing expensive electronic home rubblish increasing number " may seem that this country's economic growth is rapidly in this period, due to many people have jobs to do as well as salaries increase in this period.

Technology how impacts human behavior changing?
Technology how influences human behavior to bring changing? For example, online share purchase and sale transaction from smart phone brings share investor can do share buying or selling transation in any where and any time conveniently, non manual driving auto vehicle, bring car owner feels comfortable and spends free time to do other matter, e.g. reading, listening mucis in himself or herself car freely. electrical energy vehicle can help car owner to reduce air polluton and it can brings the drivers do not feel drive long time in any journeys in order to avoid air pollution for environmental protection responsible car drivers in our societies. Thus, they will drive long time in any journeys when they can drive electronic energy cars to replace oil energy cars.

However, online technology can also bring consumers can choose to stay at homes to buy any things from seller individual online webstore conveniently. Such as online technology can bring shoppers do not need to spend much time to visit shops to buy any things. They can choose any kinds of products from any online sellers individual online webstores conveniently at homes. Online technology excite busy consumers can make purchase decision easily as well as it can help online sellers sell any kinds of products from internet easily.

In behavioral economic view, technology can change human behavior to be improved, it can let human feels comfortable, more free time ro use, rapid making any decisions, such as apply smart phones to make share purchase or sale transaction decision, online shopping decision, even travelling any where decision in short time, when the traveller finds the most cheap hotel accommodation room price and air ticket price frm any travel agent online tourism webstore, then the potential travel customer can follow the online hotel accommodation price and air ticket price data to make decision when to buy the air ticket from the airline travel agent or make decision when to prebook which hotel accommodation room to go to the country to travel from online travel agent tourism webstores. So, technology can encourage global any country travelers to make anywhere to trvel rapidly. If the traveler can find the country's general hotel rooms and airline tickets prices had been decreasing more sightly. The traveler may make travel decision to choose the country to travel in short time, then he/she can prebook the country;s any hotel room and airline ticket to pay by visa fraom the country's any hotel and airline travel agent webstores., before one week, even one month or more easily. Hence, online technology can also encourage traveler individual frequent travel times to be increased, due to global travelers can find any hotel rooms and airline tickets prices from internet conveniently at homes. They do not need to spend time to visit any airline travel agent to enquire travel choice country's hotel rooms prices and airline ticket prices. They can compare global travel of countries choices ' all hotels rooms and airline agents air tickets prices to make prebook airline seat and hotel room decision before one week, one month even six months early.

On conclusion, online technology can encourage global travelers can make travelling any where and when traveling time desicions easily. It can excite tourism industry develops in long time. Also, such as electricity cars invention can encourage environment protection car owners do car purchase decision easily, because they can choose to drive electronic energy cars to replace oil energy cars in order to avoid air pollution occurs easily. So, electronic cars can increase electronic car purchasrs number, due to many of environmental protection attitude of car owners can choose to drive electricity cars to bring air cleans, even non -manual driving cars can encourage lazy driving and free time driving car owners to choose to buy non-manual (artificial intelligent) cars to drive , because they can spend much free time to read, listen music or do any matters in themselves cars, they do not need to drive cars, robotic (AI) auto driving machine is such one non-manual driver to help them to drive themselves cars confidently. So, non-manual driving cars can attract lazy and enjoying free time driving car owners to choose to buy to replace traditional manual cars to drive easily. Moreover, online share transaction can help any share investors to make share buying and selling decision in short time easily. When they can apply smart phones technological tool to carry on share buying and selling activities easily. They can observe any share rising or falling price suitation from smart phones in any where any any time easily. So, smart phone technology can help global any shareholders to make share purchase and sale transaction easily. So, technology can encourage human makes decision in short time rapidly.

How and why employees behaviors may influence Amazon performance?

In behavioral economy view,I believe the country's any organizational employees behavior may bring indirect relationship to influence the country's long term economic development. I shall indicate past manufacture industry social development period to explain their relationship. For many countries' past business activities had belonged to manufacturing industry, such as US, UK past before 1980 year, it focused on steel manufacturing and steel manufacturing related machine products. So, US, Uk developed countries manufacturing industries may be past main country's economic income sources. I assume US , UK past had one million number different kinds of industries. They ought had about seven houndred thousand number organizational businesses were belonged to manufactured industry. They may include:

Steel manufacturing and steel related machine manufacturing, e.g. vehicle manufacturing, home appliances, e.g.

washing machine, television, radio, refrigerate cooler, heater, air condition etc. different kinds of different kinds of steel -related manufacturing machine, they were manufactured from US, UK steel machine manufacturers. So, US, Uk the other three hundred thousand number industry may be general service industry, e.g. hotel service, restaurent, cinema, public transport service, tourism lesiure , wine bar, supermarket etc. different kinds of non-manufacturing industries business organizations were operated in UK, US past before 1980 year.

So, in UK, US developed countries industry development history, they ought have high percentage of businesses belonged to steel related manufacturing machine and steel products. Also, in the past before 1980 year, US, Uk business employers , they employed many workers are manufacturing workers. They needed to spend long time to work in factories. They were skillful workers, and they are trained to manufacturing cars, washing machine, television, heater, etc. even steel itself different kinds of steel related products to prepare to deliver to their shops to sell to US, Uk local or overseas clients.

So, I believe that past UK, US ought employ many employees, they belonged to skillful manufacturing workers, manufacture increasing steel machine or steel related machine number of products rapidly daily. So, if UK, US had had many of these manufacturing factories owned high skillful workers, then their manufacturing steel-related machine or steel both kinds of products number must be influenced to raise rapidly. Consequently, their steel machine manufacturing products would been exported to overseas or would been sold to local both markets , they may be influenced to raise sale number. They (these manufacturing workers) needed to be trained to know how to manufactur these different kinds of machine products in the efficient teams and they ought to be trained to raise their efficiencies in order to shorten time to manufacturing many kinds of steel related manufacturing machine or steel itself products rapidly. So , if their efficiencies and manufacturing performance was improved, these US, UK any one manufacturing worker and their teams ought achieve raising productivities significantly.

Hence, when past UK, US manufacturing industry development period, if these two countries' any manufacturing factories could have many manufacturing workers could be trained to be skillful and proficient manufacturing workers. Then, in past every day to these factories workers, they ought help their steel or steel related manufacturing employers to raise any kinds of machine or steel products number in every team. So, when past in the manufacturing industry development, US, UK could have many factories' manufacturing workers themselves steel or steel related machine products manufacturing skill could be trained to to improve to any kinds of these machine or steel manufacuring products quality as well as their products number could be influenced to raise by themselves skillful improvement significantly every day.

Then, what would be influenced to occur to past UK, US manufacturing industry period? In behavioral economic view, when these two manufacturing industry developed countries, such as UK, US , if they had many factories workers can be trained to improve their skill in order to achieve any kinds of steel or steel-related machine products quality could be improved as well as products manufacturing number could be also increased absolutely.

In consequence, past UK and US both countries ought increase themselves any kinds of steel and steel related machine products number to be supplied to themselves local shops to let local clients to choose any one kind of machine manufacturing products to buy easily as well as they could also export to supply overseas any countries to buy their different kinds of steel or steel related machine products to let overseas steel or steel related manufacturing machine product buyers, they can have many of these different kinds of these steel or steel-related different kinds of manufacturing machine from UK and UK these both countries easily to compare other countries.

On conclusion, I believe that past US, and UK macro manufacturing industry income GDP would increase significantly. So, they would have good economic growth performance because when many of these manufacturing workers themselves manufacturing effort could be improved. So, it explained when employees manufacturing abilities can influence economic growth indirectly.

Robots invention whether they can help organizations to raise efficiencies or inefficiencies?

In behavioral economic view, in any organizations, when the organization hopes its worker teams can raise efficiencies , the organization may choose to increase more workers number and/or it can provide training to improve these workets themselves skills in order to raise their efficiencies. For one warehouse example, when the warehouse increases many goods , they are needed to delivered these goods from the shelves to the delivering destination locations. If this warehouse supervisors feel these workers themselves goods delivery speeds are slow, which is possible due to this warehouse's workers number is not enough. So, this warehouse supervisor ought increase workers number in order to increase their goods delivery speed in order to deliver goods from the shelves to every indicated goods delivery destination in order to let any one lorry driver can transport the right kinds of goods and ensure the accurate goods number to transport to any one client home rapidly.

However, if this warehouse supervisor planed to buy several warehouse goods delivery robots to assist these warehouse workers to find the right kinds of goods from shelves and then deliver to the right destination location in the warehouse. So, these warehouse orkers can concentrate on counting the accurate goods number and ensuring the right kinds of goods in order to prepare to let lorry drivers to transport these goods to these goods of buyers themselvers homes rapidly. Consequently, in the first step, robots can concentrate on finding th right goods from shelves and delivers them to the right goods transportation of location destination. Then, in the second step, these warehouse workers can concentrate on counting the accurate goods number and ensuring the right kinds of goods in order to prepare to put them to the lorry. Consequently, when warehouse robots and warehouse workers can cooperate to work together, the most important, robots, can deal on finding the right kinds of goods and deal on delivering the accurate number of goods of job duty as well as these warehouse workers can only concentrte on counting the right kinds of goods number in order to avoid it has none any mistake of wrong kinds of goods and inaccurate goods of delivery number to be transported to the lorry and to deliver to any one buyer's home.

So, it seems that warehouse robots ought help any one warehouse worker to raise himself efficiency and avoid goods delivery of mistake occurrence easily as well as their help to warehouse workers that can let any one goods buyer feels their goods can be delivered to their homes rapidly. Moreover, warehouse robots can also help these warehouse workers to raise efficiencies because warehouse robots can help them to shorten goods delivery time between any one shelf and any one goods delivery destination of location in the warehuse because robots may help them to find the right kinds of goods from the right shelf in the short time. So, any one worker does not need to spend long time to seek anywhere is the right shelf location for the kind of goods when the kind of goods are needed to deliver to the buyer's home from lorry. Warehouse robots can help them to do this aspect of " finding the goods from the right shelf in short time job duty". So, any one warehouse worker only needed tospend less time to do the counting of any right kind of goods number and ensuring the right kind of goods job duty. Consequently, this warehouse 's any one worker, his any one kind of goods delivery time may be reduced, because robots' assistance and they may have more confidence to avoid mistake to deliver the wrong number of goods and/or the wrong kind of goods to any one goods buyer's home.

On conclusion, it seems that warehouse robots ought may help any one warehouse worker to raise efficiency for any one team in the warehouse as well as the warehouse any one supervisor does not need to spend much time to observe any one worker individual performance for " goods delivery job duty aspect" because their goods delivery job duty that had been replaced to do by these several warehouse robots. Robots can achieve the more accurate of right kinds of goods and the right number of goods delviery job performance to compare any one of human warehouse worker themselves right kinds of goods of delivery and right number of goods of delivery job performance. So, when robots can participate to cooperate with this warehouse's any one worker to do their goods of delivery job duty in this warehouse every day. Then, robots can raies any one of supervisor individual confidence in order to let they do not need to spend time to observe any one of worker individual whose goods of delivery job performane. They can concentrate on supervising any one worker whose goods transport to lorry in the final step in order to avoid to deliver wrong goods number and / or wrong kind of goods to any one goods buyer's home every day. Consequently, this warehouse's overall teams of their delviery of goods performance many be improved by robotss' participatin to goods of delivery task as well as this warehouse's oveall teams themselves efficiencies may be influenced to raise by robots' goods of delivery task participation.

Why social behavior may influence organizational strategy needs to be changed ?

Why any organizations need to know whether nowadays social behaivor how has been changing in order to implement the kind of the most right strategy to achieve the profit aim pursue in possible. I shall indicate nowadays ecommerce or online, customer shopping behavior to explain above question concerns they ought have close relationship between social behavior and organizational strategic choice or organizational behavioral changing need. On nowadays ecommerce business, or online shopping model, this kind of shopping model in global many young and old age consumers like to apply internet tool to choose any country sellers website stores in order to stay at home to buy any kinds of products from themselves webstores in global societies.

In fact, online shopping model had been popular for long time above to twenty years. Most of global sellers will make decision to design themselves webstores in order to attract global many online buyers to choose to buy their products from themselves webstores. So, it seems that social consumers purchase behaviors had been changed to online shopping from internet invention.

Hence, social consumers purchase behavioral changes may influence any organizations' strategies need to be changed from visiting shops purchase strategy model to online purchase strategy model, if the seller still concentrate on concentrate on considerate how to design itelf , but neglects to considerate how to design itself webstore, e.g. how to design attract product photos to put on itself webstore, how to arrange sale price information location to be putted on webstore and visa card payment location on itself webstore in order to let any one online buyer can feel very easier to buy itself any kinds of products from itself webstore. Then, its potential online buyers will be influenced to increase number when they can find this online seller itself any kinds of products photes and every kinds of product sale price information and visa card payment channel locations easily from itself webstore.

So, it implies that nowadays any one seller ought need to design one webstore to let any one online overseas and domestic consumers can have chance to click itself webstore to choose any one kind of product to buy conveniently when he/she does not hope to leave him/her home to go to shop, because nowadays social shopping behaviors had been influenced to change when internet invention, them it gives another online purchase method to replace visiting shops purchase method to global any one buyer in nowadays societies.

So, if nowadays any one seller still concentrate on how to design itself shop display in order to put any kinds of product on shelf in order to let any one visiting shop customer to find the kind of product to buy, but it neglects to change to choose to pursue another new technological shopping method, such as webstore purchase method in order to implement effective strategy to design the most right webstore as well as in order to attract global overseas and local consumers to find itself webstore easily from website and find its any one kind of product phots and sale price and visa card payment button in order to choose to buy itself any kinds of products in the short time. Consequently I believe that the seller will lose many customers from overseas and local when its other same or similar product sellers choose to design themselves webstores in order to let global any one product buyer can buy themselves any one kind of product when they can pay visa card to buy their products from them webstores conveniently when they stay at home habitly. Then, the seller will lose many global potential customers in long time.

On conclusion, in behavioral economic view, any consumer behavioral social changing, which will influence any in order to avoid customers number loses significantly . In future time, organizations need to make rapid decision in order to implement the most reasonable and the most useful strategy in order to avoid global potential customers number reduces or lose them in long time. So, social behavioral changing environment ought influence any global organizations need to decide how to change themselves strategies in order to avoid customers loses significantly in future time.

How and why human behavior may influence economic growth or recession?

May ourselves daily behaviors influence our global societial continue economic growth or recession? Do they have cause and effect close relationship between human behaviors and global economic growth or recession? I shall apply behavioral economic theory to analyze and explain whether ourselves daily behaviors and our global societial economic growth or recession which have close cause and effect relationship as below:

Every country itself economic development must depend on any business activities, otherwise, any kinds of business activities must need ourselves business activities or behaviors in order to achieve any business activities as well as achieve the country's overall economic development in macro view.

However, any country's overall business activites or behaviors which must depend on any kinds of individual businessmen, themselves employees daily working behavior or activity or performance in order to help them to attract or increase many clients number to acieve " earning profit" aim. So, it seems that any individual business, itself overall every department individual working behavior is one main factor to influence the company's overall business performance.

For agricultural fruit and meat food farming industry example, such as New Zealand is a farming main target industry country. It had had many New Zealanders were daily themselves own farming businesses for many years. Their farming businesses include growing fruit, sheep, cow, pig pork, meat etc. food sale business. If the New Zealand farmer owned a large size farming land, then he will choose either growing fruit or feeding sheeps, pigs, cows to be meat to to transport to New Zealand supermarkets to help them to sell to their farmers meet to New Zealanders in order to earn profit. Thus, if the New Zealand farmer owned large size of farming lands, then he needs to employ many farming employees (farming workers) to help him to carry on farming business daily tasks, e.g. picking up friuts, feeding pigs, cows, sheeps to eat food daily. These daily farming jobs are very important to influence this New Zealand farmer's meats or fruits sale number whether they can be easy or diffcult to sell in New Zealand supermarkets , if these farming workers can own encough farming knowledge or skill to know how to pick up fruits method and make judgement to know whether it is right time to pick up the kind of fruits from the trees , as well as know how feed this pigs, sheeps, cows to eat food in order to let they are better health. Consequently, their farming behaviors which can let these animals can provide the best taste and enough meat from these animals to let New Zealander to buy to eat from New Zealand any one supermarket. Even these New Zealand farming workers can know whether the kinds of fruits, e.g. oranges, apples, gapes etc. fruits whether they ought be picked up from the trees at the right time. Consequently, they can make judgement to decide to pick up any kinds of the best taste fruits to let any one New Zealander to buy to eat from any one supermarket in New Zealand. Otherwise, if they do not make judegement to know whether the kind of fruit ought not be picked up because they still need longer time to continue grow up to increase fruit size and better taste from the trees in order to let any one fruit buyer can feel better taste when they eat this kind of fruit later. If they can buy this kind of fruit to eat later, then this New Zealand farmer's his fruit buyers can buy the best taste of this kind of fruit to eat from an yone supermarket in New Zealand. Consequently, many New Zealand supermarkets will choose to buy any kinds of fruits from this farmer fruit supplier when they feel this farmer's fruits can provide more better taste fruits to compare other farmers' fruits.

Thus, due to New Zealand is one farming main income source country. It's any kinds of fruits and meats need to be export to overseas to sell , instead of local sale. It's GDP percent is very high to whole country 's overall income source. So, any one New Zealand farmer individual and any one farming worker individual working behavior will influence its economy whether it is influenced to grow or recession possible. Moreover, it also seems that farming workers' farming knowledge and skill will influence themselves farming daily activities to achieve the aim of the number of increase or decrease to any kinds of fruits whether they are better taste or the number of increase of decrease to any kinds of meats whether they are better taste to supply to any one New Zealand fruit or meat buyers to eat from any one New Zealand supermarket. So, it implies that any one New Zealand farming worker individual farming behavior may influence any kinds of fruits or any kinds of meat taste because they are transported to any one supermarket to sell in New Zealand.

Consequently, if New Zealans had many farmers can teach god farming knowledge and skill to let their any one farming workers know how to decide judgement to decide when it is right time to pick up any kinds of fruits from trees , or how to grow them on soil in order to let they can grow rapidly. Then, many different kinds of fruits can be provided to let any one New Zealanders can eat the best taste of fruits when their fruits are supplied to any one New Zealand supermarkets. Even, if they knew how to feed foods to pigs, cows, sheeps to eat daily. Then they can be more health and they can provide the best taste of meats to let any one New Zealanders can buy their meats from any one New Zealand supermarkets. Moreover, their fruits and meats can be transported to overseas to let any one country fruits or meats buyers can choose any kinds of New Zealand meats and fruits to buy to eat from themselves countries supermarkets. Then, many overseas fruit and meat buyers will perfer to choose New Zealand any kinds of fruits or meats to buy to compare other countries fruits or meats to buy when they go to any one local supermarkets. On conclusion, it seems that New Zealand farming workers themselves farming behavior may influence their farming employers any kinds of fruits or meats sale number and income because their farming task behaviors must influence whether their fruits or meats taste are the better taste or worse taste to compare their other local farmers (the farmer competitors) whose fruits or meats táste. If tthe farmer's any one farming worker can be trained to learn how to know to feed animals skill and when is the most right time to pick up any kinds of fruits from trees or how to grow them on the soil methods. Due to these farming worker individual farming behavior may influence his different finds of fruits and meats sale number to be increase or decrease, so these any one New Zealand farmer must need to depend on any one farming worker whose farming working methods, if their farming working behaviors can be the best to influence any kinds of fruits to grow rapid or any kinds of pigs, cows, sheeps animals grow up rapidly , then their sale number may be increase significantly and their taste can be improved to let any New Zealand or overseas meat or fruit buyer to buy to eat to feel from any one New Zealand or overseas supermarkets, then New Zealand's agriculture industry must be influenced to increase. In the world, any one fruit or meat buyer must choose to buy New Zealand's fruit and meat to eat in prefer to compare other countries' fruits and meats. So, New Zealand's GDP may be influenced to raise from any one New Zealand farming worker individual farming working behaviors.

Reasons why human behavior may influence economic recession or growth?

Can ourselves daily behaviors or activies influence ourselves countries' economic growth or recession? I shall attempt to explain the reasons why they have direct or indirect relationship between human behavior and economy growth or recession as below:

I shall indicate environment pollution case to attempt to explain above question. Our societies had been experiencing servious environment pollution challenge. However, environment pollution , such as air pollution is caused by air planes and vehicles emission by air planes and vehicles emission as well as water pollution is caused by plastic rubblish, or dirty water or oil or gas chemical material, these both kinds of pollution ought may bring economic recession and this both kinds of pollution are caused by human ourselves daily foolish activities.

I believe human behavior and economy and pollution which have cause and effect relationship. I shall analyze this environment pollution case to explain why they have case and effect relationship between human foolish behavior and environment pollution and economic recession as below:

When global societies had many people like to buy cars to drive to bring emission to fresh air on the roads as well as many manufacturing factories will bring emission to pollute fresh air in their manufacturing processes. Factories and cars will bring air pollution , due to factories need to pollute fresh air in order to manufacture many products and car owners need to drive their cars to go to offices or leisure places. Their cars will also bring emisson to pollute fresh air. On consequence, car owners themselves frequent driving behaviors and factory workers themselves frequent manufacturing behaviors may bring environment pollution. Technology or human behavior whether may influence economic growth or recession. Moreover, air planes also brings emission to pollute air when they are flying in sky. Also, when ships bring oil pollution or sea plastic rubblishs bring pollution to global oceans.

In fact, manufactuers and cars owners, such as factories workers manufacturing behaviours ans car owners driving behaviors and pilots driving air planes flying behaviors and ships transport behaviors, which may cause plastic rubblish, oil or gas emission to sky or sea or on the road to cause ocean and air pollution is serious. However, human ourselves need to buy cars to drive to satisfy ourselves driving leisure or enjoyment, travelers need to catch air planes to travel to enjoy leisure needs, factories workers need help factories to manufacture many products to sell to customers to satisfy their using needs. oil exploration needs to find lands to explore new oil lands.

All of these business and leisure activites may bring serious air and water pollution. However, due to serious air and water pollution will bring earth warming challenge , such as some countries temperature will be influences to rise up to 40 degree or higher br earth warming. However, earth warming is caused by air and ocean pollution. Pollution must be caused by human ourselves, driving cars leisure and factories manufacturing business activities. Hence, if human decided to continue to do these foolish behaviors, we only pursue to manufacture different kinds of industrial products or drive cars to enjoy leisure aims, but we also neglect ourselves behaviors may bring environment pollution. Then, earth warming or earth temperature will be influenced to rise up absolutely in long term. Moreover, if our future earth will be influenced to bring serious high temperature effect by human ourselves these foolish behaviors.

On consequencey, warth warming will bring serious economic losses in possible because when ourselves earth temperature had been influenced to rise up to 40 degree or high. Ourselves health will be caused poor, due to we will feel difficult breath, we must need often tried and hard to work, due to our nervous and health will be influenced to poor by pollution and earth warming effect. Also, we need to pay more money to see doctors when we had long life. Then, our societies will lose may strong labors to help manufacturers to work, e.g. factories will reduce workers number to help manufacturers to produce more different kinds of products, due to workers health is general poor. Due to lacking enough workers to manufacture products, our societies will begin to reduce enough supply number of products to sell to global consumers to satisfy their use needs.

On conclusion, in behaviroal economic view, our societies will lose many labors due to their bodies are not health by air and water pollution. Global economic and business activities will be influenced to worse by global workers reducing number reason. So, economic recession will begin to occur in possible when pollution reaches the serious level.

How employee behavior influences organizational development ?

Can any organizational department employee individual behavior may help the organization to bring long term development? When one employee individual behavior, manager won't feel whose task behavior may help organizational development, but when the department has many teams cooperate to work together , all of these team employees whose task behaviors may help their organization to bring long term development.

I shall explain how any why when the organization has many departments, as well as when every team memmber individual behavior may help whole organization to bring long term development in possible as below:

Every organization must need efficient department to cooperate to work together. They may include human resource, finance, logistic, facility management, sales, marketing , operateional , warehouse , factory manufacture , research and development, purchase, customer service etc. different kinds of departments to cooperate to work together. So, any one employee individual behavior, include manager, leader, supervisor, worker, salesperson, manufacture worker, adminisration staff, factory or logistic worker etc. themselves task behavior whether his/ her performance is worse or better , whose task behavior ought bring long term good or bad influence to cause the organization's whose efficiency, or performance , whether it can be influenced to improve significantly. For car factory manufacture workers department example, it exmploys 100 car manufacturing workers. They need to manufacture at least 50 cars in order to bring enough car manufacture number to supply to global car buyers to choose to buy (satisfaction to car buyers their driving leisure activity needs). However, if this car manufacture firm employs many low skilful car manufacture workers, their inefficient car skill may bring cars manufacture number reduces, they can not achieve to reach the at least 50 cars manufacture number, if these 100 car manufacture workers. They have half number of workers, they only manufacture 30 to 40 cars number at least daily. So, it seems that this car manufacture firm will have half car manufacture workers bring the low cars manufacture number to compare the another half cars manufacture workers, when this proficient car manufacture workers may manufacture at least 60 or more cars manufacture number daily. So, it explains that this inefficient car manufacture workers will not help this car manufacture company to manufacture enough cars number in order to supply to global car market to sell to satisfy global car buyers needs, when car buyers demand number is more thn car manufacture supply number in supply and demand view. Hence, in long term, if this car manufacture company can not employ new proficient car manufacture workers to replace those inefficient or low skillful car workers. Consequently, its car manufacture number must be influenced to reduce and it can not satisfy global car buyers driving leisure needs.

However, if this car manufacture firm also has shop to sell itself any kinds of cars, instead of manufacturing cars product. So, it needs have both main departments to help it to earn profit. The first step, it needs have proficient car manufacture workers to help it to manufacture at least 50 cars from every car worker in order to have enough cars number to be provided to global car sellers to help it to sell to global car customers. Second step, if it decided to attempt to sell itself cars. Then, it needs to set up car shops in global to different countries in order to let global car buyers may visit its global any one car shop to enquire any one car etc. salesperson about any car quality, speed, gas useful, price, safety, etc. information questions and they can attempt to sit in any one car to feel whether which car can let them to feel more comfortable to make final car purchase decision in any one shop. So, if this car company can provide good sale speaking skillful training to any one car salesperson to let his/her to know whether how to explain every kind of car function and feature, manufacture method etc. questions, then I believe that they can influence any one car buyer to makecar purchase choice decision more easily. So, it this car manufacturer hopes it may attempt to earn profit from different countries car sellers and car buyers both. It ought also provide training course to all general car salespeople to be proficient owning sale speaking skillful professional skill in order to prepare having more confidence to persuade any one car customer to make car purchase choice from any one car salesperson more easily to compare global other car sellers.

Hence, if this car manufacturer could build both car manufacturing team and car sale team more proficient. However, if this car manufacturer hopes to develop itself car manufacture busness to expend to car sale business both in success. It must need to spend long term to provide training courses to general car manufacture workers and general car salespeople both to be proficient car skillful manufacture workers and proficient car skillful salespeople in order to help they can manufacture enough car numbers and help they can persuade may car customers can make car purchase decision in short time when they visit its any one car shop.

However, this car manufacture company explains why every car manufacture worker whose manufacturing behavior and every car salesperson sale persuading speaking ability may help this car manufacture company to expand from its car manufacture market to car sale market development in sussess in possible. So, this car manufacture firm must need these two kinds of essential human resource elements in order to achieve its cars sale number and cars manufacture number increasing aim. They may include proficient car manufacture workers and proficient car salespeople both human resource elements. These both human resource daily task behavior may influence its long term task efficient performance in order to expand itself car sale business in success from itself car manufacture business easily. If it hopes to expand its car manufacture business to car sale business in success. It must need to provide training to these two departments general staffs to be proficient staffs in order to supply enough cars number to its global car shops to let global car buyers can choose its any kinds of cars to buy in any time.

Morevoer, if this car manufacture company can have good skillful of car research and development department , it aims to research and innovate any new technological cars invention in order to improve its any traditional old kinds of cars to be innovative new kinds of cars from every year. Consequently, its any new innovative cars ought attract global any one car buyer to make car purchase choice final decision more easily, because its any kinds of manufacturng cars can be innovated rapidly to compare its any one car manufacturing competitors, when its nay kinds of cars can be shorten time to innovate within three months, but its any one car manufacturing competitors need to spend more than three months, even one year to innovate themselves traditional old cars products in long term.

Hence, its car staffs research and development department staffs must need own good car product design ability, proficient car engineering knowledge , even car invention knowledge in order to innovate its any one kind of car product in short time and introduce to let its global car proficient car buyers feel surprise to its any one kind of innovative car products to compare its any one car manufacturer.Hence, these four departments: car manufacture, car sale and car research and development anr car training departments must need concentrate resource to provide enough training to any one staffs in order to achieve the best performance.

On conclusion, all these departments staffs their performance can influence car manufacture aim to chance to car manufacture and sale aim more significantly. it explains why some main department staffs whole behaviors may influence any organizational performance significantly.

Printed by Libri Plureos GmbH in Hamburg,
Germany